A DROP IN THE OCEAN

ALSO BY SYEDA SAIYIDAIN HAMEED

His Miracle, Not His Sin: The Rubaiyat of Sarmad

Born to Be Hanged: Political Biography of Zulfikar Ali Bhutto

Maulana Azad, Islam and the Indian National Movement

Islamic Seal on India's Independence: Abul Kalam Azad - A Fresh Look

They Hang: Twelve Women in My Portrait Gallery

PRAISE

'Syeda Hameed was devoted to improving the lives of girls and women, working tirelessly to change their status from second-class citizens...I am inspired and honoured to know her.'

– Joan Holmes, Founder, The Hunger Project, New York

'This book is important...because it immerses you in the brutal bigotry of our age as well as in the poetry that could redeem us... it evokes an alluring possibility: that humanity could learn to appreciate all religions as traditions of universal wisdom rather than as dogmas that demand division.'

– John Coonrod, Founder and US Chair,
Movement for Community-led Development

A DROP IN THE OCEAN
The Story of My Life

SYEDA SAIYIDAIN HAMEED

SPEAKING
TIGER

SPEAKING TIGER BOOKS LLP
125A, Ground Floor, Shahpur Jat,
Near Asiad Village, New Delhi—110 049

First published by Speaking Tiger Books in 2024

All translations of Urdu verses are by the author, except where otherwise specified.

ISBN: 978-93-5447-950-2

eISBN: 978-93-5447-782-9

10 9 8 7 6 5 4 3 2 1

Typeset in Adobe Garamond Pro by Jojy Philip, New Delhi

Printed at

Ishrat e qatra hai darya mein fana ho jaana
Dard ka hadd se guzarna hai dawa ho jaana
Bakhshe hai jalwa e gul zauq e tamasha Ghalib
Chashm ko chahiye har rang mein waa ho jaana

To mingle with the ocean is the ecstasy of a drop
When pain reaches a zenith it becomes its own cure
The splendour of the rose evokes the desire for sight
The eye should open in every state and see all

— Mirza Ghalib

Contents

Prologue		1
1.	Being Muslim, Being Indian: A Question of Identity	3
2.	Mirror to the Past: My Ancestors	26
3.	Growing Up	32
4.	In Alien Climes	46
5.	Being Wife, Being Mother	53
6.	Being an Indian in Canada	72
7.	Return To India	85
8.	Becoming a Writer	89
9.	Entering Public Life	104
10.	My Planning Commission Years	116
11.	My Many Teachers	136
12.	My Pillars of Islam	184
13.	Kashmir: The Desolate Paradise	193
14.	India-Pakistan: Dooriyan Nazdeekiyan	217
15.	Inteha: Conclusion	237
Notes		243

Prologue

Ibteda: The Beginning

In these times, when the world is in unprecedented turmoil, I want to tell my story. The Quran says, '*Kullu nafasin zaiqatul maut*' (Every soul must taste death). These lines have echoed in my heart; an incentive to write for those I love. For future generations…not only my children and grandchildren but hundreds of children and grandchildren that my life has given me. Tonight, as I begin, I feel a restless churning within my body as though something has to be expunged. It is my story; it has to break out of my conscious and unconscious mind and be placed before the reader.

Munir Niazi's line '*Hamesha der kar deta hoon mein*' (I am always too late) has become the inspiration for this memoir. Write before it is too late, speak before the lips are silenced, and remind them before they forget that not long ago another world existed. What Faiz Ahmed Faiz said about 'bol' (speak) is an apt summing up of my thoughts:

Bol ke lub azaad hai tere
Bol, zabaan ab tak teri hai
Bol ye thoda waqt bahaut hai
Jism o zabaan ki maut se pehle
Bol ke sach zinda hai ab tak
Bol jo kuchh kehna hai keh le

Speak for your lips are free
Speak for your tongue is your own

Speak for the shortest time is long
Speak for truth still lives.
Speak whatever you need to say
Before the death of speech and body

1

Being Muslim, Being Indian

A Question of Identity

It is early in the morning of May 3, 2018 when I sit down to write this. After the rain has washed it, the world is stirring, I can hear the birds and see the spread of light over the dark. My fajr prayer has been offered even before the sound of the Azaan. I open the *Divan-e-Ghalib* and find these lines that match my present state of mind.

Dil mein zauq o vasl o yaad e yaar tak baqui nahin
Aag iss ghar mein lagi aisi ke jo thha jal gaya
Mein hoon aur afsurdgi ki aarzu Ghalib ke dil
Dekh kar tarz-e-tapaak-e-ahl-e-duniya jal gaya

No desire for union no memory of the beloved
An all-consuming fire took it all from my house
O Ghalib! How I yearn for sadness
For my heart is smouldering with the fake warmth of this world

How do I feel as a Muslim when I look back now at the last ten years since the country was swept with the tidal wave of a right-wing regime?

Aligarh Muslim University rises on my mindscape. Alma mater of three generations of my ancestors where each of them found a place in the university's Roll of Honour. Khwaja Sajjad Husain, Khwaja Ghulamus Saqlain, my grandfathers, and my father Khwaja

Ghulamus Saiyidain. In 1925, my father, the then 21-year-old newly appointed head of the Education Department in Aligarh Muslim University, spoke at a debate on the occasion of the Golden Jubilee of the Mohammedan Anglo-Oriental College, the precursor of AMU. The cream of Muslim intelligentsia was present on that occasion. Father, recently returned after his academic achievements in England, was given the honour of opening the Grand Jubilee Debate. The topic on which he spoke ninety-three years ago remains as relevant today as it was then for all Indians. He moved that Indian Muslims should not organise themselves on communal lines but must work together with the nationalists of other communities for the freedom and progress of the nation as a whole. After his short and persuasive speech, there was a vigorous attack from the top brass of Muslim politicians who were seated on the stage. Luminaries like Muhammed Ali Jinnah, the Agha Khan, and Sir Ali Imam took on my father and patronisingly dismissed the arguments of the youthful mover of the motion as 'irresponsible idealism'. The climax of this debate is described by my father's young cousin Khwaja Ahmad Abbas, who was sitting at the back, watching the proceedings. 'I remember Saiyidain seated in a corner seemingly overwhelmed by the powerful and authoritative voices of the elders, but furiously taking notes.' In his tribute to his Bhaijaan, as he called my father, Abbas writes, 'He succeeded by the sheer weight of his arguments and persuasive power of his eloquence to trounce…his formidable opponents. Mr Jinnah took at least ten years to recover from the shock of the defeat which he suffered in the presence of the most representative gathering of Muslim intelligentsia.'

On May 2, 2018, almost a century after that historical moment, Aligarh convulsed under a storm unleashed by right-wing forces with strong political backing. The issue was the portrait of the very same man who sat on the stage in 1925. M.A. Jinnah was among the dignitaries whose portraits were hanging in the university gallery. All of these men had been given a lifetime membership to the Students Union. This piece of history was used as the trigger to stoke communal fires in preparation for the by-election in UP. It did not matter that the portrait had hung there for ninety years. The local MLA, like Rip Van Winkle, waking from a decades-long sleep, collected a lumpen brigade to surround the university for the anti-national act of displaying Jinnah's portrait. The protest was calibrated to coincide with the visit of the former Vice President of India, Hamid Ansari, for a public oration on the occasion of the confernment of the same lifetime membership on him.

The events that followed are a matter of public record. I recall an experience narrated by a friend who was caught in the midst of a menacing crowd at the university gate, Bab-e-Syed. Hordes of marauders of the Hindu Jagran Manch were heading towards the place where the former Vice President was staying. Their purpose? To ignite the communal flame and start a Hindu-Muslim *fasaad* (riot). My friend saw the indifferent Aligarh police standing by. It was the sight of the crowd that chilled her. 'It was their eyes that made my body freeze. There was palpable murder emanating from them.'

When AMU students saw that the mob was not being stopped effectively by the police, they resisted them. Six members of the mob were overpowered and handed over to the police but instead of booking them, they let them off. When the students decided to go to the police station to demand an FIR against the six members, the police lathi-charged them and used tear gas.

~

I was a little girl when my father started reciting the poems of Dr Mohammad Iqbal to me. By the time I was five, I had learnt to read Urdu but had no understanding of his poems other than enjoying the simple verses he wrote for children. I listened to my father recite lines from Allama Iqbal's poem 'Ram'. The story of the Ramayana was in my literature texts; we enacted scenes from the epic at school functions. That Iqbal, a poet best known for writing on Islamic themes, should write about Ram did not appear the least odd to me. I had been told by my *buzurgs* (elders) that Hindu and Muslim writers often wrote about each other's faith; that was part of our eclectic Indian tradition. Several decades later officialdom blared from all platforms that Ram was a Hindu deity who could be celebrated only by Hindus. On the other side, Islamic subjects were becoming taboo for non-Muslims.

Iqbal's poem 'Ram' begins with lines that explain the ascendancy of Indian philosophical thought over all other schools of philosophy:

Labrez hai sharab-i-haqiqat se jam-i-Hind!
Sab falsafi hain khitta-i-maghrib ke Ram-i-Hind!
Yeh Hindiyon ke fikr-i-falak ras ka hai asar,
Rif'at mein aasman se bhi ooncha hai baam-i-Hind!

The cup of Hind overflows with the wine of truth.
Philosophers of the West are mesmerised.
The high philosophy of Hind's thinkers,
Has taken her star to the greatest heights.

Iqbal ranges Ram along with great world philosophers and imams. This is the highest pinnacle which the poet can accord Ram.

Is des men huey hain hazaron malak sarisht,
Mashhoor jinke dam se hai duniya mein nam-i hind!
Hai Ram ke wujood pe Hindustan ko naaz,
Ahl-e-nazar samajhte hain usko Imam-i-Hind!

This land has fashioned thousands of angels
They have proclaimed Hind before the world.
The existence of Ram makes Hind proud
The discerning eye sees in him Imam of Hind.

Having declared him Imam, Iqbal lists his three outstanding qualities: bravery, purity, and passion. Each one of these has a special place in his poetry; also, they are the highest qualities to which human beings can aspire.

This poem epitomises the seamless journey of writers and artists from one faith to another. It was the diet on which I grew up. This is the India I loved. The Secular Divine…no one can take away from me the memories of reading Iqbal's poems on Ram, Nanak, and his numerous works on the Vedas and Upanishads. Nor can any rightist diatribe erase the gentle voice of my father patiently dinning these thoughts into my youthful mind.

Inspired by patriotic poetry quoted to me by my elders, I wrote a poem but on a different note. On August 28, 1996, four years after the demolition of the Babri masjid, I wrote this poem dedicated to my India. Its title: 'Happy Birthday, Motherland!'

> Behind me
> Fifty years of Independence
> Linked with broken promises
> And before me…
> Fifty years of anarchy?
>
> I sit upon the cusp
> And watch the dreaded beast of 2047
> Slouching—its pitiless gaze on me
>
> Fifty years from now
> Will nothing ever change?
>
> Will there still be then
> The toiling, scraping, starving father
> The mother raped and ravaged everyday
> The child with bulging belly, sunken eyes
> Skin, bones and sores, pretending to be human?
> Can I still stop this cycle of despair?

I will unclasp my hands, unbend my knee
And reach out to bludgeon those
Who lie, who cheat—oppress, mislead
To whom we gave the power they wield
Against us with the barrel of a gun

And if you hold my hand in yours, my friend
Together we will haul them by the forelock
And hang them in the open marketplace
(Something rancid about money-filled suitcases
That needs purging by drawing tainted blood)
We have the power
We have the might
We need the will
To break this spiral of misery

Stretch out a billion hands
Reclaim your homeland

Then together we shall sing
Happy birthday, motherland

Seventy-five years have passed since the Partition and sixty-five years since my brush with its prickly aftermath. Today, I am much older than the 'sixty-year-old smiling public man' from W. B. Yeats's poem 'Among Schoolchildren', a poem which epitomised ageing for me.

People label me with the epithet 'prominent Indian' not 'prominent Indian Muslim'. I have travelled the length and breadth of this country proud and free with a single identity, Indian, a person whose spirit is embedded in every stone, leaf, and blade of grass of my *dharti* (soil). As expressed in Allama Iqbal's poem 'Naya Shivalaya':

Khaak e watan ka mujh ko har zarra devta hai

Every grain of dust of my country is my deity

That is (or was) my description.

Sadly, today communalism has become too deeply embedded in our daily lives. I finally understood how deeply entrenched it is, through an incident that is very personal and which, for some, may seem trivial. But it hit me hard.

On June 12, 2022, I visited a friend who was ill and had been in and out of hospital. I had known him since our school days; he was in my class from the sixth standard until the end of our schooling. Over the years we had kept in touch. His wife had also become a friend. I was leaving Delhi for a few weeks so I decided to drop in to see him before I left.

He always liked to talk politics but I veered away from the subject, knowing that his political ideology was the opposite of mine and I did not feel like arguing. We spoke about how my cousin, Anwar Abbas Anwar, and I had been brought up like twins and attended the same schools in Delhi and Mumbai. He and my host had been good friends since our days in Modern School in Delhi. Anwar had gone to Karachi many years ago and settled there with his family. For the last few years he had been ill. My friend asked if I had spoken to him recently. I told him that I would go to see him in Karachi as soon as I returned from my trip to the US and Canada. I added that I would try to go via Wagah because there was no flight from Delhi to Lahore or Karachi and going via Dubai was too expensive.

That is when decades of communal baggage gently tumbled out. My hostess said, 'You should have no difficulty going there because I am sure you have something there.'

'Something?' I asked.

'Yes. I mean a house or some place,' she said.

I could have let her remark pass, but something within me said, 'Why do you say that? What can I have there? My family stayed in India when the country was partitioned in 1947. Do you say this because I am a Muslim? Do you think all Muslims have "something" there?'

She looked embarrassed. 'I mean you used to go there quite often… so…'

'Yes, I did go there. So did Mohini Giri, Nirmala Deshpande, Kamla Bhasin; forty-three women took a bus of peace to Lahore in 2000. Except for me and one woman from Kashmir, no one was Muslim.'

There was an awkward silence. Then my host spoke. 'Syeda, you know around me there are many Muslim bastis. People from all trades live there. They are all my friends.'

In drawing rooms when I am present such conversations rarely take place. This time it was in my face. I was not only a witness but also the unwitting target. This reminded me of an incident many years ago when I was a Member of the National Commission for Women. There was a meeting at Jamia Millia Islamia University. The subject was Gender in South-Asian Perspective. The next day it was reported in a leading English newspaper. I was quoted and described as a Member of the Women's Commission from Pakistan. Later the reporter apologised in a published statement.

Once again, I recall the words of a poet which reflect my feelings more than a thousand words could do:

Gulsitan ko lahu ki zaroorat padi
Sab se pehle hii gardan hamari kati
Phir bhi kehte hain hum se ye ahl-e-chaman
Ye chaman hai hamara tumhara nahin.

When the garden needed a shower of blood
Our neck was the first to be severed
The dwellers of the garden remind us still
This garden is ours it is not yours.

~

Looking through the historical prism of seventy-five years, today I search for the kind of leadership which we looked up to in the post-Partition years. The leaders were from all communities and for all communities. We did not think in terms of Muslims for Muslims, or Hindus for Hindus. I often wonder where are the women and men, who will pull us out of the second abyss into which we have sunk post 9/11, post Gujarat 2002, and now post…post….

The self-appointed and self-anointed 'Muslim leaders' who appear in the visual and print media, are not Maulana Azad, Badshah Khan, Saifuddin Kitchlew, Abbas Tyabji, Rafi Ahmed Kidwai, and Aruna Asif Ali; sadly the 'leaders' of today hurt the very community they profess to represent. Many events come to mind. The assault on Taslima Nasrin in 2007 in Hyderabad by the MIM (Majlis Ittehadul Muslimeen) is an early incident in this self-strangulating chain. Now that party has entered the election fray in a big way. Since 2014 the assault on Muslims is unending and relentless. Islam is vilified by Hindutva brigades and we Muslims retaliate by using it to inflame passions, often distorting its basic injunctions. In all Quranic teachings about peaceful co-existence, the Prophet's own life (Sunnah) is full of incidents that show him as the most tolerant human who walked the earth. According to historians like Al-Tabari (923 AD), the Prophet would walk home through a certain street in Mecca every day after leading the prayers. Whenever he walked past a two-storied house, a basket of waste was dumped on his head. An old woman who lived in that house wanted to show her anger at his teachings by this act. The Prophet just brushed the rubbish off his person and walked on. One day when the waste was not dumped, the Prophet learnt that the woman was ill. It is recorded that he walked up to her bedside to offer help. Islam enjoins '*Lakum dinakum walia din*,' meaning 'To you, your Faith, to me, my Faith.'

I was just four years old at the time of Partition. I was in Pune with my parents and sisters, hence I was relatively insulated from the killings in Punjab and Delhi. Men and women of my family and our friends who stayed back decided to devote themselves to lifting the morale of those Muslims who were left to pick up broken lives in their ravaged hometowns. As a child, I saw the trauma of Indian Muslims. They took a long time to come out of the fear and insecurity of post-Partition India. Despite the regular communal flare-ups, they struggled to find their way into the mainstream of life. They received confidence and solace from Mahatma Gandhi, Pandit Jawaharlal Nehru, Maulana Azad. They also found mentors such as Dr Zakir Husain and Rafi Ahmed Kidwai, educationists like my father K.G. Saiyidain and philosophers like Dr Abid Husain, who pulled them out of despair into the new emerging paradigm of the nation. With stern secularists at the helm, communal incidents remained subdued at least for the first decade. My uncle, Dr Abid Husain, one of the triumvirates who established Jamia Millia Islamia, started a weekly journal, *Nai Roshini*, to encourage Muslims to become partners in building a new India. My uncle and mentor, K.A. Abbas, journalist and filmmaker, used films as a medium for social reform. His subjects ranged from food security (*Dharti ke Lal*), water scarcity (*Do Boond Painni*), left-wing extremism (*The Naxalites*), labour unrest (*Rahi*), displacement (*Sheher aur Sapna*), casteism (*Char Dil Char Rahein*) to name a few.

In school, my 'Muslimness' never came in the way of singing 'Hindu' prayers during Assembly with the same fervour as Allama Iqbal's '*Lab pe aati hai dua ban ke tamanna meri*'. My Muslimness never came in the way of attending the iconic Narendra Sharma's dance classes. Enriched with liberal education of the finest kind from artists like Kanwal and Devyani Krishna, and poetry and theatre from the superb educator, Ved Vyas, and the one and only Mr Kapur (MNK), legendary principal of Modern School and the presiding deity of India's *Ganga Jamuni Tehzeeb* (a *sangam* or co-mingling where Islam and Hinduism 'give and take'), I went into the world armed with confidence and humility. My world thus learnt, lasted for thirty years—first as a student, second as a wife and mother. After moving to Canada in 1967, I returned to India in 1984 filled with fervour and determination to 'give back' to my homeland. I was comfortable in the belief that after many years in foreign climes, I had returned home where the bones of my loved ones were in nearby *qabristans* (graveyards). For me, *Ghar Wapsi* meant just that.

~

The first serious blow to my pride at being Indian was dealt by the *shahadat* (martyrdom) of Babri Masjid on December 6, 1992. Its blow-by-blow demolition was watched by the Prime Minister, Narasimha Rao, in Delhi and Chief Minister Kalyan Singh in Lucknow; the Centre and the State, both under oath to protect the religious places of all communities. PM Narasimha Rao watched the demolition on TV screens from 7 Race Course Road in Delhi and CM Kalyan Singh, from his bungalow on Kalidas Marg in Lucknow.

I watched as stroke by stroke, Kar Sevaks did what they did. Youths with orange headbands stood atop the dome, their pickaxes held up for TV cameras, before thrusting them into the stubborn fifteenth century stone. Media persons stood at the base of the mosque sending minute-by-minute news bites. Leaders reached the spot to be seen, to cheer, and to lead the mobs. Triumph was written all over the faces of three of them. They are engraved in my mind: L.K. Advani, Uma Bharati, and Murli Manohar Joshi.

Twenty-eight years later, these people have become too old and too vulnerable to infection, to help lay the first stone of the Ram Mandir. I wonder what they must be feeling now, sitting sequestered in their homes. Iqbal Ansari, son of the original litigant Hashim Ansari (now deceased) was also invited to the grand ceremony held on January 22, 2024. I will attend, he said. Gayatri Devi, who lives close to the mandir, was also determined to go but for a different reason—to give peace to the soul of her husband who fell to *andha dhund* (blind or random) police firing during the demolition.

I recall the day after the demolition, December 7, 1992, when I tried to drive myself to work. Jamia was then a sleepy place, a university campus that was identified as a 'Muslim' institution. At a gurudwara near my house, I was stopped by random groups of young men who did not ask about my religion or harm me but warned me of *khatra* (danger) and asked me to turn back.

As I drove back, I thought of Jamia's Silver Jubilee in 1920, when Mahatma Gandhi, Jawaharlal Nehru, and Maulana Azad sat on a wooden stage, side-by-side with Jamia's founders, Dr Zakir Husain, Prof Mohammad Mujeeb, and Dr Abid Husain, and lauded the secular character of an institution that called itself Jamia Millia Islamia.

Each stroke of the pickaxe was a blow to that secular character which was the credo of each person present on that stage. With the razing of Babri, the country stepped on the path that would lead a decade later to Gujarat in 2002, to lynchings, pogroms, riots, killings, incarceration, to the Ayodhya Judgment 2019, and finally to the Bhoomi Pujan. The list goes on.

Ramchandra Gandhi, the grandson of Mahatma Gandhi, wrote a small book called *Sita's Kitchen: A Testimony of Faith and Inquiry*[1] after he visited the site and saw a lowly *belan* and *chakla* (rolling pin and board) marking the spot which read, 'Janmasthan Sita-ki-Rasoi' which means 'Birthplace: Sita's Kitchen'. Where was this *rasoi*? What is real? What is mythical? It's all *astha* (faith), we are told. Whether you believe or you don't, one just has to watch one's words and actions. A slight slip can stamp you anti-national, especially if you are a Muslim.

~

The second blow was dealt by the Gujarat 2002 riots. The then Chief Minister of Gujarat and current Prime Minister of India,

Narendra Modi, watched over the massacre of Muslims from his imperious perch. The image of Qutubuddin Ansari, begging for life with folded hands before the raging Bajrangi mob, will live in public memory long after all perpetrators and victims are dead. That morning when we opened our eyes we saw in most newspapers the face of this man. His eyes were glazed with fear and tears. Who was he imploring? His assailants or the police? One paper called him a 'Muslim seeking mercy from the rioters'; another said he was a 'resident of Ahmedabad imploring the police to save him'. His eyes will haunt me until my dying day, he may have been a Hindu, a Sikh or a Christian, he may have been my son, my brother, my next-door neighbour. Having lost their lives and livelihoods, the surviving Muslims of Gujarat lived in relief camps and ghettos through the years following 2002. They still remain on edge.

I was part of a six-member team of women that visited the broken city days after the carnage which broke loose unabated and unchecked, from March 27 to March 31, 2002. We visited seven relief camps in both rural and urban areas (Ahmedabad, Kheda, Vadodra, Sabarkantha, and Panchmahals districts) and spoke to a large number of women survivors. We also spoke to activists, members of the media, administrators, and leaders of the BJP. We were shaken and numbed by the scale and brutality of the violence. Despite reading news reports, we were unprepared for what we saw and heard. We found compelling evidence of the most extreme form of sexual violence against women during the first few days of the carnage. The violence against the Muslim community was pre-planned, organised, and targeted and the crimes against women were grossly under-reported. For me, these incidents and the ghosts of Gujarat refuse to go away; they persist in my mindscape.

Ehsan Jafri, former Congress Member of Parliament, was seventy-six years old in 2002. His house was surrounded by a mob that was baying for Muslim blood. His fault? That he had chosen not to move into a Muslim ghetto and remained in a mixed Hindu-Muslim neighbourhood, and that a few weeks ago he had campaigned against the party in power in his state, specifically against the CM. For six hours he called the police, his influential friends, Congress colleagues, and even the Chief Minister, begging for help to save his family and those who had come to his house seeking protection. No one came. Jafri and all those who had rushed for protection to his home, were consumed by the raging mob and blazing fire. Over several hours, with police standing by, a mob lynched and burnt Ehsan Jafri, along with his family members and neighbours, forty in total. Today, twenty-two years later, the country is ruled by the dispensation that supervised the lynching and killing of Ehsan Jafri and over 1,000 Muslims within seventy-two hours. In 2022, at a public tribunal, Ehsan's son Tanvir deposed before a large gathering. Everyone's eyes were moist after his testimony.

There was also the story of Juzar S. Bandukwala, a physics professor from Maharaja S. Sayajirao University of Baroda. The attack on his house was led by an aspirant for a ticket to the Assembly, a BJP corporator. Bandukwala's cardinal sin was having campaigned during the last election for one Prajapati, an opposition candidate from Sayajigunj constituency, who won with the support of Muslim votes. The professor heard the police say to the mob, 'You have fifteen minutes to come through the window and do what you want.' Professor Bandukwala jumped out of a window and hid in a neighbour's house while his house was ransacked and all his possessions smashed. All this carnage was in the name of revenge for Godhra. The *Gujarat Sandesh* headlines screamed, '*Khoon ka badla khoon*'.

'*Jo hum sey takraey ga*/*choor choor ho jaega*', anyone who dares to oppose us will be smashed to smithereens. So went the anthem of the juggernaut which was unleashed by the then Home Minister L.K. Advani when in the early 1990s he had sallied forth on his Rath

Yatra exhorting innocent masses to partake in his 'holy' mission. Today what his oath unleashed has spun out of control; no one knows when and how this ghoul will stop its dance of death.

~

Globally, after 9/11,[2] Islam became identified with terror and Muslim boys were freely branded terrorists and anti-nationals. Kashmir, as always, was smouldering, it was a slow, consistent, and never-ending fire. Then came Muzaffarnagar[3] in 2013, another Muslim carnage. The corollary to demonising Islam was the giant wave of the BJP victory in 2014.

Khushwant Singh in his book *Need for a New Religion in India*[4] wrote on the eve of the General Elections in 1991, 'What matters most is whether or not India will continue to remain a secular state committed to socialism or become a Hindu Rashtra wearing a secular mask with an agenda of its own, including building a mammoth Ram Mandir at Ayodhya, preserving the Ram Setu and other relics associated with Hinduism. The choice is between an India of the dreams of Mahatma Gandhi and Jawaharlal Nehru on the one side (secular), and those of Vir Savarkar and Guru Golwalkar on the other (Hindutva)… We have to choose between remaining what we are or opting to become a Hindu Rashtra.'

For fifteen years, I worked on various national bodies, including apex bodies like the National Commission for Women and the Planning Commission. The only way I could function was to be given a free hand to work for all Indians regardless of their gender, caste, class, religion, or ethnicity. Dalits of Dharmapuri, Kathodis of Udaipur, Muslims of Mewat, and Gonds of Bilaspur; all of them were my equal concern; they were my sisters and brothers. I, a Muslim woman, identified myself with a Dalit, a Gond, a Bhil; many identities roiled inside my being.

However, today my world crashes around me each day when I read the news which captures random voices across the country, voices which direct me to go to Pakistan or to a Qabristan. This directive or invective is ghettoising the world into exclusion enclaves. Along with this message are bands who appear with weapons to show that these slogans are not empty threats. Groups of middle-class women and youths go from door to door asking for donations for the Ram temple. Muslims are watched and their response to the door-knocks is noted. Police are duty bound to protect those who are threatened but they often quietly look on; sometimes they go a step further and join the marauders. Today, I am living in an India I cannot recognise anymore.

Violence and failure are being hidden behind a rhetoric of false nationalism. The nationalism that Mahatma Gandhi talked about, which Jawaharlal Nehru professed, which Maulana Azad spoke time and again, has been expunged from textbooks and is parallely being expunged from collective memory.

The question before hate merchants is what to do with us Muslims. This huge population of *dadhi-topi* (beards and skull caps). All cannot be hacked and burnt, drowned, or ethnically cleansed. But they can be beaten into submission, therefore hate crimes are allowed a free run.

The tsunami of violence continues to hit the country. Back in 2007, I visited Rajsamund in Rajasthan. I was dreaming of turning it into a tourist circuit. My animated talks with district officials in the evenings after spending the day at the many scenic spots in the region were promising. All that seems like a distant dream now. In 2021, the bones of a migrant labourer, Afrazul Islam, were placed in a kafan in Malda in West Bengal. It was a hate gift from Rajsamund—Afrazul had been hacked to death by Shambhu Lal Regar, an unemployed marble worker from the district, who then uploaded a chilling video of himself hacking Afrazul to death, and circulated it on social media.

Between September 15 and 19, 2008, I visited Mayurbhanj, a tribal district in Odisha, to review the NRHM (National Rural Health Mission) and malnutrition situation, especially among tribal children. I was also on a tribunal on hunger in Odisha organised by a Supreme Court Commission on Right to Food. But all this got overtaken by the issue of the killing fields of Kandhamal[5] and the sufferings of the Christians at the hands of Hindu tribals, instigated by the BJP, the Bajrang Dal, and the Vishva Hindu Parishad.

I interacted with residents of the relief camp at Bhubaneshwar which housed women, men, and children from thirty-five villages, there were 437 in all. I met voluntary organisations and other victims who had escaped the carnage but were not in the camps. I also met some eminent citizens (academics, professionals and journalists) who had returned from a visit to the worst affected sites in Kandhamal the night before. All this happened in one day; the next morning I left for Mayurbhanj. In Mayurbhanj, when I stood in what had been the home of Reverend Graham Staines,[6] the Australian missionary, I realised what had really happened in Kandhamal and how deep the roots of this malaise were. Staines had been working in Odisha since 1965 as part of an evangelical missionary organisation, the Mayurbhanj Leprosy Home, caring for people who had leprosy and looking after the tribals in the area who lived in abject poverty. The right-wing Hindu group, the Bajrang Dal, claimed that Staines and his wife were forcibly converting tribals to Christianity, and though no evidence of this was ever found, on the night of January 22, 1999, he and his two sons, aged ten and six, were burnt alive in the station wagon in which they were sleeping on their way back from the village of Keonjhar.

On the wall of Staines' cottage in the Leprosy Ashram was his photograph in a kurta pyjama, smiling with his arms wrapped around his two small boys, Philip and Timothy. Someone handed me a slim paperback that bore the title *Burnt Alive*. Outside there was torrential rain. It was as if the universe was awash with tears at the tandav of violence which had been unleashed on innocents; violence which knows no boundary, no season, and no reason. Kandhamal had spawned copycats all over the country—Koraput, Chikmanglur, Jabalpur, and Mangalore. Watching the horrible atrocities against Christians, I thought of the Grey Nuns who were my first teachers in school. My professor from the University of Alberta, Dr Marion Norman, herself from the University of Chicago, and a Loretto nun, under whose watchful eye I completed my PhD.

Around the same time, in my own neighbourhood of Jamia, two 'alleged militants' Atif and Sajid were gunned down in an encounter on September 19, 2008, by the police in Batla House, Jamia Nagar. It was also the month of Ramadan. Fasting brought its own sense of both hardship and fulfilment, but this Ramadan brought violence right to my doorstep in Jamia.

Jamia is a large area with more than twenty residential bastis, mostly middle and lower-class Muslims. One basti, closest to my house, is Batla House, described in media reports as an 'epicentre of terror'.

Over time I have seen the changing face of Jamia—from a small band of teachers and students where everyone knew everyone, it has become a big university in every sense of the word; a happening place where the academic and cultural world of the capital began to converge. Around it grew many bastis to which Muslims moved from all over Delhi, sometimes by choice, sometimes because landlords forced them to do so. Its gullies and mohallas grew exponentially. Densely populated, in some quarters it began to be called 'mini Pakistan'. Civic amenities remained next to nil. Garbage dumps were ubiquitous. Private schools and private clinics began mushrooming while public institutions lagged far behind.

There was another change. From a haven of peace and learning, it started transforming into an area of struggle and strife. Strikes by students, road accidents, agitations for *bijli-pani* (electricity and water), and more recently the watering ground for gun-toting armed police. Jamia turned into a microcosm of the macro violence in the country.

Kaifi Azmi wrote:

> *Basti mein apni Hindu o Muslim jo bas gaye*
> *Insaan ki shakl dekhne ko hum taras gaye!*
>
> In our neighbourhood since Muslims and Hindus began living
> We longed to see the face of just ordinary humans.

On October 3, 2008, fourteen days after Atif and Sajid were killed in the Batla House encounter, their Ghaibana Namaz (funeral prayers) were read in the qabristan of Batla House where thousands of mourners wearing black armbands participated and raised protest.

Talking to neighbours and friends and reading Urdu newspapers, I understood the prevailing desperation all around me. This piece from the Urdu press sums up the mood: 'Muslims are now being accused of even killing Muslims; whether it is Modasa, Malegaon, Phool Mandi, and Mehrauli. Administrators and police have decided—behind every blast is a Muslim "hand" or "module". Sometimes ISI, sometimes Lashkar-e-Taiba or Indian Mujahideen. Most police persons feel that a Muslim when delivered from his mother's womb is a terrorist. Proof or no proof, Muslim youth are thrust into jails. Media applauds police action and important centres of learning like Azamgarh are branded "nurseries of terrorism". Diatribes are hurled; "Muslim children being indoctrinated! Time for the Ummah to do *Atma Manthan*!"'

Regarding the encounter of Atif and Sajid, there is no one in these bastis of over two lakh people who believes the police version. Two weeks after the encounter, a jaloos of ten to fifteen thousand ordinary women and men (Hindus, Sikhs, Christians, and a few Muslims) was taken out on Eid on October 1, 2008. They marched from Jantar Mantar to Gandhi Samadhi protesting against the false allegations against Christians and Muslims. The media blocked the event. The media, which had kept a watchful eye on governments, from Indira Gandhi to Rajiv Gandhi to Vajpayee, has simply looked the other way in the past few years.

I have tried to put myself in the place of all the actors in this national tragedy. Incidents of terrorism and many-pronged violence are anchored in communalism, caste, and ethnicity. The political parties have a single agenda and their clock is ticking. The beat constable with all his past baggage has a job to do. The youth, the mother, the car mechanic, the street vendor, and the ragpicker, all are victims of terror. One violent incident on the heels of another; where does one run?

In 'Ode to a Nightingale', John Keats wrote:

> My heart aches and a drowsy numbness pains my sense
> As though of hemlock I have drunk

As an undergrad at Delhi University I read the poem for the first time, its intense romanticism sent me into a trance. Five decades later its words have become embedded in my mind but it leaves me in a different kind of trance; albeit with the same sip of hemlock.

In English news, the expression 'beaten to death' is used whereas in Hindi/Urdu media, it is '*peet peet kar maar daala*'. These expressions refer to the poorest Muslims who are caught and killed for 'cattle-related crimes'. Another crime for which killing is fair game is 'daring to love'. Killing is fair retribution for any Muslim man who dares to fall in love with, much less marry, a Hindu. It is taken for granted that conversion to Islam is the only motive! Whether it is the mutilation of the bodies of jawans at the Pakistan border, the ISIS terror modules that keep cropping up every few days, or the violence in Islamic countries, invariably I am the one who feels guilty. The same guilt covers millions like me with shame. I am pinned on the wall for all ills including the ignorant indictment of the Muslim Personal Law. In recent times, it is the hijab which has come under fire as an identity marker which is now being universally targeted.

Day after day, I live out these lines of the poet Faiz Ahmed Faiz:

Nisaar mein teri galiyon pe ai watan ke jahan
Chali hai rasm ke koi ne sar uttha ke chaley
Jo koi chahney wala tawaaf ko nikley
Nazar jhuka ke chaley jism o jaan bacha ke chaley

My land! My adored land
A new ritual has come into force
That no one will walk with head held high
If a devotee comes for Parikrama
His eye should be glued to the ground
His body and soul held furtively.

~

The Urdu media headlines carry the news from Bulandshahar: '*Maummar aadmi ko peet peet kar maut ke ghaat utaar diya*' that is, 'Elderly man beaten to death in Bulandshahar.' In the same order, the next headline: '*Assam mein mavaishi chori ke ilzaam mein do Muslim naujawanon ka peet peet kar qatl*' ('Two cattle thieves lynched in Assam'). Another story is from Pahasu Tehsil in Bulandshahar where a Hindu girl and Muslim boy eloped. Members of Hindu Yuva Wahini had taken the boy's uncle Ghulam Mohammad to a wooded area and beat him to death. In Assam's Naugaon, two young men are accused of stealing cattle. Abu Hanifa and Riyazuddin Ali are chased and severely beaten up with lathis by villagers. By the time the police rushed them to hospital they were dead. Very quickly such news fades away, whether Golaghat or Bulandshahar. When slashing and slaying take place, newsreels momentarily go into a bloody spin but it is soon forgotten. Can anyone now recall the lynching of 'cattle stealers in Assam's Golaghat'?

Now in 2024, I am compelled to say that my primary identity has become that of a Muslim woman. I was brought up in a totally different *mahaul* (atmosphere) where I learnt to live joyously with many parallel identities within me: Muslim, Indian, woman, and a few more. These multiple identities, I was taught by my elders, were a matter of pride and celebration. My love for India remained intact despite brushes with communal incidents right from the 1950s. I did not know the word Hindutva then; post-1992, it is branded deeper and deeper in my brain.

That home in which I grew up now seems like a fading story. Something which has died many deaths with the death of the *zamir* (conscience) of middle-class Gujarat and many other states which are perched on the communal precipice. I do believe that there would be many beautiful stories like K.A. Abbas's 'Sardarji' (where a Sikh at the risk of his life rescues a Muslim family from a bloodthirsty mob) happening even now in every state. Despite the pitched battles raging in cities, despite the lynching of the poor and the wretched, there are the heroic women and men quietly watching out for any life they can save. This is the India in which I as a Muslim, as a woman, and as a mother still have hope, however dim it has become now.

Despite the connivance and collusion of the government, despite the pat excuses and the blame—a game which no one believes anymore—despite the glib excuses given by politicians and bureaucrats in the full glare of television cameras, there is still hope in the masses of women and men still untouched by the communal poison, who may one day rise in a mighty wave, who knows?

In 2020, the student-led movement was started. It was spontaneous—to save India from the curse of CAA (Citizenship Amendment Act)[7] and NRC (National Register of Citizens). In the capital, Jamia was the hub. On a certain day, for five hours thousands of students, activists and local people were tear-gassed, lathi-charged, hounded, and chased. The state used all its repressive machinery to crush the movement. With wet pieces of cloth on their faces the youth tried to brave the onslaught. Suddenly hordes of them ran back in a frenzy while being chased by armed attackers. Girls, boys, Hindus, Muslims, Sikhs, and Christians from Jamia and elsewhere were pitted against the brutality unleashed by the state. Some of the injured were rushed to Holy Family Hospital, and more than 100 were herded into police vans. This peaceful demonstration, now bloodied, was raging within a few metres of my house. Despite the blood-letting, my spirit soared. I felt vibrant in my old age because I watched the students as they refused to budge from their stand. Let victory be theirs, I prayed.

In our college days, I used to swear by a poem by W.B. Yeats, the poet and revolutionary, it was called 'The Second Coming'. Today it is a prophetic voice, about Ahmedabad, Muzaffarnagar, Hashimpura, Maliana, and many such places in this nation where once there was room for all faiths:

> Turning and turning in a widening gyre
> The falcon cannot hear the falconer
> Things fall apart; the centre cannot hold
> Mere anarchy is loosed upon the world
> The blood-dimmed tide is loosed and everywhere
> The ceremony of innocence is drowned
> The best lack all conviction, while the worst
> Are full of passionate intensity

From this cosmic chaos, Yeats predicted in this poem, a Second Coming. In a Christian context, it is the Second Coming of Christ. I cannot predict like the Irishman did, but I pray to the Supreme Power of all faiths that from the ashes of these communal carnages will rise a phoenix. This immortal and mythical bird symbolises the good and the honest. My prayer is that it will exhume the poison from the earth, the air, and the oceans in and around this land. This will be The Second Coming.

2

Mirror to the Past

My Ancestors

In 622 AD, when his enemies from his own clan, the Quraish, hounded the Prophet out of Mecca, he performed Hejrat to Medina and from that year commenced the Islamic calendar. When the Prophet arrived in Medina there was much rejoicing in the city. 'At which door will he disembark?' was the question whispered among the adoring crowd. The Prophet, ever kind, ever sagacious, said simply, 'I will enter the door where my camel sits.' Every man and woman in the crowd prayed that the camel would choose their threshold. The animal, fatigued from the long journey, circled the city and folded its legs before the humble dwelling of Abu Ayyub Ansari. That blessed Medinite was my ancestor, whose name is recorded in the earliest Islamic history. Our lineage is narrated in the 'Shahnama-e-Islam', a long poem written by the poet Hafeez Jalandhari in 1929.

Below is the scene from 'Shahnama-e-Islam'. The Prophet performs Hejrat and enters Medina. His camel stops before the house of Abu Ayyub Ansari:

Sahaba se kaha jab tak na ho masjid ki tayyari
Hamare mezbaan honge Abu Ayyub Ansari
Falak ne rashk se dekha us Ansari ki qismat ko
Abu Ayyub ghar mein le gaye saamaan e rehmat ko

The Prophet addresses the crowd which is clamouring to host him.

> He told his companions until the mosque is laid
> Our host will be Abu Ayyub Ansari
> The skies looked with envy at the kismet of Ansari
> Who ushered Allah's blessing into his humble home.

I had first heard and then read this story in numerous oral and written accounts by several family members, most notably my father, my uncle K.A. Abbas, and my father's sister, Saliha Abid Husain. I also read about it in the Prophet's biographies, one of them by Lesley Hazelton.[8] The conclusive proof was shown to me by my father's cousin from Lahore, Dr Shubbar Hasan. His most prized possession was a family *Shajra* tracing our ancestry from the first human couple, Hazrat Adam and Hazrat Hawwa (Adam and Eve). Every time I visited him, he took it out of his safe and allowed me ziarat of the *Shajra*. He allowed me to scan my family's portion, one page of the total sixty pages. Dr Shubbar passed away five years ago, I have no doubt that the *Shajra* has been safely preserved by his children. I learnt that this same ancestor Abu Ayyub Ansari, became a close companion of the Prophet. He enjoyed a privilege that many of the Ansaar (Muslim residents of Medina who welcomed Muslims from Mecca), craved for. He also had a distinguished military career, which brought him fame. Abu Ayyub was one of the men who fought valiantly outside the walls of Constantinople during the first Arab Siege in 674-678 AD. I was also told by Dr Shubbar and his brother, Dr Mubashir Hasan (former Finance Minister of Pakistan), that this ancestor's descendant, Khwaja Abdullah Pir e Herat, became the most revered Sufi of Istanbul. Many years later, I resurrected Abu Ayyub Ansari's *Munajaat* (Prayers) from my archives. In 2022, it was published as *Invocations and Prayers of Khwaja Abdullah Ansari*.[9]

In 2007, while I was visiting Kabul, Zelmai Rassoul, advisor to

President Karzai, presented me with a book of photographs of Herat monuments, *Herat Deroz Imroz* (Herat Yesterday Today) edited by Majid Fadaeian and Reza Nazarahari. There, in shades of blue and turquoise was the mausoleum of Khwaja Abdullah, my ancestor. This monument of the 'Old Man of Herat' is now a UNESCO-preserved monument. In its stunning photographs, devotees are seen praying at the mausoleum. The photographs created in me a desire to see the monument for myself, but despite several requests, I could not prevail upon my hosts to let me go there. I have written an account of this, my one and only journey to Afghanistan.

From the lineage of Khwaja Abdullah came Merak Shah, Badshah-e-Herat. Begum Saliha Abid Husain, my aunt, in her classic book, *Yaadgaar-e-Hali* refers to him as 'Farmaanrava-e-Herat' (Sovereign of Herat). His son Khwaja Malik Ali decided to undertake the long and arduous journey to Hindustan to spread the word of Islam and the Sufi Tariqah (Sufi way). His journey took him to Panipat, then part of Punjab. This was in the mid-twelfth century during the reign of Sultan Ghiyasuddin Balban of the Delhi Sultanate, who was known for his great regard for scholars and ashraaf from Iran and Turkestan. At that time, another Sufi scholar and teacher, Hazrat Makhdum Shah, had already settled in Panipat.

Given the fact that these descendants of Pir-e-Herat, themselves were fountainheads of wisdom and learning, the Sultan gifted them the most fertile lands in the pargana of Panipat and revenue lands in the district which would support their scholarly pursuits as well as land within the city of Panipat for residential purposes. He also appointed them qazis, narkh-e-bazaar (controllers of market prices), and keepers of shrines (there were many shrines) and the responsibility to read the Eid Khutbas. In the chronicle, *Hayat-e-Nau Risala Makhzan* (Hali Muslim School, Panipat, 1933), the editor, Shaikh Badrul Islam Fazli, writes: 'It seems the ruler gave Khwaja Malik Ali all of Panipat as Jagir.'

Many decades later, in 2013, I visited Jeddah as part of an official delegation appointed by Justice Aftab Alam on behalf of the Supreme Court of India to draw up a plan for the accommodation of Hajj pilgrims. I almost did not make it. The night before I was to leave for Jeddah, I fell sick. I had a raging fever and spent most of the night vomiting. Should I go and make a nuisance of myself? Or should I call it off, the choice was more agonising than the illness. 'Syeda, go ahead, you will be fine'—my friend and guiding light Dr Qasim's assurance made up my mind. I placed his medicines in my handbag and shakily left for the airport. I slept all the way to Jeddah. Two biscuit crackers were all I ate and by the time we touched down, I had gotten over whatever sickness I had.

I was standing before the first House of God ready to begin my *tawaaf* (circumambulation). I, a child of the man who wrote *Musaddas-e-Hali*, stood there reciting the lines:

> *Utar kar Hira se soo e quom aaya*
> *Aur ek nuskha-e-cheemia saath laya*
>
> Descending from Hira stood facing the quom
> Proverbial touchstone he brought in this form

I was looking at Khana-e-Ka'aba for the first time in my life. From the window of my hotel room on the twentieth floor I saw the scene which I have no words to adequately describe. There was the black cloth-covered perfect cube structure around which thousands of small human figures were moving in an endless tawaaf. Their movement never ceased. For the next two days, I was witness to this human wave moving every moment of the day and night. Sometimes I too was part of this wave; sometimes I was its *shahid* (witness). It occurred to me that perhaps this was the moment when my life should come to an end, it is said that the best time to die is in the precincts of the Haram Sharif.

The huge crowds were daunting; but while I was overawed, my

legs were steady and I was not scared. Around me were men and women of all ages, from all parts of the world. It struck me that every single face was uncovered, people were moving shoulder to shoulder with one another, words of prayer on their lips. I especially noticed men and women from Africa, from East and West Asia, and from South Asia. There were old people in wheelchairs, there were children holding onto their parents, there were infants carried by their fathers and mothers, and there were groups of women holding each other. All wore identical clothing, the men in lungis and chador; both unstitched. Women wore a black abaya which covered them from head to toe, and a black hijab or head scarf, leaving their faces uncovered.

I had always dreamt of performing the Haj or the Umra with my children: my two sons and my daughter. None of them were there. But I was blessed with four 'sons' who took me through the tawaaf like guardian angels. One was a young lawyer who had accompanied me from Delhi, another was the Deputy Counsel General of India, and the other two were young men from the Haj Consulate. One or another was at my side throughout the tawaaf and later on, at the Sai'ee. At the Sai'ee, we are required to follow the route of Hazrat Hajra,[10] when she ran back and forth between two mountains, the Safa and Marwah, looking for water for her newborn infant, Hazrat Ismail. Following her trail, we are required to run on the very same stretch that she ran while making sure that the child remained within her visual range. Finally, a water spring began to bubble in the desert where the child Ismail had kicked the earth with his little heels. The spring which gushed forth became known as *zamzam,* eternal water which has never dried despite the passage of thousands of years. Over the course of the walk which we calculated was six kilometres, there was a chair to sit on when I felt tired and whenever I was thirsty there was aab-e-zamzam to drink.

The mini world of the KSA (Kingdom of Saudi Arabia)

meanwhile swirled around me. It was a world where unlike, in the Ka'aba precincts, the men and women were in strictly divided worlds. It struck me that women were an undifferentiated mass of humanity. Instead of individuals, they were black-veiled forms gliding around the polished floors surrounding the Haram. While the men were beautifully dressed either in traditional white and gold abayas or western suits or casuals; the only visible part of the black-veiled women were their eyes. In restaurants, malls, and on the roads, there was no colour for the women, little girls, and toddlers. In the House of God, their faces were uncovered but not so in the House of Man. But the holy city of Medina which I visited next, as is customary, is another story. It was love that took me there while it was longing that took me to Makkah (Mecca). In Medina, I searched for my roots, the home of my ancestor.

I was told that all the landmarks of that historic arrival of the Prophet are within the precincts of the Masjid-e-Nabavi, close to the place where the Prophet is buried. Being a woman, I could not get close to the green dome which covers the graves of the Prophet and his companions. But I was given a sign that this was indeed my homecoming. My hotel overlooked the Medina Haram. The number of my room happened to be the year of my birth.

There it was, the year of my birth engraved on the door. Did I need any more benediction?

3

Growing Up

I was born in the land of lakes and deodars on October 1, 1942. Since both my parents were non-Kashmiris I could not stake my claim as a state subject, that privilege given only to those who were permanently settled in Jammu and Kashmir, as it was then,[11] before 1942.

My birth caused disappointment all around. At the time of delivery, instead of being at her maternal home, my mother was in Srinagar where my father was Mushir-e-Taleem (Director of Education). I was born at home, with the help of a British doctor, Mrs 'Gabbey'. This is the name I recall, though I suspect this was a 'desi' take on the English original. Despite prayers, supplications, charms, and amulets showered on my mother, I was disobliging enough to be born as her fourth girl. I am told that on the day of my birth, the men of my family were glued to the radio, which was relaying war news. An attendant brought me out of the delivery room wrapped in a blue towel. 'It's a girl!' Dr Gabbey announced to no one in particular. A stony silence greeted the announcement. Many years later, I was told that my father was pleased and made it a point to show it but my mother just covered her face with her dupatta and turned away from the doctor and her newborn. She had once again proven herself incapable of bearing a male child. It was a personal setback since her only brother's wife had already borne him three sons. Two were still to come; making it a total of five boys on that side of the family. That evening some visitors came to offer their sympathies. I also heard that a highly educated and respected 'Inspectress of Schools' called Mrs Jalaluddin swooned with grief when she learnt about my gender.

My family came to live in Delhi in 1951. Before moving to Delhi, my father had served as the Educational Advisor in Bombay State for a couple of years. At the time, Maulana Azad was independent India's first Education Minister and was looking for the best minds to formulate the country's education policy. He wrote to B.G. Kher, Chief Minister of Bombay State, requesting that he spare my father for the Government of India since education needed special nurturing.

Most of our relatives had been forcibly sent to Pakistan after our ancestral town, Panipat, had been emptied of all Muslims by government edict during the communal killings of 1947. My paternal grandmother hand-wrote a note and stuck it to her door. 'We are leaving for a few days to visit my son (Khwaja Ahmad Abbas) in Bombay. We will be back soon to our home'. They had lived in that city for eight centuries. For our family, that day marked the end of their watan, their homeland, Panipat. All this I had heard from elders. My father along with his brothers and sisters, under the influence of Mahatma Gandhi, Maulana Azad, Jawaharlal Nehru, and Zakir Husain, decided to stay in India despite some attractive offers from Pakistan.

In 1947, when they left, Panipat was a flourishing *qasba* (district) of Punjab, with a large population of Muslims. The distinguishing feature of this cultured, Sufi-dominated town was the primacy of women. Our homes were known by the name of the woman of the house, for example, *Bi Maimuna ki Haveli* (much later, I was pleasantly surprised to see the same formulation in Marrakesh: '*Riad dar Maimuna*'). My mother and my aunts' decision to remove their burqa was accepted and respected by the men of the family. These

Panipat women were agents of their own fate. When several of them reached Pakistan, they did not revert to the veil. Nor did anyone ask them to wear or remove it; neither the state nor the family.

I grew up in a country where families had been cleaved by Partition. I watched my buzurgs long for their loved ones who were now on the 'other side'. My generation across the divide would have witnessed the same longing in their elders. In my life, I have witnessed seven decades of this separation during which two generations have passed away. Deaths, births, marriages, and festivals went by minus those from 'the other side'. Neatly handwritten letters expressing longing and pain were sent from both sides.

Like the protagonist of the poet T.S. Eliot's 'The Love Song of J. Alfred Prufrock', I too have been a witness to all:

> For I have known them all already, known them all:
> Have known the evenings, mornings, afternoons,
> I have measured out my life with coffee spoons.

In Delhi, my parents admitted me first to the Convent of Jesus and Mary for three years and then to Modern School. Prior to Modern School, my schooling was a subject of continued controversy between my parents. My mother preferred to send me to a convent school where I would be educated under the watchful eye of the nuns and imbibe discipline and high moral values. Not that I was in any way a wild child, but that was her strict feudal outlook on education. My father, being a liberal educationist, wanted to see me in a co-educational school, especially where academic and extra-curricular activities were given equal emphasis. I recall that when we lived in Bombay, I had to attend two schools to fulfil the requirements of both parents. I attended J.B. Petit School in the forenoon and Gamadhiya School in the afternoon. That proved too much for me and ultimately even for my parents, so I was sent to Alexandra School, which was closer to my house.

In Delhi, we were provided sarkari accommodation in Sujan Singh Park, a mixed neighbourhood consisting of old residents and newcomers from West Punjab. I started playing in the park with the neighbourhood children. One day someone asked me the question which I had learnt to dread due to my reading of new Urdu writings born of the Partition trauma of writers and poets. One of the girls asked, 'What caste are you?' So far I had successfully avoided the issue by mumbling my name. But now I was caught.

When the children discovered that I was a Muslim by 'caste', they said that no one would play with me. The humiliation of having to go home and relate this to my father still rankles. Meanwhile, the children's grapevine sent the word around that there was a Muslim girl in their midst who was not to be played with. Some days later, a Sikh neighbour came calling on us with his little daughter. 'Sati will play with you,' he said. She was to become my one and only and best friend at the time. Thus, the tragedy of total ostracism was averted. But my father suggested that while the incident was still fresh, I write it up as a story for the children's section of the magazine, *Shankar's Weekly*. I called my story 'You Have to Learn to Make Friends'. A young Argentinian artist from Buenos Aires, Brigitte Frankfurther, read it and it moved her greatly. She took up her brush, illustrated it, and sent it to me as a little book. With these beautiful illustrations, the book was published by Rajkamal Prakashan. In 1951, this little book won the Jawaharlal Nehru Prize in the International Writing Contest of *Shankar's Weekly* and created a mini storm. It was translated into several languages and published in many countries, including the UNESCO Courier. It was also quoted in the Institute of Social Sciences in a discussion on 'Techniques of Understanding'. Dr Zakir Husain, a close family friend and mentor, wrote a foreword for it that still encapsulates the trauma, the dilemma, and the anguish of the Indian Muslim. Dr Husain wrote:

'A child goes out to play in a garden and is stung by a wasp. That is an experience, but it leads nowhere. A child goes out to play with other children and they do not want her. That is an experience which, if misunderstandings are not soon cleared, could have agitated the mind and disturbed the values of life. But little Syeda Saiyidain has converted her experience into a story and the story into a truth of life. She has told her true story with such natural simplicity and beautiful directness that it goes straight to the heart. Shankar's Weekly takes the story to all parts of the world. In the heart of one person, very far from Syeda and quite unknown to her, it awakens a strange love and comradeship of experience. Miss Frankfurther of Argentina makes the story into a work of her own art. She illustrates it in a manner that murmurs of childhood and awakening and love and makes a present of it to the author. The result is before you. May the simple childlike beauty of this story help people to understand each other better and to realise the reality of a comradeship that extends beyond space and time.'

It was thanks to this story that I met the then Prime Minister for the first time, Pandit Nehru gave me the award at a glittering ceremony that made front-page news. At the awards function, I performed a solo play about Peter Rabbit, a favourite tale for kids. When I went to receive the award, I forgot to remove my 'ears'. Nehru smiled and said, 'You have large ears!' Then, handing me a large box, he added, 'This box is bigger than you!' For many decades I treasured the walkie-talkie doll, but much more, those words and the smile that accompanied them.

That was also when I received my first 'fan' mail. The fan wrote that he had been 'moved to tears'. Since he happened to live in the same block as us in Sujan Singh Park, my father and I went up to his door and rang the doorbell. I was painfully shy. That was my first encounter with Khushwant Singh. As I was to discover later, he had just completed his two-volume *History of the Sikhs*[12] and understood the spirit of all religions better than most people. I might add that sixty-five years later I am still ringing his doorbell; except now he is not there to answer my call. Khushwant Singh quoted from my story in some of his writings and always reminded me that it was my best piece of writing.

Although this rather tragic story had a happy ending and I ended up making new friends, the self-consciousness of religious identity never left me until I entered Modern School. Mr M.N. Kapur was the alchemist who turned my trauma into triumph. In Modern School, I became an ordinary kid, not a 'Muslim girl' who, in the eyes of other kids, was shamefully different. Today, I salute the memory of this wonderful human being for giving me the first chance, literally, to be an ordinary little girl without any religious label.

Those growing-up days were, to quote Charles Dickens, 'the best of times and the worst of times.' India had just woken up from a 150-year-long slumber to shake off her colonial shackles and offer a lead to the colonised world. It had a domino effect and as colony after colony, all over Asia and Africa, declared independence, the mighty Empire crumbled to dust, and the sun finally set on its horizon. In the process, some national leaders rose and forever captured our imaginations. Gandhi with his dhoti, lathi, and undaunted spirit dominated our mental landscape. I was a small girl when Gandhi was assassinated. I am told that no stove was lit in the entire country that day. We children were told there was a death in our family. Later on, my school saw Tagore, Nehru, Azad, and many others walk on the red bajri to the old gymnasium which was the fulcrum of all activity. Sarojini Naidu, Aruna Asif Ali, Mridula Sarabhai, Rajkumari Amrit Kaur, and later Indira Gandhi, all crossed the school's threshold while we played, sang, acted, painted, danced and, yes, needless to say, studied hard. They all came through the gates of our school and indulgently watched us display our modest skills during school functions. We were told snippets of history, some of which were unforgettable; like Frontier Gandhi Badshah Khan's lament before his colleagues when they decided on partitioning the country. 'You have thrown us to the wolves,' was what he said. We walked with Vinoba Bhave and learnt the Sarvodaya philosophy which promulgated non-violence and love.[13]

Having been nurtured in a school where we were judged only on merit, I slowly lost my 'Muslim' self-consciousness. We shared tiffin from each other's homes, devouring the kababs and besan ki kadhi with equal relish. We had heard stories about 'Hindu paani' and 'Muslim paani' being sold at railway stations during Partition but that was anecdotal. Our upbringing on Nehruvian principles was perhaps an urban elite phenomenon. Regardless, we drew into ourselves the values scattered in the mahaul of the school as lungs draw in air. At the time, none of us had the vaguest idea about where life would lead us or where we would lead life!

At home, the atmosphere was not very different; it was almost as if home and school were a continuum. We were a modest, middle-class family. Middle-class had a very different connotation back in the 1950s compared to the burgeoning Indian middle-class of 300 million who are now coveted as a market for global consumer goods. My father was a senior bureaucrat who never allowed his staff car to take his children to school or college and if he did, he noted that the mileage be billed it to his personal account. We, like other students from the middle class of those days, did not have much money but an abundance of intellectual capital! In our home, we had the best of poets and artists coming and going. I recall listening to Sahir Ludhianvi recite his famous poem on the Taj Mahal:

Ek shahenshah ne daulat ke sahara lekar
Hum gharibon ki mohabbat ka uraya hai mazaaq.

Emperor who, buttress'd by infinite wealth
Has mocked our very love, our impoverish'd, destitute love.

Raghupati Sahay, known in the literary world as Firaaq Gorakhpuri, recited for us his immortal lines about national identity comprising of many qafilas which came to make Hindostan their home:

> *Sar zameen-e-Hind par aqwaam-e-alam ke, Firaq,*
> *Kafile aate rahe Hindostan banta gaya.*
>
> On the soil of Hindustan, O Firaq
> Caravans from all over the world kept coming, and so was
> Hindustan made

I recall hearing Zehra Nigah's haunting voice singing her famous and very personal poem about compromise in married life at the Shankar-Shaad Indo-Pak Mushaira held on the lawns of Lala Shri Ram's house on Curzon Road:

> *Mulayam garm samjhautey ki chadar*
> *Ye chadar mein ne barson mein buni hai*
>
> Warm and soft, this blanket of compromise
> It has taken me years and years to weave

Faiz Ahmed Faiz Sahab wrote this couplet from his book *Zindaan Nama* on my notebook:

> *Dil na ummeed tau nahin naakaam hi tau hai*
> *Lambi hai gham ki shaam magar shaam hi tau hai.*
>
> The heart has not lost hope it is only failing
> Evening of suffering is long but it's only the evening.

I sat spellbound in the presence of Helen Keller with her companion Polly Thomson, 'seeing' beautifully with her sightless eyes and hearing each word as we spoke with her stone-deaf ears. Another precious memory is of going to Maulana Abul Kalam Azad's house on King Edward Road to wish him on Eid-ul-Fitr and being struck by the beauty of the man, every bit like the fairytale Irani Shehzada, whose stories I heard from my grandmother during summer nights on the lawns of our house in Lutyens' Delhi. Later, I winced whenever I saw stereotypical photographs of him (black beard, black cap) displayed on political posters with other leaders. They did not do justice to his striking persona which Abid Raza Bedar described as 'Irani Shehzada'.

That school with the sprawling lawns and glorious flowers which Mrs Kapur personally nurtured with the diligent gardeners, each of whom she knew by name, was for many of us, life itself. Geeta, the erudite, Birindra, the humorist, and Neera, the beauty, were my best friends. Our school was docketed in the dream of a new nation-state. Nationalism was the flavour of the day; Ahimsa, Panchsheel, Non-Alignment, the birthing of new nations one after another, a new vista was opening before our bedazzled eyes. We revelled in the thought that we were children of a Nehruvian India. We wore khaddar with pride and sang hymns from all religions in the morning assembly with fullness of heart. Our beloved teacher Mr Ved Vyas taught us to sing:

Aman ke hum rakhwale sab ek hain ek hain
Hum zulm se ladne waley sab ek hain ek hain

Protectors of peace, we are one
Fighters against repression, we are one

We imagined ourselves to be guardians of peace and combatants against all kinds of oppression. That feeling continued in myriad forms throughout life.

It was these ideals that helped me to navigate my life's journey. Had someone looked into a crystal ball and explained to me the trajectory of my life, I would have been struck with disbelief. Now that most of the journey is over and I look back, I see that my school and home, in equal proportions, led me to a lifelong struggle for gender justice and prepared me to embark on what Robert Frost calls 'The road less travelled'.

~

I joined Miranda House in 1959, amidst some tension in the family. The decision about Miranda was my father's. Ammi did not agree. St Stephen's College, a boys-only institution (it became co-educational only in 1975) was a stone's throw away, and the thought of boys' and girls' colleges in such close proximity made her visibly unhappy. But that was the precise reason why Papa was keen that I should study at Miranda. Campus life is important for rounding off the personality, he used to say. As for me, I cannot say that I was too happy when I entered college on the first day. My first impression was overwhelmingly one of arriving at an institute of fashion. Being an English Honours student, I somehow found myself placed among the college elite. All the seniors who were our principal 'raggers' were stunningly turned out. I wished I could close my eyes and find myself back in the dog-eared comfort of school. My former school friends all seemed to be in the same boat, in their simple clothes and faces sans make-up.

In those years, the Miss Miranda Beauty Contest was a major event on the college calendar. Every year, all the freshers were made to parade up and down on a stage before a hall full of jeering seniors and a small panel of judges selected the finalists. Someone told me to dress smartly in a sari. I dare not tell anyone at home about this competition, not because they would have stopped me but because such events were looked down upon by my family. So I did the best I could—which was a white and pink chanderi cotton sari belonging to an older sister which I wore for the occasion. But when some seniors insisted that I use make-up, I drew the line. So with a face scrubbed clean with soap, I followed the others onto the stage. There was some IQ testing but I can't recall the questions. What I do remember is that

I was declared 'Miss Miranda No. 4.' Miss Miranda 1959 was June Chettur (later known as Jaya Jaitly), No. 2 was Saloni Sehgal (related to the Nehru family). I cannot recall who No. 3 was. But the sharpest memory I have is of being teased for months by my school friends and family who later found out as 'Here goes No. 4!'

These may have been initial hiccups but this fashion-plate image of Miranda House remained a bogey for me during my college days and for many years afterward. Then as we moved into the classrooms and took hold of Palgrave's *Golden Treasury*[14] of poems, a whole new world opened up before me. To quote the poet John Keats:

> Then I felt like some watcher of the skies
> When a new planet swims into his ken

I have affectionate memories of my teachers in college, Kamla Acharya, Mrs Eisaloff, Maya Muttoo, Vasantha Menon, and Shanti Dutt. Mrs Eisaloff rises in my mind. Later she reverted to her maiden name, Krishna. I never knew her antecedents. Had I known it wouldn't have made any difference to my admiration of a woman who cared not for what people thought, who lived life on her own terms. Tall, thin, with nicotine-stained fingers and a hoarse voice, she smoked in the staffroom and wore cotton saris with narrow borders and sleeveless blouses. She must have been married to a Russian at one time. She was single, she was inspiring, she taught Milton, Dryden, and John Donne. We started with a love affair with the works of Keats, Shelley, Byron, and Coleridge. But soon we were over this juvenile crush and moving towards the majesty and grandeur of Milton's *Paradise Lost*, the high tragedy of Shakespeare's *Othello* and, the bitter satire of Swift's *Gulliver's Travels*. One by one we dropped our subsidiary subjects, History and Hindi, and lived and breathed nothing but literature. Along with the immortal works were the mortal 'help' books—David Copperfield summarised in ten sentences or ten pages, whatever fitted into your time slot, or

Dryden's *Absalom and Achitophel* reduced to a mofussil teacher's dull prose. One could never turn down help no matter which quarter it came from.

It was quite early that I began to take part in college debates, and proved to be quite a creditable debater. Whenever the need arose, my friend Veena Mago and I were sent to represent the college in inter-college debates. Memorable in a different way was an all-India debate we attended at the Engineering College in Patiala. The arrival of two Mirandians created a commotion on campus. Completely unaware of the effect we were having, Veena and I were all set to unroll our bedding in the guest house which was located in the centre of the campus. Earlier a young man had come to receive us at the station and take us to the guest house. With great hesitation, he asked if he could use our 'convenience'. Neither Veena nor I understood this euphemism for a toilet and the poor man left in a great hurry. That night, as we learnt later, no one slept at the college. We were told that the boys had surrounded our guest house and spent the night chanting love spells in the vain hope that these two celestial beauties from the never-never land of Miranda would bestow a little love on them! Oblivious of the incantations and rites being performed outside, Veena and I were fast asleep. We carried away the first and second prizes plus the trophy and evidently left a deep and lasting impression on Patiala, not the least due to our debating skills!

The single most important component of college life was the No. 9 University Special. I was among the lucky ones who boarded the bus at Teenmurti, which meant I had a place to sit. I soon started noticing a tall fellow who used to saunter over to the bus at the same stop. I was too modest to have thought that he noticed me but I started wishing that the bus was not so empty so that I would have a reason to sit next to him. None of my friends agreed with my assessment of his looks, but I had a crush on him. Later a plump girl cornered him and to quote a famous Hindi film song, '*meri baat rahi mere man mein'*. Later he was to join Hindi films, the very first one being my uncle Khwaja Ahmad Abbas' *Saat Hindustani*. Many of my friends have since changed their minds about him, but I have always felt in my heart that I was the one who discovered Amitabh Bachchan!

It was the one year that I spent in the hostel that I really got into the swing of college life. My father was invited to spend a year in Kashmir. As I was in my third year, I remained behind and was admitted to the hostel. Whenever anyone had to go on a date it became a sort of joint venture. Clothes, accessories, and cosmetics seemed to find legs—we never knew or cared who took what or what belonged to who! When any of us went out looking beautiful, albeit a bit sheepish, we all felt genuinely elated.

The Jose episode happened that year. Jose, the ultimate romantic, was a student from Mauritius. He played the guitar and tugged at the heartstrings of one of our very good friends. Love knew no barriers, so one night Jose slipped into the hostel and entered the room of the young lady, which in fact was a double-seater room. Miss Kurien, our formidable warden, had evidently received an anonymous phone call. So in her nightgown and nightcap, she immediately rushed to Room 19. The terrified girls opened the door but to her utter surprise, Kurien found nothing. It was the strumming of the guitar that led her to the closet—and there was Jose still serenading the girl of his dreams. The two girls were in the doghouse, Jose almost expelled, the hostel abuzz with the 'scandal'. The story made it to the newspapers. The older generation frowned and said, 'Alas Miranda! Going to the dogs.' The youth laughed and said '*La vie en rose*.' And love continued to creep in through the crevices and cracks of the college walls.

The university finals meant total sleep deprivation. While we nodded and pinched each other awake, there was our dear junior, Anju (Anuradha Lal), feverishly grinding coffee granules with sugar to produce cup after cup of gourmet coffee. Her nightly vigil was only in sympathy for her friends' predicament. Sitting through eight exams—an ordeal of twenty-four hours—was something that I would rather forget. Now in the autumn of my life, I wonder what is it that I have to show? Ghalib summarises the sum total of his life's possessions in this famous couplet:

Chund tasveer-e-butan hund haseenon ke khutoot
Baad marney ke mere ghar se ye saaman nikla

A few photographs of beautiful ones, a few letters they wrote
After death, this was the sum total of my possessions

Memories of Miranda flash through my mind. Many friendships have endured, persons like Geeta, Birinda, Veena, Nina, Kiran, Reva, and Anju. And the boys! A whiff of romance or back-slapping camaraderie. Kiran (killed in the Indo-Pak war in 1965), Vimal, Vinod, Ravi, Ashok...endless. Together we have sipped and supped on life during our salad days. In Miranda, we learnt to read books of poetry and prose and also gleaned wisdom from the Book of Life. Since then we have stumbled and faltered many times but have never lost the capacity to recover our balance.

4

In Alien Climes

Being the youngest child of my parents, I went everywhere with them. In 1962, my father was invited to the University of Wisconsin as a Visiting Professor in the Department of Education. I got admission in the graduate school in the Madison Campus of the university. We rented a small house close to the campus. Teaching being his first love, Papa was in his element. I basked in the warmth and attention I got from my parents, fellow students, teachers, and neighbours. In the mornings, Papa and I left for our respective classes as Ammi saw us off at the doorway.

Within the first few weeks, I noticed that Ammi was growing quieter and more withdrawn. Leaving her little grandson Shahid in India had been very hard on her. He was her first 'son'; she had been given this child at birth by my sister Zakia who had two sons already with one to come later. Ammi missed all her loved ones more intensely than either Papa or I did. We tried to cheer her up. However, within four months of arriving at Madison airport, my world fell apart. Ammi was gone.

The death of a beloved wife, and a loving mother, all in a country far away from home shattered both Papa and me. Ammi's illness started with excessive sleep and progressed into memory lapses, at which stage she was admitted to the university hospital. My sister Bilquis, the best and brightest of us all, left her two small children behind and arrived from India. My beloved friend Akhtar Khan (actor Dilip Kumar Sahab's younger sister) flew in from New York. Those evenings when we returned from the hospital to an empty house, Akhtar's soulful voice rendered ghazals while the three of us listened with tear-filled eyes.

Sau baar chaman mehka sau baar bahar aiyee
Duniya ki wohi raunaq dil ki wohi tanhai

Hundred times bloomed the garden hundred times came spring
The world ever splendid the heart ever lonesome

I recall us sitting together evening after evening; outside it was stark winter and the sounds and sights of Christmas were all around.

Ammi was diagnosed with brain cancer. The university community rallied around us throughout the crisis. She went in for a very complex, highly risky surgery. She came out smiling, but death stood right beside her hospital bed. Three of us watched. It was my first direct encounter with death. Papa and I carried her body back to India so she could be laid to rest in her own 'mitti', her own soil.

Many years later, my dearest sister, Bilquis, the same sister who came rushing to Ammi's bedside, died of the same disease that has taken most of our family—cancer. She was the same age as Ammi when she passed. But we did not bring her back from Canada. She was buried in alien soil. A few years later, when my husband, Syed Mohammad Abdul Hameed died, his final resting place was not to be where he was born nor where he had first migrated. Born in Hyderabad, he had migrated to Karachi post-Partition and was buried in Edmonton, Alberta. I left pieces of my heart in the Islamic section of a beautiful graveyard of my adopted country.

Graduate School in Wisconsin was left midway. We returned, ironically, to the same flat in Sujan Singh Park where I had my first communal encounter. Papa's house in Jamia, which is where I am as I write this, had not yet been built. The flat in which we lived on return from the US was allotted to my sister's husband by his company Bharat Heavy Electricals Ltd. Within a few months, many offers came from the US for my father to take up a teaching position. On hindsight, I feel that his decision to go back was partly due to me. I had to complete my degree in the US and this was the only way. So he accepted the position of Scholar in Residence at the Centre for Advanced Studies at the East West Centre at University of Hawaii in 1964. My credits were transferred from the University of Wisconsin and finally, I got my Master's degree from the University of Hawaii in 1965. Back home, no one could imagine the rigours of academia in a place called Honolulu, known by most for Waikiki Beach, scuba diving, and Diamond Head (Le'ahi). I spent two years there, the first with Papa in the university accommodation. After he returned to India, my second home was with three friends, two from Lahore, Chhammi and Shelley, and the third, Sally from Massachusetts. Chhammi (Saman Mahmood) was studying linguistics, her sister Shelley (Shahla Mahmood) was my best friend who became a lawyer and founded the Aurat Foundation in Lahore. Sally was introduced to me by the sisters.

That summer after the first semester, I registered for a camp in New York called Encampment for Citizenship. No one told me what to expect at this camp nor did I ask. At age twenty-one the sense of adventure was paramount. Flying from Honolulu to San Francisco and taking a Greyhound Bus from there to New York was a very exciting thought and affordable at $99 coast to coast. Better yet was the thrill of meeting my father in San Francisco at the start and end of the journey. He had been invited as a visiting professor by Stanford University. Sixty years later his grandson Morad is a Trauma Surgeon and his great-grandchild, my granddaughter, Sofie, is studying architecture at the same university. My everlasting memory of that bus journey from California to New York is that every two hours the bus stopped at a highway 'all-nighter', all called 'Howard Johnson', where all of us dutifully disembarked to use the toilet and eat ice cream. During the entire journey, the two-hour routine remained unchanged. Salt Lake City, Reno, and the Grand Canyon, the bus rolled over the entire length of the country. How I got to the camp in the heart of the Bronx after reaching New York is another story. Most of the students, boys, girls, and instructors, were black African Americans. I had never seen so many African Americans in one place. I was fascinated. In my family colour consciousness was strictly forbidden. My elders used the most beautiful epithets for 'dark complexion': 'Gandumi' and 'Malahat'. It is difficult to find English equivalents. They used these epithets to compliment dark skin, but that was my family preference; all around me, colour and prejudice existed then as it exists today. From birth to death a person is identified by his or her colour.

The Encampment for Citizenship was founded in 1946 by Algernon D. Black and Alice K. Pollitzer, as an opportunity for young adults of many religious, racial, social, and national backgrounds to learn the principles and techniques of citizenship through lived experience. The oldest photograph I saw of the founders had Eleanor Roosevelt along with others. The camp was held in a large public school in the Bronx. I spent six weeks in an intense atmosphere where human emotions were stripped bare; there was much crying, as though centuries of pain were being washed away. In locker rooms, dorms, and decks, we bared our souls before the cohort. These were boys and girls I had never known before nor was ever likely to meet again.

The Encampment gifted me two treasures which I carried with me throughout my life. One was a girl my age, Marsha Chapman, and the other was an instructor much older than me, Ernest Boaten. Marsha was from Canyon City, Colorado, and Ernie was from Accra, Ghana. She had studied at the famous Antioch College and he was teaching at Goddard College in Vermont. A bond was created between the three of us which was to last our entire lifetime. I met

Ernie again when I returned to New York on my way home after completing my MA. We sat on a slope in a park, Palisades, I think it was, watching the skyline with flashing billboards at a distance. He told me about his NY life and his loves, and I told him about mine. That was the last time, I never saw him again.

Marsha has remained with me, dotting my life with her visits and letters. She was in Delhi at my ancestral home, she was in Edmonton, my first home in Canada. I was with her at her adobe house in Taos, Albuquerque. I have her beautiful handwriting, and her letters on fine blue stationery still arrive in my letter box; she has never written me an e-mail or called me on WhatsApp; no computer, no cell phone. She has remained in my life, but Ernie has gone. I found that out much later from Marsha. We cried separately and together. In death, once again, he created an undying bond among the three of us. Later, there was Serge Augustin, a social worker originally from Haiti with whom I worked in my very first job in Canada at the General Hospital in Ottawa. He understood my bewilderment at this strange new world into which I was thrown. Knowing him made me breathe easier in this alien place. It was a bond that transcended borders and boundaries.

After six weeks at the camp, I returned to stay for a few days with my beloved foster parents, Kapur Sahib and Amrita Aunty. They had come to NY for a short assignment. I think of them as my foster parents, although there was no formal reason. The Kapurs were also visiting their daughter and my best friend Geeta who was studying at NYU. They were living in an apartment in Manhattan near Greenwich Village to be close to her. I tried my hand at cooking in their small kitchen while Mr Kapur sprayed air freshener all around. I was puzzled until they explained that spices, especially Indian spices, were taboo in NY. People were not allowed to use them in their apartments lest the smell spread to the neighbours' apartments! My return journey from New York to San Francisco was again on a

Greyhound bus except this time I had Geeta by my side. We recalled our school and college days and conjured dreams for the future. We threaded through the country, same drill, same landscape until we reached California and made our way to Palo Alto. We stayed with Papa, who was completing his assignment at Stanford University.

My academic trajectory was from a Master's in Hawaii to a PhD in Alberta. At the University of Alberta, our department was in Athabasca Hall. I used to share a third-floor office in a wooden building complete with creaky stairs with two other grad students, Paul McIsaac from Halifax, Nova Scotia and Karen Grover from Alberta. I became friends with Karen, who told me that she was christened Thelma, but she did not like her name so she became plain and simple Karen. Paul, I was always in awe of. Deeply thoughtful, brilliant mind, reserved, mostly silent. He spoke very little to me or to anyone for that matter but slowly a bond developed which was again unspoken. I invited him home to meet my husband. He brought along a friend, Ken, who did most of the talking. The three of us shared the office for a few months. His PhD was completed, and he returned home to Nova Scotia, one of Canada's Atlantic provinces. There he began teaching at Mount Saint Vincent University in Halifax. Very soon he became chair of the department. We exchanged handwritten letters occasionally. Before leaving, he had made a deal with me. We would share any unusual experience with each other which would make us laugh.

Then came the summer vacation and he wrote to say he was going for a holiday to Amsterdam. The next thing I knew was that the hotel in which he was staying caught fire. I still have the card sent by his parents for his memorial ceremony. Paul McIsaac 1943-1970. He was born a few months after me and his end came fifty years ago. I am still alive and the memory of him sitting on my right in the office we shared at Athabasca Hall is the most cherished memory of a deep unspoken friendship in my student days.

Despite a few setbacks, for the happiest times of my life, I look back on my student days. The best part was when friends of all nationalities, religions, colours, and castes, peopled my life. For example, my best friend in the US was Shelley whose mother was a Sikh married to a Punjabi Muslim from a place called Wah, West Punjab. In her generation too, love had overcome manmade barriers.

5

Being Wife, Being Mother

As a teenager, I visited Lahore and Karachi only once with my parents. I recall feeling very surprised at the love and affection showered on me, having grown up listening to snippets of anti-Pakistan rhetoric outside my family circle. Pakistan trailed me all the way through school and college right up to graduate school at the University of Wisconsin, where I met Pakistani students on a neutral ground. They seemed so much like us in every way. It was a new experience meeting young Muslim men. Although my school was co-educational there were hardly any Muslim students, neither girls nor boys. I was conscious of the wordless boundaries drawn by my family. Friends from all communities, yes, but marriage (or love) is only within my faith. In school and college, I had many admirers. But admiration was where it stopped. For my generation, falling in love meant marriage. I was aware that my father would be hurt if I expressed a desire to marry a non-Muslim and that I would rather stifle my feelings than hurt my father. There was also an unwritten warning: marriage within Islam but not to a Pakistani. The reason was India and Pakistan's everlasting conflict meant separation from loved ones if the baraat crossed the border. Even back then, Indo-Pak marriages were rare.

At the Wisconsin campus, I was suddenly surrounded by fellow students from all over the world. So I began to dream of finding the love of my life. Campus student gatherings reminded an incorrigible romantic like me of legendary swayamvaras from Hindu epics, where I imagined myself placing my garland around one of the many dashing young men around me.

Then one day at the Students' Union, a man detached himself from the crowd and walked towards me. He looked every bit the tall, dark, and handsome hero that classic romances describe. As he drew closer, I saw my dream come true. To put it simply, I fell in love…right there on the spot. Syed Mohammad Abdul Hameed was a Fulbright student from Karachi doing his PhD. After this first brush, Hameed and I began to meet off and on. Together we faced the trauma of my mother's death. I found immense solace in his company. All that ended when, soon after, I left for home with my mother's body. As time passed, both of us went our different ways.

For the next three years, we had no contact, but I always cherished his memory. Once, on an impulse, I wrote an aerogram to him at the only address I knew. By then, he had left Wisconsin for Ottawa in Canada. I was told later that my letter was pinned on the bulletin board of his rooming house. A good Samaritan took it off and redirected it to his Canada address. That was the beginning of a new phase of my life. A few romantic letters were exchanged between us. Then as if on an unknown, indescribable impulse, he proposed marriage and, on the same wave, I said, 'Yes'. Imploring letters came to my father. Papa did not say much, Indo-Pak relations were at their usual low ebb.

It was five years after we had met for the first time in Madison that we decided to get married. Our wedding date was fixed as April 9, 1967, at a time when there was a simmering animosity between our two countries because of the war in 1965. A visa for him was out of the question. Not only was he a Pakistani (albeit born in Hyderabad), but much worse, after migrating from Hyderabad, as a teenager, he had served briefly on ground duty in the Pakistan Air Force.

Warring nations have never stood in the way of true love. I made a plea to my father. That was a year after I had completed my MA and returned from Hawaii to Delhi. I had joined Lady Shri Ram College (LSR), University of Delhi, as a lecturer. My announcement that I was going to marry Hameed shocked my friends. Although no one actually said it, the reaction was evident. 'How can she think of marrying an "enemy"?' My father was sad about 'losing' his youngest child to a 'hostile' country but pleased that his future son-in-law was highly educated and came from Hyderabad which he cherished for many reasons, most important amongst them was his love for Nawab Mehdi Nawaz Jung, a scholar, philanthropist, and later Governor of Gujarat. Hameed was the son of a school principal, hence, from the same field as Papa. But the question was, how to get him across the border?

For the sake of his daughter, Papa was constrained to use 'sifarish' and seek a favour. He approached his friend and mentor, Dr Zakir Husain, the then President of India, to get a one-week visa for Hameed to visit Delhi for the nikah. My baraat consisted of two persons, the bridegroom, and a sole baarati, Professor Gopi Chand Narang, who had taught Hameed Urdu, as a second language requirement for his PhD, at Wisconsin. The irony of it strikes me now after all these years as I am writing this. A Hindu from Baluchistan, teaching Urdu to a Hyderabad-born Pakistani in the US! My one and only baraati! As I write this, I am grieved that he too, a grand symbol of Ganga-Jamni tehzeeb, has gone; with him perhaps the tehzeeb is also gasping for breath.

My husband and I felt we belonged everywhere in South Asia. (It was much later that I met Kamla Bhasin, who was to become my lifelong friend, who had only one identity—South Asian.) Hameed started the Afro-Asian Forum to envision a world beyond geographies. Borders became irrelevant for us. Our three children were born in Canada. We found a way out of the India-Pakistan deadlock by opting to become Canadian citizens. Since we could not soften the borders and move back and forth, we pitched our tent in Canada, a country I loved but which in a small corner of my heart always remained for me 'alien'.

~

Hameed's father was a school principal from Hyderabad. His home and his father's school were near Moazzam Jahi Market in the inner city near the famous Charminar. He told me that his mother's name was Ayesha and that she died when he was a child. When our daughter was born, he named her Ayesha after his mother. His father remarried; the second wife was from a feudal background and went back to her parental home for reasons he did not explain. The third wife bore him two daughters and one son. The fourth wife was a domestic help, that is all I know. He had three half-siblings—one brother and two sisters. Hameed told me that being his father's favourite child, he was given special treatment by the mothers—all to win the patriarch's heart. He must have seen through this facade of affection early in life. Women in that patriarchal setup would have been 'kept in their place'. Another recollection which I heard from Hameed was about his father's childhood. It was his father's love for art that took him to Bombay's J.J. School of Art. He had a beautiful singing voice, but none of this was tolerated by his austere and rigid father and he was subjected to some corporal punishment from time to time. To placate his father, he diverted his musical talent to Quranic Quirrat and his art to Quranic calligraphy. Fascinated, I listened to these stories as if it was fiction, never understanding how it would have impacted my husband's young mind.

My upbringing was different. All my buzurgs were faithful and practising Muslims but their Islam had a quality of universality and gentleness which I learnt later, was also the sunnah of the Prophet. Subconsciously, I imbibed my family ethos. When I became involved with human rights and social reform, I understood what my great-grandfather, Maulana Hali, and his generations, both women and men, were propagating right from 1905. Hali wrote the first ever feminist verses in Urdu called 'Chup ki Daad', meaning 'Admiration for the Silent'. He raged at the patriarchy, which deprived women of their right to education, health, choice of husbands, and widow re-marriage. A hundred and twenty-five years ago his words lambasted men of all castes, creeds, and religions. Addressing the women he wrote:

Jab tak jiyo tum ilm-o danish se raho mehroom yaan
Jaisi thein aayein bekhabar waisi hee jao bekhabar
Jo ilm mardon ke liye samjha gaya aab-e-hayat
Thehra tumhare haq mein woh zehr-e-halahal sar ba sar
Aata hai waqt insaaf ka nazdeek hai yaumul hisaab
Mardon ko denna höga inn haq talfiyon ka wan hisaab

Deprived of education in the garb of 'innocence'
In ignorance came thither, go ignorant from hence
Knowledge, which for men was thought elixir of life
For you it is pure poison, deadly, lethal and rife
The Day of Judgment dawns, the reckoning is in sight
The world will be pilloried for depriving you of rights.

On May 27, 1967, six weeks after I got married and had left for Canada, I wrote a letter to my father:

'Living away from you has taken the joy out of my life. I hope my daughter does not become so attached to me. Everywhere I look, I see you. Your photograph on my dresser is so handsome, kind, and comforting. There is no doubt that I love Hameed but he is alone against all that which was my beautiful past. I want to write. I have even tried but my poems are becoming very morbid. I have just received your letter with an overflowing heart. So if this seems a sad reply, it is not always so. Life is a kaleidoscope.'

My father came to visit us in Ottawa, the first of his two visits. We took him on a spectacular drive through the Laurentian Mountains. He fell in love with the colours of the fall. Fifty-four years later and I can still see the happy look as he recited a couplet of his favourite poet, Allama Iqbal.

Phool hain sehra mein ya pariyan qataar andar qataar
Ooday ooday, neelay neelay, peelay peelay pairahan

Are there flowers in the glade or fairies row upon row?
In purple, blue, yellow swathes of colour

While he was there, we received another visitor, Dr Clovis Maksoud, who I considered my adopted brother. He was a close family friend, and loved by all of us. He was an academic turned diplomat, a public intellectual, a Lebanese Christian who had become a part of India where he lived for many years as Ambassador of the Arab League, and a close friend of Indira Gandhi. I loved hosting him and my father in our modest two-bedroom flat in downtown Ottawa. There were other visitors during our year-long stay. Dr Zakir Husain, whom we loved and respected as a family member, made his presidential visit to Canada and stayed with his old friend, Governor-General Roland Michener. He invited my husband and me to visit him at the Governor's House. After sixty years, I have two treasured possessions: a photograph with him and a beige tussar sari he gifted me.

~

My sons, Morad and Yavar, were born in 1968 and 1972, respectively, and my daughter, Ayesha, in 1974. When I was pregnant with Morad, my husband said to me that he hoped for a girl in my image. But I gave birth to a robust ten-pound son! My male gynaecologist, Dr Beck's remark is my first recollection when I regained consciousness from the Caesarean section, 'Congrats, you have a little football player!' A Canadian could not have given a greater compliment. Later I realised that my husband's desire to have a daughter had no firm basis. Holding his firstborn, he declared to all in the hospital room that from now he wanted only sons!

When I first set my eyes on Morad, I had just come out of general anaesthesia in the maternity ward of the University of Alberta Hospital. I saw his face and I can still feel my own gasp. His face was my mirror. He was lying, neatly bundled beside me. It had been a breach delivery. It took eight days for the stitches to heal before I could be discharged from the hospital. Hameed brought us home, both mother and child, wrapped and bundled. A memory that lingers is placing him on a white sofa before a large bay window overlooking the front lawn in which the grass had begun to turn brown. It was October 12, 1968.

Over the years, how did I see my older son? Introspective, and sensitive, he used to tease me by saying that his sensitivity was the result of his regressive genes! He was thoughtful, gentle, and he always had the right words for the right moment. One summer in Delhi, my children and I were at the Jamia Qabristan to recite Fatiha at their grandparents' graves. As we waited in the drizzle for Mohammad Yunus, who was like family, to arrive to recite Fatiha for his son, Adil Shahryar, Morad must have felt the immediacy of death. 'The land on which peoples' marble is placed,' he said to me, 'is incredibly fertile.' He remarked how lush and green the place was. Death, Morad said, was just a flash in this evergreen process of incarnation and reincarnation.

I think of another side of Morad: to put away his clothes, to pay his bills, to open his cheques, and to eat his packed lunches may not always happen. But he can pick up the brush and carefully clean the cobwebs. He has beautiful hands and a mane of dark curly hair. Tall like Yavar, a little stooping (which Hameed continually checked). Always a smile and word of encouragement for those around him.

'Mother, I was just thinking about you,' he said once as I came in, sweaty, rushed, and irritated.

'About me? What?'

'How beautiful you look and how much I love you.'

Sitting in my father's home in Delhi years later, I wrote about my children in my diary. At the end of the piece on Morad, I wrote: I hope people can appreciate his quality and I hope I don't fall into the trap of wanting to protect him. A man who has just finished studying five months of human anatomy. A man who has been running from work to school for two years. Surely, he doesn't need his mother in that sense. Am I pig-headed?

~

My second son, Yavar, was born on Canada's Dominion Day on July 1, 1972. Morad was the firstborn but Yavar was equally the joy of our life. He grew into a responsible young man, as well as a poet and an artist. One year, when I was away in India, he was invited to deliver his class valedictory address in Grade 12. He wore his father's sherwani and delivered a beautiful speech. Why didn't I return for the event? It remains one of the deepest regrets of my life. Through handwritten letters exchanged with him and with my sister I learnt how hard he had worked all year. Cleaning the house, mowing the lawn, hauling the garbage, washing dishes, folding laundry, and shovelling snow. Then he would sit down and compose a beautiful poem, play his guitar, paint, act, or run a marathon for the city. Initially, he had considered a career in community medicine or public health, but then he was accepted for a joint Master's degree in law at the North Patterson School of Carleton University and the University of Ottawa. So he became a lawyer.

In 2009, I timed my return to Canada so that I could be in Ottawa for Yavar's birthday. He received me at the train station since I had flown directly from Delhi to Toronto and taken the train from there. We drove straight to his office where I asked him about the landmark case he was fighting. Abousufian Abdelrazik was a Sudanese Canadian who was arrested in Sudan, while he was visiting his ailing mother in 2003. He was denied re-entry to Canada based on a United Nations anti-terrorism listing. The Federal Court of Canada later concluded that this arrest likely took place at the request of the Canadian Security Intelligence Service (CSIS). Though never charged, Abdelrazik was beaten, threatened, and tortured during two periods of detention totalling a year and a half. Blocked from returning to his home in Montreal, Abdelrazik went public with his story and took refuge in the Canadian Embassy in Khartoum, where he remained a virtual prisoner for fourteen months. Finally, a groundswell of public support from across Canada and a Federal Court ruling forced the government to issue permission. It was his lawyer, Yavar Hameed, my son, who fought the case with unswerving grit. He flew to Khartoum and returned home with his client.

That night I wrote in my diary: Yavar is on the brink of something big, something which will make him rise to great heights one day. I am so proud of him. His name will be up there with global crusaders for human rights.

From his office, we drove to his apartment which was across the street from the hospital where I had worked when I first stepped on Canadian soil in 1967, General Hospital on Bruyere Street. It has another name now and looks nothing like it was thirty years ago, but its sight revived some precious memories. Looking around Yavar's well-kept apartment, I was happy to see that my three gifts were beautifully displayed. Three carpets that I had given him over the years: one from Peshawar, a Killam, one from Baku in Azerbaijan, and the third from Bokhara in Uzbekistan. The next morning, Yavar drove me to the airport. I wrote in my diary, 'I am going to Edmonton with a heavy heart; it is always painful to leave Yavar.' I told him, 'Yavar, you will become our torchbearer towards better climes and hemispheres. I will arrange my work so I can spend a few months with you every year.' Happiness flushed his face. At the end of my life, I say with regret that it never happened.

~

After Morad and Yavar, I gave birth a third time. My daughter Ayesha was born in 1974. When I saw her for the first time she was lying in an incubator, with shades over her eyes. 'Infantile jaundice,' my friend Dr Srishti Nigam told me. Standing at the glass partition of the nursery of the now-defunct Charles Campbell Hospital in Edmonton, I cried as I saw her lying under the UV lights and I prayed. At that moment, it seemed as if she was mine, only mine, my daughter, my soul. An image of me in every sense.

Without intending to do so, Ayesha has followed my trajectory but has gone much further than I could ever aspire. My love for theatre was passed on to all of my children. The boys did theatre at home and in school. Theatre was twined into Ashi's life. She staged a Christmas play on her school stage. Her recounting of it in one of her letters is hilarious (her humour, she says she did not inherit from her mother who is boringly serious). Here is an excerpt from her letter:

'On the day before the function, a classmate and I sat down to write the script. I had a rehearsal where all vocals were off stage and the people on the stage pantomimed. We selected a plump, mature girl to play Mary but finally… the general census was that I should take Virgin Mary's role. The first scene was the "sweeping" when Gabriel (off stage) warned me of Jesus's birth. There I was brooming away and Gabriel's voice was nowhere to be heard. So I went on swishing at the floor when a voice called from the audience "Hey, you missed a spot!" Finally, Gabriel spoke. When we were to lay the child in the manger, a girl discovered that the doll was in the box already. So she flung it across the stage to me. Finally, the play ended with more laughs. I am glad there was the whole winter break for people to forget it. The funniest part is that a few people have ecstatically praised my poise (?) and the fact that I carried myself so "Maryishly" (?!?)'

Ashi, who rides high among global art circles today, used to read the books I had left behind in Canada. 'I have your copy of *Of Human Bondage* on my bedside table. I really loved the book; looking at its inscription it seems you read it at the same age I am now.' Our bond has remained firm despite all the time spent apart, despite the distance between India and Canada. Handwritten letters from her (and from my sons) are my most precious possessions.

'I missed my 9:30 bus and as I sprinted to Michener Park I thought of how you chased my school bus and hated doing it. I can rather sympathise with that today. My bag was heavy and the silly mug I had strapped to the back of it rattled. Life is rather like that. You can run and run fast. But your silly mug will always rattle around.'

Humour laced with philosophy or philosophy laced with humour, that is my daughter.

~

In my early days in Canada, I wanted to pass on my family traditions to our children. Moharrum was embedded in my soul—ten days of mourning for Imam Husain, the grandson of Prophet Mohammad. So I started observing Moharrum in Canada. During my childhood, I saw a devout, liberal, and compassionate religion all around me. Parents prayed, fasted, recited the Quran, and observed the month of Moharrum with deep reverence. All this I was part of but without much understanding or real involvement. The commemoration of the ten days of Moharrum every year was something which captured my imagination. Listening to soz-salaams, nauhas, and marsiyas made me cry during and sometimes even after the Majlis ended. Sometimes I was angry. Why was Imam Husain and his family tortured? Why the denial of water in the burning desert of Karbala? Why was the throat of the six-month-old child Hazrat Ali Asghar pierced with an arrow? When the Imam brought him to the battlefield in his arms, the child was dying from thirst. One sip of water was all he asked for. Images flashed before my eyes of the Imam hauling mutilated bodies of his beloved family members and friends. Each persona of the Ahl-e-Bait (Imam's family) became 'my family'. I thought of my father as Imam Husain, my mother as Hazrat Shehr Bano, my chacha whose name was also Abbas, as Hazrat Abbas (Imam's brother), my aunt Saliha as Hazrat Zainab. Their selfless love for each other was my benchmark.

My husband was a Sunni but was very respectful of the Shia tradition. In deference to my Shia faith and practice, he built with his hands an imambara in our house. The symbol of Moharrum is the imambara; literally 'House of the Imam'. It has emblems and banners—gold, silver, brocade and silk or wood, metal and cotton—depending on the means of the *azadaar* (mourner). Islam prohibits photographs, only symbols are permitted. The imambara that Hameed built was a wooden structure on which the emblems could be installed. On wooden spikes placed within the structure, he helped me install my mother's heirloom silver alams. I had brought them with me to a new land where I wanted to continue my family tradition. At the end of the Majlis, when we all rose up to recite dirges for the Imam and his family, to the rhythm of *matam* (lightly beating the chest) my husband stood up along with us, a practice which Sunni Muslims usually never follow. While Shias say 'Ya Husain' to the beat of striking their chests, Sunnis stand respectfully at the back with their hands folded. Later he told me that he performed matam so that the children would not get confused, not knowing which parent to follow.

I was not a regular namazi, I would usually offer namaz whenever there was a crisis in my life. Since the end of 1971, I began offering namaz regularly as solace for the loss of my father who had died in Delhi that year. He passed away when I had just left Delhi with Hameed and Morad to return to Canada. This was seven months before Yavar was born. When they were very young, my daughter and sons imbibed the habit. I have a photograph of Morad and Yavar, aged five and two, sitting with me on the prayer mat.

Yavar and I once read together Abdullah Yusuf Ali's translation of the Quran—two Surahs, Surah Qayamat and Surah Dahr. This would have been around 1996. I was able to understand some Arabic vocabulary, and through explaining its spirit to Yavar, I began to understand it better myself. That year I had planned to go to NY and Boston but decided to stay back in Alberta and study the Quran with Yavar. Morad had in the meanwhile got married to Salmana, whose family, like ours, had migrated to Canada but the marriage did not last and both were now remarried. Their son, Aazar, lived with his mother. I feel it was the gift of Allah for the month I had spent studying the Quran with Yavar that I got the joy of playing with my grandson Aazar whenever he came to visit.

~

My husband was a curious combination of a dreamer and a pragmatist. He was political, philanthropic, religious, liberal, and patriarchal. It was later that I realised that in many matters he was quietly transferring his ambitions to me. Hameed's upbringing was very different from mine. His was of a patriarchal family as most families were and still are. But he never lacked ambition for me. He made me do things which I would never have done on my own, such as stand for the City Council elections (more about this in the next chapter). In retrospect, I feel I was the crux of the agenda he had chalked out for himself. I always thought of him as an 'Aazar', the father of Prophet Abraham, who was a sculptor. Inspired by this biblical reference, George Bernard Shaw wrote his famous play *Pygmalion* which played on stage for years, finally becoming the classic musical film, *My Fair Lady*. Professor Higgins, like Aazar, wanted to mould the perfect statue. Unlike Aazar he had as his model the little flower seller Eliza Dolittle. Such stories are semi-tragic because 'statues' have a will of their own. I feel Hameed had the desire of an Aazar to make the perfect 'statue'. I was his clay. He made me do this, he made me do that. Although it worked for a while, it could not be sustained. The clay became animated; displaying a mind of its own. That became the breaking point which caused anguish everywhere.

It was in the early 1980s, that my husband expressed his wish to spend the remaining years of his life in India. I never questioned his decision though we had built a good life in Canada. Hameed was teaching at the Faculty of Business at the University of Alberta where I had earlier taught as a Sessional Lecturer. My job as Director of Colleges and Universities in the Government of Alberta was permanent, the children were in good schools. I had many anchors in Canada; life was on a roll. But deep in my heart, there was a desire to return to India, to keep up the tradition of my ancestors. Hameed would have sensed that. When he spoke about returning to India, he said, 'I am doing it for you.' His decision was in part a throwback to his earliest memories of growing up in Hyderabad under the care of a loving father. Although Hameed never visited his birthplace after we returned, there was a latent desire that drew him to India.

One day in the dead of winter, in a temperature of minus 30 degrees, Hameed and my sister Zohra said goodbye to me and our three children and caught a flight to explore the 'return of the Hameed family to their homeland'. They went first to Karachi, where they were hosted by my father's closest friend, Rahat Chhatari. From Karachi, they flew to Delhi, where my nephews, Arif and Ahmed, had booked them at the Imperial Hotel, on Hameed's instructions.

After a few weeks, they moved in with my sister and brother-in-law, Zakia and Kazim Zaheer. In April 1984, the children and I joined them in what had become an overcrowded apartment. My old school still had regard for me, and Morad, Yavar, and Ayesha were admitted to Modern School the same year. In 1985, we all returned to Canada. It was to be the last time we stayed together as a united family.

In 1978, a decade after we got married, Hameed and I had begun to drift apart. The reasons are many and unspoken, it is hard for me to write about them. I am placed on the anvil by my dear ones as well as judgemental observers. The assessment depends on who looks and with which lens. I thought about leaving, he may have thought the same. But we were the ideal diaspora couple with three beautiful children. Neither of us could deprive them of a parent. On the surface, all was normal, the turmoil was within.

In 1979 came Hameed's first heart attack. After ten days, we brought him home from Miseracordia Hospital. I had set up a room for him on the ground floor so he could avoid the stairs. I recall that he preferred to be looked after by Zohra, so I withdrew quietly in deference to his wishes. Another heart attack was followed by a massive heart surgery in Los Angeles.

It was soon after we brought him home that he decided there would be two homes for the Hameed family – one in India, and one in Canada.

From 1985 onwards, we ran two households. This, too, was Hameed's decision. He said, 'You live in Delhi and visit Canada in the summers, and I will live in Canada and visit Delhi in the winters. We will have the best of both worlds!' And for five years, from 1984 to 1989, when Hameed passed away, this remained the pattern of my life. In retrospect, it was a strange arrangement, but at the time, I took it in my stride, and there was no one to give me sage advice or warn me of the pitfalls of such a lifestyle.

Initially, I was supposed to return to India and set up home there with all three children. But the way things worked out, the boys stayed behind with their father, and I went alone to India with Ayesha. This too was Hameed's decision. The school term in India begins in July. When it was time for us to return, I booked four tickets, for myself and the three children. As the time drew near for our departure, Hameed suddenly said that Morad needed to stay back since he was seventeen and had to gear up for higher studies. He declared, 'I designate Yavar to look after his mother and sister.' Then he had another change of heart. He said, 'I don't want to separate the boys, brothers should not be separated. You cannot take Yavar, only Ayesha will go with you.'

Something inside me died. It broke my heart to leave my sons behind, but I was too scared of Hameed's heart condition to make a scene just as we were leaving for the airport. Tearfully, I left with my daughter for India.

In Canada, home was the house on Lansdowne Drive in Edmonton which Hameed and I had bought in 1986 on the recommendation of our friend, Dr Shristi Nigam. Zohra stayed behind to run the house and look after Morad and Yavar. Over the years, that house became an 'adda' where family members congregated from Delhi and other parts of Canada. The only permanent dweller was my sister Zohra, who looked after my 'Canada life' after I left for India with Ayesha. Zohra has since passed away.

In India, I tried to pick up the strands of a life that had lain dormant for seventeen years. It was lonely and tough. From India, Ayesha and I kept returning to Canada innumerable times to be with the family. No one wants to read about a woman's journey back to her land of adoption where her children are growing up under the care of their father and an aunt who has become a surrogate mother. It is an old story, repeated through history, the separation of a mother from her children.

My husband had declared that he would spend his winters in Delhi, and I would go to Canada in summer. But he could not keep his end of the bargain. After spending one year in our family home in Delhi, he was not able to bear the strain of transcontinental travel. His health was deteriorating steadily and he could never return to India. However, the boys used to visit Ayesha and me in Delhi. At the end of one such visit, as Ayesha and I were leaving the airport after seeing them off, my heart dipped with anxiety and pain. It was August 29, 1986. Morad and Yavar had spent a few weeks with us. My daughter and I stood behind the glass barriers in the airport lounge with mounting sadness. When I reached home, I wrote these lines:

Sons and Farewells
You
standing uncertain
on polished floors behind luggage carts
among a throng of travellers.
We
flapping broken wings against glass partitions.
I suddenly know
why lines on my father's face
became deeper furrows
each time I stood on airport ramps
to wave goodbye!

All joy ebbs out of me
like a splinter
which carefully drawn from the flesh
leaves a clean, light trace of blood.
It was, after all, an alien emotion.
Myopically watching
your long strides

eternalizing the distance between you and us
as you orbit into other spaces,
We gather our broken wings
which are now
scattered along the concrete pavements
of all the world's airports:
(the quill and the stone
bleak testimonials of meetings and partings)
and begin our weary walk
towards an empty car.

For Ayesha, too, the separation from her brothers was hard, but she never complained. My daughter has exquisite taste and immense grit. There are so many murky potholes into which she may have fallen but she has risen and touched the apex of her dreams. I know in my heart that she adores her mother, but she is also angry and resentful, blaming me perhaps for her splintered childhood. Parallel emotions. I wonder: will she ever return to the fold of her mother's embrace?

~

In the context of my sons Morad and Yavar, I draw parallels between my life in Canada in the 1970s and my life in Delhi fifty years later. Bear with me.

My two sons were born in Canada. Fifty years later two sons, not mine, were born in Orissa and are now working in my house in Delhi. They are Mohan and Hemant, from Koraput, the tribal belt. Their village is Ambagouda in Jeypore tehsil. I have a clear memory of visiting Koraput during my Planning Commission days. My report of the visit was called 'Reality Bites'. There were two reasons for this title. While addressing a gathering in one of the villages I was stung by a bee. That sting and the sting of starvation and malnutrition in the village created this title.

Mohan was tall, thin, a phone addict, and forgetful. He was diagnosed with tuberculosis and we nursed him through it. His younger brother Hemant was stronger, calmer, and faster. He looked after his brother and did whatever work was required. Their grandfather, Dhannu Bagh was my driver in 2004 when I started my Planning Commission term. The first thing he did was plead the case of his son Suresh for the post of my peon. I said 'yes' and thereby began a relationship which has lasted ever since. I demitted office in 2014 but ten years later he and I remain close. Suresh's original name is Sukru which he rarely uses. Mohan and Hemant are the sons of his older brother Detari Bagh, who died of liver disease caused by alcohol. I have not seen their mother but now I am their local mother (or grandmother) trying to train, scold, and care for them. I swing between sympathy and irritation.

Both sets of boys have lost their fathers. One loss is described above. The second was my loss, and the loss of Morad, Yavar, and Ayesha. Our loss was due to heart disease brought about by food habits imbibed in childhood and excessive tension. Hameed used to tell me that as a boy in Hyderabad, he sometimes ate a dozen eggs at a time. For breakfast, there was liver, keema, paratha, and *bheja* (brain), the favourite breakfast foods of his family.

In 1989 came the final heart attack and he passed away in Edmonton. I grew more involved in my life in India, built a career, and carried on. Canada has remained a second home.

6

Being an Indian in Canada

It was in the year 1921 that the first woman was elected to the City Council of Edmonton, the capital of the province of Alberta in Canada, where I spent a chunk of my life. The woman was Izena Ross. Unfortunately, the story of the housewife turned alderman has largely been lost to history. She was one of three women who ran and the only one to win a seat. Her election got the male aldermen worried, lest they be stopped from smoking in front of a lady. Izena soon laid that one to rest. She served a one-year term before losing a re-election bid in 1922. Later, she served on the Edmonton Public School Board for a decade, from 1935 till her death in 1945. I searched the Edmonton Journal archive but found no other biographical details. There is very little online about Izena beyond a few news clippings, and only a small park in Edmonton has been named in her honour. In 2021, to mark the hundredth anniversary of her election, the Alberta YWCA (Young Women's Christian Association) launched the 'Searching for Izena' project. It was then that the phone rang one morning when I was at my desk, writing these memoirs. On the other end, it was Katherine O'Neill, CEO of the YWCA. 'Did you run for a City Council election in 1974?' she asked. I was astounded. I had just finished writing about my first foray into politics. The phone call opened a flood of memories.

Earlier in the day, I had listened to the first woman Vice President of the US, Kamala Harris, the first Black and the first South Asian woman to be elected to this office. I heard as she spoke her piece before the nation. Passion, energy, and joyfulness. I loved what I saw.

It was forty-seven years, almost half a century ago when it happened to me.

I was thirty years old, the mother of three. My youngest, Ayesha, was only a few months old. I had been in Edmonton for six years, having arrived in 1968. My PhD was complete. I had taught in my own department at the University of Alberta, as a Sessional Lecturer for two years. Hameed was a professor in the Faculty of Business at the same university.

One day, out of the blue, my husband proposed that I should contest the forthcoming local election for the City Council. His colleagues and friends joined him in persuading me. For me, it was a blind move because I had no idea what I was in for. Initially, it came as a shock. But I was always game for something new and exciting. So, I went along with him and his bunch of friends. I had a sense that in placing me in the race he was fulfilling his own longing.

At the time, the total population of the city was 500,000. It was divided into six wards. Ward 1, which was mine, had a total of 40,000 voters. I ran on the URGE (Urban Reform Group Edmonton) ticket. URGE's main plank was the environment. I was surrounded by 'people like us', feminists, both women and men, university professors, several from the South Asian diaspora. My husband and two colleagues from the Department of Sociology took charge of my campaign. All three of them were in their early forties and had, at some time in their lives, nursed political ambitions. Today, looking back, I feel I was their mascot; thrown in the midst of something which I understood only from a lens which I loved: theatre. Politics to my mind was theatre!

So there I was, a South Asian, Muslim woman running for City Council on the ticket of the Urban Reform Group in Edmonton. And what was Edmonton? It was the capital of a province that had been the bastion of ultra-conservatives where the 'dyed-in-the-wool' SOCRED (Social Credit Party of Canada) had ruled for a long time.

Switching from saris to pantsuits, I went from door to door asking for support. I confined my door-knocking to residential areas surrounding the university. Many homes that opened their doors, were welcoming, hospitable, and encouraging. It was late fall and the temperatures were sub-zero. I was so cold that one moment inside the warmth of an open doorway was read by me as one vote! I had blocked out of my mind the remark of a small boy who came with his parents for dinner at our house. For his book on a 'three or four day work week' Hameed had interviewed 'blue collar' workers; the man who came for dinner to our home with his family had facilitated his field research. His child turned to his mother and said, 'Hey Mom, the lady forgot to cut her hair.' Then looking carefully at me, he remarked, 'Look, there's something funny in her nose.' My long hair and my mother's diamond nose stud became my shame for that moment. But all these warning signs were lost in the euphoria of the election.

The results were declared. I had got 6,194 votes. The highest tally went to Ches Tanner, an Independent, with 17,222 votes. All those who won were Independents. All URGE candidates lost because the environment, which was our main plank, had very few takers in those days when development was the mantra. Our manifesto stated 'no freeways'. In that part of the country, to rephrase Shakespeare, development was all; hundreds of trees were smartly cut to make way for what became the city's pride, the Whitemud Freeway.

But I was not at the bottom of the list from Ward 1. Ernie Hayne scored only 2,332 votes! So I hadn't done too badly; people told me, 'It was a decent showing.' Some said, 'It was not her, it was the platform of Urban Reform which Albertans rejected.'

I was disappointed but did not bother to analyse the result; electoral politics was not to be my future.

I have preserved my election cards and posters from 1974 among my favourite mementoes. I took them out with pride when I was asked to speak at the centenary celebrations for Izena Ross. After that one attempt at electoral politics, my interest in global politics deepened but I never contested an election again.

Almost half a century later, on September 20, 2021, it was my lawyer son, Yavar who contested a parliamentary election on an NDP (New Democratic Party) ticket. His constituency was Ottawa, West-Nepean. He polled 11,163 votes, much better than his mother.

My PhD coursework and shared office at the University of Alberta was in an old heritage building. Athabasca housed my English department where I began attending classes wearing my silk saris. That was the only dress I was comfortable in. On the left side of my nose flashed my mother's diamond. Fifty years later it is still there. People on the campus looked at me with curiosity. Some remarks were hurtful, but I won't recall them. What I do remember is the remark of a Canadian professor from the English department who sensed my discomfort, 'Syeda! If they react to your sari, it is their problem. You please continue to dress as you wish.'

That sentence has stayed with me ever since.

~

Whether in Canada or in the US, I have always been reminded of my colour and Asian identity at various stages of my life.

One particular incident happened very early on in my Canada days. It was in the early 1970s. On a bright winter morning, I was going to work, driving very carefully because the previous night it had snowed heavily and the roads had not been cleared. It was a typical prairie winter morning in Canada when the bright sun was deceptive; one thought that the world outside is as warm as it appeared from the windscreen of the car. But the cold hits one as soon as one steps outside, so I was wearing my (fake) fur coat as a precaution. Life was filled with new promises; we had bought our first house and second used car.

That morning, the car I was driving was a second-hand Cadillac which a friend had given us for a trial run. It was a leaf green colour with a good music system. Like most South Asians sunk in nostalgia, I had been playing Mehdi Hasan's ghazals, thinking longingly of mehfils back home, while negotiating the snow-covered roads.

Suddenly, my car veered to the side and loose snow crunched beneath the wheels. I rammed the brakes. The puncture happened right in front of a school. The sign read Harry Ainlay High School. I would see groups of students hanging around when I passed it on my way to work every day. Snow had been shovelled on the side of the pavement when I got out of the car, pulling my coat around me against the icy wind. Some students were standing outside, fifteen or sixteen-year-old girls and boys, eating, smoking, and oblivious of the cold. Those days mobile phones did not exist, so I looked around for a phone booth to call my husband. There was none in sight.

I don't know whether it was my fake fur or second-hand Cadillac that attracted their attention. I saw a bunch of boys looking straight at me. Being a teacher, I was used to sixteen-year-old schoolboys, so I smiled and asked if there was a phone inside that I could use. That one sentence of mine seemed to trigger something. I sensed rising tension. They were looking at me intently, unsmiling. Then came the first slur. Someone shouted, 'You damn Paki, go back.' The group seemed to enjoy this phrase and took up the refrain. Suddenly I found them flinging coins at me and my car. 'Take the money and go.' Then came a shower of leftovers of their sandwiches and muffins. They landed on me and the bonnet of my car. 'Why don't you go, damn you!' By then, I had lost my courage and felt the first trickle of warm tears over my frozen face.

That Harry Ainlay High School incident was my George Floyd moment forty-five years ago. In the Canada of 1974, my neck was not placed under the knee of a muscular policeman for nine minutes. I was let off easily, I was only heckled. I was a brown Paki, a target of teenagers of a high school in an upper-class, mostly white neighbourhood. I managed to call my husband. He came, six feet tall, well-built and the teenagers melted away. Later, I was invited to the school for some sort of apology.

It was the first blow to the self-esteem and self-confidence with which I had entered this predominantly white conservative part of Western Canada. After this incident and its fallout, I spent another ten years there doing useful and challenging work but that moment had sunk the first seeds of disillusionment which would tear out in nettles from the frozen ground when the weather warmed. A decade later, in 1984, when I headed home, it was as if to the comfort of the womb.

~

Many years passed during which I lived in India but followed a pattern of visiting Canada once a year, sometimes more often. Travel is always tedious, but when I was appointed to two important public offices, first with the National Commission for Women and later with the Planning Commission, my travels became easier since I held the rank of Minister of State, with all the accompanying protocol. After my term ended, I surrendered my official passport in 2014. The perks ended too, and I became an 'ordinary' traveller once again.

Now a member of the hoi polloi, I travelled again to Canada with my sister Zakia, on a cheap discounted ticket and a personal passport. At the first immigration check, I realised that I was viewed on this trip within a frame of three identities: a woman, a South Asian, and a Muslim. I was as usual travelling in a sari. It also became obvious that this triple identity was a challenging combination for the security and immigration personnel who queried me at every stage of the journey.

At the Toronto airport, a security guard beckoned me, palm up, gesturing with four fingers. Her gesture was reminiscent of a feudal beckoning the serving classes. That was her signal for me to come up and subject myself to a body check. I complied. Patiently I allowed her to search my hair and remove my hairpin. She then proceeded to probe my shoulder for the safety pin I had used to keep my pallu in place. I read her name tag, 'Pammi', confirming her Indian origin.

Meanwhile, Zakia, who was dressed elegantly in a churidar set and Pashmina shawl, was trying to convince another security guard to allow her to place her small nail set (which she had inadvertently left in her hand baggage) in her checked suitcase. With the same four-finger gesture this other woman motioned to me. I had just got free of 'Pammi' and was waiting for my sister to get over her ordeal. 'What language do you guys speak?' she asked when I went across, pronouncing each word slowly. I wanted to say 'Hindi, English, Persian, Arabic, French (which was required for my PhD), and Spanish (which I had learnt when I visited my sister who had lived in Venezuela).' But I said nothing, allowing her the pleasure of baiting us. The nail set was tossed out.

On the return journey, I had to transit through Frankfurt. Once again, the search ritual was re-enacted. When it came to the body check, the German security guard kept running the probe over me again and again. I panicked when she made me sit on a stool in her little cubicle. I had recently seen the film *Reader* which was about torture in the Third Reich. She then asked me to remove my shoes. She picked them up with a pair of tongs and walked off somewhere. I could not understand the concern since the shoes had gone through many checks without any problem. What had gone wrong now?

Then, I saw that she had placed them on the moving khaki tray for a second check. Finally, she said, 'OK, you are good,' throwing the shoes at my feet.

I returned to India. The sight of our own immigration officials was a relief. They were unsmiling, slow, matter-of-fact but not insulting. They were especially courteous to people in the foreign visitor's line.

There is an old story of Khalifa Haroun Al Rashid, the Caliph of Baghdad who was immortalised in *One Thousand and One Nights*, who used to go among his people in the guise of a common traveller. He saw hunger, sickness, and death and listened to the public's opinion about his policies and programs. I had gone one step further. Like the Khalifa, minus official 'robes', I had experienced the travails of the ordinary Indian woman traveller with a Muslim name. At all security posts, my presence invoked scrutiny, suspicion, and a certain degree of hostility.

Whenever I returned to India from one of these trips, I would think, I can never go through this again. But the longing to see loved ones made me return year after year. As the poet Asadullah Khan Ghalib wrote:

> *Dil phir tawaaf-e-koo-e-malaamat ko jaaey hai*
> *Pindar ka sanamkada veteraan kiye huey*
>
> The heart returns to wander in places where insults are heaped
> Having emptied the idol-temple of my ego

~

Post-2014, most of my trips to Canada and the US were to visit family, but sometimes for work. In 2005, I became associated with The Hunger Project. THP, as it is called, started with an idea which was born forty years ago in the mind of a young woman who wanted to free the world of hunger. Her name was Joan Holmes, a woman I have grown to love and admire. But my experience in New York is also a record of discrimination inflicted knowingly and unknowingly by North American and European society on people of coloured description. New York is the THP head office and where our annual meetings are held. On one such trip, I had been in the city for nine days. During that time, I received warmth and love from colleagues and friends. But as W.B. Yeats said about Byzantium, 'This is no country for old men' so also this was no country for a coloured Asian woman. Two incidents happened in succession after which all I wanted was to leave NY. Some would put it down to ignorance, but I see it as a form of arrogance—of those who consider themselves superior and, hence, not obliged to learn about other cultures.

One evening, we were to dine at one of the most exclusive restaurants in the city. The place was overflowing with elegant men and women. I dressed in a beautiful sari but wore simple accessories since I did not want to overdo it. We placed orders for the hors d'oeuvres. I asked for a small lobster salad. When the order arrived, it turned out to be not lobster but tofu and soya. 'I asked for lobster,' I said firmly. Only then did it occur to me that in their eyes, a sari-clad woman could only be a vegetarian. My guess was confirmed by the next course when they refused to serve me clam soup. Since this was a place frequented by the creme de la creme of NY, I felt that they needed to learn to respect differences. My friend and I remonstrated with the staff. An argument began in the politest of tones. The *maitre de* insisted that by serving me a vegetarian meal he was saving me from the gelatine which could contain meat. He won. I gave up, having lost my interest in reform as well as my appetite.

Meanwhile, I was expecting a friend to pick me up for the theatre so I informed the receptionist to alert me when she arrived. But when my friend came and asked for me at the reception, she was told that 'two women in saris have just left'. 'Where are you?' I heard her shout into my phone probably from the street. There was too much noise so she couldn't hear me. Turning to one of the waitresses, I asked her to run down and stop her, or else I would miss the play's opening.

When I was leaving the restaurant, I realised what had 'gone wrong'. Two Indian women had indeed left the restaurant. Both were visibly Indian but while one was in evening trousers, the other wore a churidar kurta. But the staff had set minds; when they saw two Indian women they only saw saris, no matter what they were wearing!

As I was preparing to leave, the breaking news was violence in downtown NYC. A sniper had been shot in New York while trying to swing a hatchet at a member of the NYPD (New York Police Department). A man with a gun had killed a guard on Parliament Hill in Ottawa, Canada, before being shot to death. There was a shooting at a school near Seattle with two dead and a few critical. The assailant was a teenager who was a very popular student. I tried to draw my lessons, to extrapolate, and make sense of all this. At the same time, I was glad to be going home.

In India in 2023, the story is not very different to that of North America. Many like me are tortured and lynched; our houses are burnt, our youth booked under draconian laws. So what was then is also now, the difference is of degree. The world I have lived in for over seven decades has remained unevenly balanced; the gigantic pandemic which afflicted us came as the great leveller.

The year 2023 is a long time, half a century, from my experience of being heckled at Alberta's Harry Ainlay school for my 'Paki' colour. But have things changed? Have they grown worse?

Here is my latest story which speaks for itself.

In 2022, I was returning from a three-week visit to Canada and the US. I reached JFK Airport five hours ahead of my departure time. All went well until I reached the American Airlines check-in counter. The agent asked me for something that sounded like 'airsweeta form'. I requested her to repeat it. She was irritated but spoke the same word, and said it was a requirement. 'Can you help me get it?' I asked her.

Now she was angry, 'I don't know a thing about it. You go down in the lift and find out. And please move, I have others in the line.'

Later, I learnt that it was an 'Air Suvidha Self Declaration Form' which was a mandatory declaration that needed to be completed by travellers planning to visit India during the ongoing COVID-19 pandemic.

It was an ordeal trying to find the answer because whoever I asked just shrugged and walked on. Eventually, a woman in uniform passed by. 'Can you help me?' I pleaded. She stopped, took a look at my distraught state, and smiled kindly. For the next two hours, she wandered around with me trying to find someone who could assist. Two young agents, both African-American like her, looked at my ticket vaccination certificate and smiled at the photograph on it of PM Modi. They took my phone and began to work on it. After a few attempts, they uploaded the form, and even filled it out but it was not accepted. By then it was time for their break, so they took their leave, assuring me that I would get an email soon. I went back to the disagreeable agent at the airline counter, back to the queues, but with my guardian angel at my side. Finally, my turn came, this time it was a man at the desk, only to hear, 'No. Go back or stay at a hotel until you figure it out.' We went back to a desk in the basement where a nice young girl tried to print out the form. 'I will fill it by hand,' I told her with hope. Back to the check-in counter, to the same man, 'Nope. We only accept soft copies. No paper please.' By this time, I was ready to collapse with exhaustion. Four hours of struggle was taking its toll. Suddenly, a young Indian couple who had been watching me, said, 'Aunty, let us help you.' Their fingers flew over my phone, their phone, and within five agonising minutes, they had uploaded the form, filled it, and got confirmation. This time the man took my luggage and gave me the boarding card. My friend who was holding my baggage cart in place in the queue disappeared without a word before I could thank her. I don't know her name but I will call her Scarlet because she showed me two red glass bangles on her wrist which a grateful Indian passenger had given her. Fighting back my tears I walked to the gate just in time for the boarding announcement.

After we were seated one agent singled me out and asked for my details. 'Why?' I asked. 'Oh, we were not sure you had boarded,' he replied. There was a palpable difference in the service between this flight and the one I had taken three weeks ago, on the same airline. That was to NY with mostly white passengers; on this flight, we were all Indians. A woman sitting near me confirmed my feelings. I asked the hostess for a feedback form. 'Sorry we don't have paper; you can go online.' I tried but could not get the Wi-Fi despite travelling in business class. The hostess said she would find out and tell me. She did not return and I did not ask again.

The world after seventy-five years remains unchanged in this respect. Despite the enormous human resources South Asia has provided to North America, despite the assertions made by our leaders at international fora, we remain second class in their reckoning. Every time I tell myself, 'This is the last time I will come to this part of the world,' I return to be slighted because I long to see the people I love.

I am reminded of my uncle K.A. Abbas. For all of us, blacks, browns, and subalterns, the lyrics of a song from his 1957 film *Rahi* (about the tea garden labourers of Assam) written by his friend, the poet Prem Dhawan, holds out the hope that Martin Luther King Jr spoke of in his immortal words, 'I have a dream':

Julam dha le tu sitam dha le
Hamare bhi to din hain aaney waley
Lagaye ja tu kodey hamein tan tan ke
Har ek ghao boleyga zubaan ban ke
Labon pe lageinge kab talak taley
Hamare bhi to din hain aaney waley

Torture us, oppress us

Our day will come, at last!
Lash our bodies with your whip
Every wound will speak out
Until when will our tongues be locked?
Our day will come at last!

7

Return To India

After I returned to India in April 1984, it seems as though two periods of my life, each of thirty-eight years—1947 to 1984, and 1984 to 2022, have been fused. I cannot recount them in any chronological order.

My father had built a house in Jamia in the late-sixties and moved there in 1969. After his death in 1971, it was encroached upon by various people and had become a wreck. A wily contractor had taken possession and slapped cases against us. Fourteen years later, when I saw Saiyidain Manzil, as we had called it in my father's memory, it looked very different from what it had once been. It was my sister Zakia's perseverance that finally got the contractor out and the house restored. This was where I made my home when I returned to India with Ayesha.

With the help of a contractor, Tarsem Singh, my sister Zohra started renovating the house in early 1984. When I arrived two months later, I watched Tarsem Singh work, and my respect for him grew. With him, I went to my hometown, Panipat, to buy drapery and upholstery. Jamia in those days was Delhi's poor and distant limb, so electricity and water supply were erratic. Hand pumps were still used in many houses. Having grown used to the cold climate of Canada, we ordered a massive generator so that not just the lights and fans but an air-conditioner could function 24x7. Borewells were dug 60 metres deep to ensure a regular water supply. The original house had been designed around an open grass courtyard, Spanish villa style. However, being near the Yamuna River, there was a huge mosquito infestation. So our first structural violation was to pull out the grass and pave the courtyard.

In many ways, 1984 was a landmark year in my life. My uncle, Mohammad Yunus, became a mentor to me. He was a veteran freedom fighter, a distinguished diplomat, a nephew of Khan Abdul Ghaffar Khan, and very close to the Nehru family. Through him, I began to work with Mrs Indira Gandhi. On Yunus uncle's recommendation, I went to her residential office on Akbar Road. The interview was short, she even walked outside to see me off and I became what I described to myself as her 'correspondence secretary'.

I found her to be a beautiful person, deeply appreciative of my modest efforts to draft her routine correspondence. It was an informal arrangement between her office and me. I did not meet her every day, files were sent to me and after I completed my work, and were picked up from my house. I didn't have to go to South Block except for a few times. On those rare occasions, I met P.C. Alexander,[15] Gopi Arora,[16] and H.Y. Sharada Prasad.[17] These three IAS officers all took me under their wing. Wajahat Habibullah,[18] also in the IAS, who was working closely with Mrs Gandhi at the time became a good friend. We were of the same age and had family connections. Mrs Gandhi told me that I should plan to work in her office premises after her return from Bhubaneshwar. I was elated and promised myself that I would strive to live up to her expectations. Then came what was literally a dead end for me. It was the day after her return from Bhubaneswar on October 31, 1984, that she was shot dead by her security guards. My dream world crashed before I could step into it.

Rajiv Gandhi took office as Prime Minister after the assassination of his mother, Indira Gandhi. Uncle Yunus suggested that I meet him and offer to help him in the same capacity as I had assisted his mother. One morning, a couple of months after Mrs Gandhi's assassination, the phone rang and rang. It was Uncle Yunus. After scolding me for not answering my phone, he informed me that my appointment with Rajiv Gandhi was scheduled for 11:30 a.m. that day. So I went to Rajiv Gandhi's office on 10 Janpath Road. I made it on time, but it was almost forty-five minutes before I was asked to step in. Rajiv was seated at his desk, he had the same stunning looks as his mother, and the same welcoming smile, whereas, I was nervous, quiet, and reserved. He said, 'We will start on the same basis.'

I said, 'That will be best. Where will I be located?'

'Jawahar Bhawan,' he replied.

'What about the work?'

'The more substantive correspondence someone else is dealing with, you deal with the routine,' came the reply.

'How do I get in touch with you if I need to?'

'We will be in constant touch; I will be in and out of Jawahar Bhavan. On Monday, speak with P.C. Chidambaram and Mani Shankar Aiyar.'

I had read that Chidambaram was a lawyer with a Harvard education and had been a minister with every Congress government, and he was in charge of RG's office (later rose to the rank of Finance Minister). I was asked to talk to him first and then with RG's other assistant, Mani Shankar Aiyer.[19] So the three of us met and I was told my duties. 'We will call you,' they told me. That was the last word. Then for weeks, the phone did not ring. In my heart, I was uncomfortable at the thought of working with these colleagues after experiencing the kindness of the people around Indira Gandhi. But I was more uncomfortable at the dead silence from the PM's office.

I spoke to Yunus uncle and suggested that since I had not heard back from Chidambaram or Aiyer, I should perhaps work for some cell of the party, specialise in any given area, and slowly become an indispensable part of the party machinery. Yunus uncle was angry. He gave me a tirade about some 'ghatiya log' in the party who would stifle me, 'Don't even consider the party route. You will live to regret it.' He went on to say, 'Mrs Gandhi sent me to work for the party. D.K. Barooah who was then president of the party almost smoked me out. So Mrs Gandhi said "Enough is enough."' It came as a shock that despite Yunus uncle's unwavering loyalty to the Nehru family and his outstanding work for the country, there were people in the party trying to throw him out. However, Mrs Gandhi stepped in and in 1975 he was appointed as a special envoy to the Prime Minister. In this capacity, he promoted trade between India and the rest of the world through regular trade fairs. He established the Pragati Maidan in Delhi and went on regular trade exhibitions around the globe to promote Indian trade and much more.

Yunus uncle's advice was to wait. 'Political kaamon mein der ho jaati hai. When your name comes from the highest quarter, your entry will be more graceful.' He said that I should not be disappointed at the delay. It was all a matter of timing. Then he went on, 'Don't listen to people, there will be many, who say, "Rajya Sabha mein aiyeeye." They only flatter, they are not your well-wishers.' After this stiff dose of advice, I decided to make no further move. I never saw Rajiv Gandhi again.

Maulana Altaf Husain Hali, my great grandfather (top), my father, Khwaja Ghulamus Saiyidain (below left) and my mother, Aziz Jahan Begum (below right).

All photographs courtesy the author

My three sisters: (above, left to right) Zakia, Bilquis and Zohra, and (below) three Mirandians: (left to right) Birindra, me and Geeta Kapur.

Entering married life: With my sister Bilquis at my nikah (top left), my husband Hameed (top right) and (below) with Hameed on our wedding day.

Two continents, two homes: Our house in Edmonton, Canada (top of page) and (above) the Imambara at Saiyidain Manzil, my home in Delhi.

A passion for theatre: Performing Amir Khusro on stage (left); and (below) recreating Ammi's world: an exhibition of my mother's doll collection at the Indira Gandhi National Centre for the Arts.

GenNext: With Morad's son Aazar (top left), my granddaughter Sofie (top right) and with Aazar's wife Yusrah (below).

The children grow up: Yavar with Sarah on their wedding day (top left); Ayesha (top right), with Morad on a recent visit to Stanford, California (above).

My Canada life: Hameed and me with, in descending order, Morad, Yavar and Ayesha (above) and (below) standing for the City Council Elections in 1974, my only foray into electoral politics.

Solemn moment: Dr Manmohan Singh adminstering me the oath of office as Member, Planning Commission, on 1 July 2004.

NCW days: Marching with Dr Mohini Giri, then Chairperson, National Commission for Women (top of page) and (above) with Mohini in Orissa. I was Member, NCW, from 1997 to 2000.

Precious moments: With Kamla Bhasin in Morocco (right) and with Bismillah Khan in Benares (below).

Touring my beautiful land: With NCW colleague Padma Seth in Sikkim, 1998 (above), and (below) in Chizami, Nagaland, 2005.

With the women of Hariya ki Garhi, Distt Mathura in U.P. (above) and, (below), in Gyanpur Village, Bhadohi distt of U.P. Aug 17 2006.

Women from either side of LoC discuss peac

Shujaat Bukhari

SRINAGAR: Over 50 women from both sides of the Line of Control met here on Friday to discuss the possibilities of finding common ground for pushing through peace moves in the troubled state. They called for widening the scope of confidence-building measures (CBMs) on both sides.

Organised by the Delhi-based Centre for Dialogue and Reconciliation (CDR) in collaboration with the women studies centres of Kashmir and Jammu universities, the three-day conference was inaugurated by Syeda Saiyidain Hameed, member, Planning Commission.

She said the arrival of 17 women activists from Pakistan and Pakistan-administered Kashmir showed that no power could thwart the process of interaction.

"Ease travel curbs"

Amartya Sen with NCW member Sayeeda Hamid (centre) and advocate Kapila Hingorani at Pyare Lal Bhawan. *Photo by HEMANT CHAWLA*

Fighting for peace and education: Meeting women activists from Pakistan as Member, Planning Commission (top of page) and (above) with Amartya Sen at the release of the Public Report on Basic Education (PROBE) in 1997, as Member, NCW.

Midnight vigil for peace: With (l to r) Justice Rajindar Sachar, Mahesh Bhatt, Kuldip Nayar and Tara Bhattacharjee, Gandhi's granddaughter, at Wagah Border on the night of August 14/15/2010.

Holding up a candle for peace at Wagah border—this was an annual event on the night of August 14/15 (above) and (below) late journalist Praful Bidwai, Sonia Jabbar, singer Hans Raj Hans with me at Wagah, 2000. Hans Raj Hans performed that night for an audience of 10,000 on both sides of the border.

8

Becoming a Writer

It was Mohammed Yunus who advised me that my best bet would be to write. 'Books will make you famous,' he said in his straightforward Pathan way.

I was living on the campus of Jamia Millia Islamia, in the house built by my father—and continue to live there to this day. My father had a deep commitment to Jamia due to his long-standing friendship with its founders. In the early years of the twentieth century, three brilliant young men, Zakir Husain, Mohammed Mujeeb, and Abid Husain, while they were students in Germany, dreamt of creating an institution like Jamia Millia Islamia, as a national alternative to Aligarh Muslim University. Jamia came into existence in 1920 in the presence of Maulana Mahmudul Hasan, in Aligarh, and later moved to Karol Bagh in Delhi and then to Okhla, then a wilderness with zero amenities.

The house holds my father's library containing a wealth of books in three languages, Urdu, Persian, and English. It has a large collection of the works of Maulana Azad, Maulana Hali, and Allama Iqbal. It also holds the archives of my mother Aziz Jahan, the rarest of rare Urdu books. The house is also an archive of many stories of writers and poets who came here during my father's lifetime. I immersed myself in this world of books and began writing again.

I wrote poems, stories, and columns on current social issues as well as film reviews for different daily newspapers and magazines.

On the advice of Yunus uncle and Khushwant Singh, I began to translate works from Urdu into English. My translated works began appearing in print. First among them was Mohammad Yunus' *Letters from Prison* (1986). This was followed by Khan Abdul Wali Khan's *Facts are Facts: The Untold Story of India's Partition* (1987), which according to Khushwant Singh was 'the most provocative and well-researched thesis on the genesis of Pakistan.' It was initially written in Pushto and then translated into Urdu by Naseem Wali Khan (wife of Khan Abdul Wali Khan), and finally rendered into English by me.

Subsequently, I translated the book by S.M.H. Burney (a civil servant, later Governor of Haryana) *Iqbal: Poet-Patriot of India* in 1993. Then came the book which created a storm in South Asia and later in many parts of the world. *The Quilt & Other Stories* by Ismat Chughtai (which I co-translated with Pakistani writer Tahira Naqvi) was published in 1994. After that, my cousin and soulmate Dr Sughra Mehdi, Professor of Urdu Literature at Jamia Millia Islamia, and I collected and translated Urdu short stories by women writers of the twentieth century. The book *Parvaaz* which may be translated as 'Soaring' appeared in 1992. We included only those stories which were written by and focused on women, this was done to highlight feminist themes in stories by women writers.

Then out of the blue, I was asked by two of my two mentors, H.Y. Sharada Prasad (then media advisor to Indira Gandhi and later Rajiv Gandhi) and Yunus uncle to edit four centenary volumes to commemorate Maulana Abul Kalam Azad's birth centenary (1988-1989). I felt very humbled and ill-prepared. Thanks to my mother's library which I devoured as a child, my English and Urdu were at par, but I was no scholar and had studied the language only at home. My one redeeming qualification was my family's firm link with Azad.

In our household, we had grown up on Maulana Azad's *Tarjuman-ul Quran*. His influence was an important part of my growing up years, even before my father worked for him, rising to the position of Secretary of Education, between 1951 and 1958. The first time I met Maulana Azad as a small girl was when my father took me to his house on King Edward Road in Delhi to wish him Eid. He left a deep impact on my childish mind. I can still remember him reclining on a sofa with a slim silver cigarette case on the table, his gentle smile, and his reserved manner. My family's deep reverence for him and listening to them talk about him throughout my growing years encouraged me to accept the assignment. At the time, I never imagined that he would one day become an integral part of my life.

I entered the portals of the Indian Council for Cultural Relations (ICCR) in 1986 to start my work on the volumes of Maulana Azad. The ICCR was founded by Maulana Azad in 1950, so it was befitting that his work should be translated within its walls. I spent countless days at the ICCR library which housed 8,000 volumes Azad had presented to the Council.

'This is our librarian, Gulzar Naqvi,' Veena Sikri, the DG ICCR, said as she escorted me to the library which housed Azad's world-famous collection of books. Gulzar Naqvi, the iconic librarian, introduced me to the two cherished entities of his life: the Azad Collection and Usha, his wife and colleague, who I liked from the moment I saw her. That was the start of a friendship that would last beautifully, seamlessly for life.

In those ICCR days, Gulzar (later I dropped the Sahib, he was just Gulzar, or Gul-o-Gulzar, as he was fondly called by many friends) was my anchor. From showing me Maulana Sahib's handwritten copy of *Tarjuman-ul-Quran* to sharing the delicious lunches Usha used to pack for him, his gentle presence brightened my days in that formidable library. When we developed mutual trust he told me, 'Syeda, I am a *mujavar* (keeper) of Maulana Sahib's most precious collection. Sadly, people here neither understand nor care.' He used to tell me about Maulana Azad's dream behind the creation of ICCR. I learnt from him Azad's plan of intellectual exchanges especially with West Asia which resulted in Sanskrit translations of Persian classics and vice versa. He told me how Azad directed the exchange of scholars from the region to deepen the understanding between and among neighbours. This dream, Gulzar said, had over the years changed to naach gaana; not that there was anything wrong with song and dance but hadn't the cultural pendulum swung too much on one side, he asked. He gave me references which I read to verify all that he had told me. With his help, I completed my assignment and four volumes on Azad were released on his birth centenary in 1990. An important part of the volumes was a complete Bibliography of Azad by Gulzar Naqvi. On the first page, he wrote a couplet that not only reflected Azad but also him, as we remember him today, in retrospect:

Meri tasveer ke ye naqsh zara ghaur se dekh
Inn mein ek daur ki tasveer nazar aaye gi

Look carefully at the contours in my painting
You will see an image of times gone by

The four volumes published by ICCR appeared in Hindi, Urdu, and English with a message by President R. Venkataraman, who wrote, 'Azad's early eclectic training made him a powerful votary of international understanding and world peace. The ICCR of which he was the founder and first president bears shining testimony to his worldview.'

When the volumes were released by Vice President Shankar Dayal Sharma in the presence of Prime Minister V.P. Singh, and the programme was covered by Doordarshan channel, Khushwant Singh's review appeared the next day in the *Hindustan Times*, on November 17, 1990: 'Those who watched Doordarshan coverage of the release of Maulana Abul Kalam Azad's four volumes of selected writings and speeches by Vice President Shankar Dayal Sharma in the presence of Prime Minister V.P. Singh were shown many dignitaries including Najma Heptullah who has built her political career on her relationship to the Maulana. None of the speakers made any mention of the one person who had laboured for two years to translate and edit these four volumes. Nor did any of the newspapers which carried photographs and texts of the speeches. This often happens in our country; people who do the work are pushed into the rear; people who push themselves in front of cameras and give press conferences steal the credit. The person so callously ignored was Dr. Syeda Saiyidain Hameed.'

Khushwant went on to write: 'Not many people know that much of the material in these volumes has never appeared in English before. The Maulana was very fussy about letting people handle his writings and refused to let anyone try translating his *Ghubar-i-Khaatir* because he thought it was untranslatable. Among other incidents in his life, it tells of the Maulana's love for music (he used to play the sitar sitting on the terrace at the Taj Mahal on moonlit nights) and his love of tea. Syeda has done the job so well that it reads as if it had been originally written in English.'

After the publication of these four volumes, an international conference on the 'Contemporary Relevance of Sufism', a subject that deeply interested Maulana Azad was organised by ICCR in 1992. It resulted in a book with the same title in 1993 which I edited.

From all over the world arrived Sufi scholars and practicing Sufis. Thirty years ago, they said some of the same things that are being spoken today. They lamented the growing haplessness of the common person in an increasingly violent global scenario and presented the Sufi Tariqah as the only way to remain sane. It was Azad's writings more than my personal Sufi background which introduced me to Sufi philosophy.

I had never known this aspect of Azad, but once I knew it, I could see how it was all-pervasive even in his magnum opus *Tarjuman-ul-Quran*. Although I knew about my own Sufi forefathers, who arrived in India more than 850 years ago during the Sultanate period from Herat, then part of the Persian Empire, it did not touch me at the time in the manner that Azad's writings did. It was when I read Azad's essay on Sarmad Shaheed that Sufism in all its splendour opened up before my wonder-struck eyes.

Sarmad, whose Islamic name was Saeed, was an Armenian from Kashan in erstwhile Iran. He came to India as a trader and entered the country through Sind's famous port city, Thatta. There, he first experienced temporal love, which brought him closer to the spiritual. He found his way to Shahjehanabad, the seat of the Mughal Empire. It was there that he met Prince Dara Shikoh, the eldest son of Emperor Shah Jahan. It was his inspiration and patronage that led to Prince Dara's Persian translation of Sanskrit texts, including the Upanishads, which was titled *Sirr-i-Akbar* (The Great Secret). Sarmad became Dara's tutor and his influence grew to such an extent that it shook the Mughal Empire. Those were the days that Aurangzeb was plotting his move against his father. Of Dara, Azad writes that the humility with which he met the Muslim divines was matched only by the devotion with which he bowed his head before Hindu saints and sadhus.

A true lover of God is misled
Both by religion and lack thereof
A moth does not choose
Between a burning candle
Whether in the mosque or the temple.

In Aurangzeb's eyes, Sarmad's greatest crime was his growing influence among the populace and his closeness to Dara. He desperately needed an excuse for ordering his execution of this Master of Tariqah. What better excuse could he find than the use of the instrument of Fatwa?

Whenever Sarmad was asked to recite the Kalima, he always

stopped at the first two words. 'La Illah' (There is no God). 'Say the rest,' they ordered. 'I can't. I am still at the Stage of Denial,' he replied. The Mullahs then gave their verdict. The executioner moved forward with his sword. Azad writes, 'These godly men of worldly ways did not understand that Sarmad was far above their pedantic discussions of Kufr and faith. Self-impressed with their writs of execution, they often climbed on the pulpits of their mosques or madrasas to think about the heights to which they had risen and still aspired to rise. But Sarmad had reached the pinnacle of love from which the walls of the mosque and temple are seen standing face to face.'

At the time of his execution, Sarmad was so deeply immersed in his communion with God that he looked up only once. That was the moment when his executioner moved forward, flashing his sword. He is said to have smiled, looked straight at his executioner's eyes, and spoken the following words:

> Come, O come I implore you
> In whatever guise you come
> I know you well

In his lifetime, Sarmad had never recited the Kalima beyond the first two syllables, 'La Illah.' The historian Valeh Daghistani writes that after he was executed, a group of elite passers-by reported that they saw Sarmad's lips move in recitation of the entire Kalima: 'La Illaha Illallah…' (There is no God but God).

Sarmad Shaheed and Maulana Azad are both buried close to each other in front of Jama Masjid, The Saint and the Maulana, the Martyr and the Chronicler. These are little-known aspects of history that need to be remembered today.

In 1991, I came out with the first translation of *The Rubaiyat of Sarmad*[20] into English. It was the first time Sarmad's quatrains and

Maulana Azad's essay 'Sarmad Shaheed' have been combined in a single volume and rendered into English.

~

Before I end my recall of these four volumes I want to talk about a man I met during this research who was an image of Maulana Azad. I had gone to Kolkata in 1992 to meet Maulana's closest living relative, his older brother's son, Nuruddin Ahmed. The memory of this meeting continues to haunt me till today.

It was a warm April evening when I sat beside his bed. The road outside was named Bright Street. But to me, it seemed the darkest street in the city. A naked bulb suspended from the ceiling filled the room with a sickly light. The air was streaked with the smoke from a mosquito coil. I noticed a few dusty bottles of medicine on the newspaper-covered bedside stand. The man lying on the bed covered its entire length. His hair was long, his beard tangled, and his nails uncut. The sheet flung over his emaciated frame was blackish-grey with Kolkata grime. His long fingers were laced over his chest.

Maulana Azad had one older brother, Ghulam Yasin Abu Nasr Aah, his senior by two years. Abu Nasr resembled his father Maulana Khairuddin in every way and was designated the successor to his Sufi seat (Gaddi Nasheen). Unfortunately, he fell seriously ill during his trip to Iraq in 1906 and died the following year in Calcutta at the age of twenty-one. Abu Nasr's literary and linguistic achievements placed him among the elite scholarly circles of his time, and his writings were published in several literary journals. He was married to the elder daughter of one of his father's disciples. (Azad was married to the younger daughter, Zuleikha.) Nuruddin was a posthumous child of Abu Nasr. He grew up in his grandfather's household which consisted of his mother, his aunts, Fatima Begum and Hanifa Begum (Azad's sisters), his uncle Abul Kalam Azad and Zuleikha Begum, his mother's sister, and Azad's wife.

In Azad's writings, there is a brief account of his brother, but not a single word about Nuruddin. We know that he stayed with Maulana, first in Kolkata at Circular Road, Ballygunge, then at King Edward Road in Delhi. He was at Maulana's bedside when he passed away on February 22, 1958. During Maulana's tenure in Delhi, he served briefly as a Librarian at ICCR. A note preserved in the Council's archives dated July 1, 1957, states that Nuruddin served as a librarian for a nominal salary of Rs. 1. The note was sent to the Vice President, ICCR, by my father, K.G. Saiyidain (then the Secretary, Education) and returned for action on July 2. The position lasted a few months.

'Maulana had a superb memory,' Nuruddin's voice was barely audible. I placed my ear close to his mouth, 'When he was at Ahmednagar prison, he used to write to me to send him such and such book. It is on the top shelf, seventh from the right, he would write. There it was, exactly, I could not believe what I saw.' The resemblance this man bore to Maulana Azad was stupefying; the same fair complexion, chiselled nose, long fingers, and precise personality. Whether his eyes dark or light, I can't recall, but the fact was that except once he never looked at me. The eyes were focused inwards, the sockets were white. The unmistakable stamp was the handsomeness I associated with his uncle. Maulana Sahib, as I recalled him, not the Maulana of press photographs. I touched his hand with reverence. I could hardly keep back my tears.

I had often been told that Nuruddin possessed rare documents of Azad. Perhaps the complete *Tarjuman-ul-Quran* of which only eighteen parts had survived. People described him as a recluse. It was rumoured that he kept a trunk filled with Azad papers underneath his bed. I could not of course, search there, but I did see some old rusty trunks lined along the side of the wall where he lay. I also saw yellowing heaps of newspapers piled at the foot of his bed. What I did not see in that room was a single scrap of fresh-looking paper.

My focus of interest on entering the room was no longer the papers I had heard about, but the man who was the image of Maulana Sahib. I forgot my original mission to discover the lost Azad papers. It did not seem decent to violate the privacy of a dying man by posing the question. Questions, however mildly put, always display the curiosity of the eager questioner. His dignity foreclosed the issue.

That evening when Ahmed Saeed Malihabadi Saheb, son of Azad's lifelong associate Abdul Razzaq Malihabadi, introduced me to Nuruddin, the 86-year-old man remembered my family members. His eyes moved to my face at the mention of my father's name. I remembered that my father had initiated his appointment letter to ICCR. I asked him two questions. 'The unidentified man standing next to Mohammad Yunus, beside Maulana's body lying in state (a famous photograph taken at 6 King Edward Road), was he my father's brother Khwaja Azhar Abbas?' He agreed, 'Yes, that's who it was.' Could he identify his grandfather's house? He could not. Maulana Khairuddin had died in 1908. Nuruddin was born much later. 'Would you write to me?' I asked. 'Yes, he would, but only if I wrote'. By the time I left the room, I realised that I was not the one asking him questions but answering his. I told him about my work, family and future plans. He seemed interested in my work with a genuineness I rarely encounter. His family members who had remained present during the first part of the evening, now went about their work. I noticed his eyes watered, and although he gave me tea, he refused to drink more than a few sips of water. I accepted his hospitality but did not dare to offer him anything to relieve the squalor of his surroundings. His dignity defied charity.

The next day, I visited the Maniktala graveyard. I had read that Azad went straight to Maniktala after being released from Ahmednagar prison. His wife, who had died during his prison term, was buried there along with his father Maulana Khairuddin, and brother Abu Nasr. I had often thought of Maulana's desolate homecoming in 1945. The long drive from Howrah station to the graveyard, culminated in a small floral tribute and Fatiha at the modest grave of Zuleikha Begum.

Maniktala had become a dumping ground for dead auto parts and scrap material. It hardly seemed a place worthy of burying one's dead. My friends told me that it was being used for manufacturing desi liquor. People were often caught using the great Sufi Pir's mausoleum as their gambling den. Our little group received menacing stares from scraggly-looking men and boys hanging around. Standing among piles of junk and weeds, I recited Fatiha at the graves of Maulana Khairuddin, Zuleikha Begum, Abu Nasr, and all other marked and unmarked graves.

When I returned to Delhi, all I wanted was to do something for Nuruddin Ahmed. First I thought about writing a story. The dismal condition of the closest living relative of one of the architects of India's freedom movement would make a stirring article. It would move the hearts and minds of the authorities, who would fall over themselves and each other to give dignity to the dying. On second thoughts, would the news media carry my article about a man who was eighty-six, dying, and who didn't really care? Probably not. In any case, time was running out and I couldn't wait for the editors to clear their backlog. So I decided on direct action.

I wrote letters. I spoke to people. Could Nuruddin get nursing care at home? Could his surroundings be cleaned up? Could Orient Longmans be asked to speed up royalty cheques for *India Wins Freedom,* Maulana Azad's story of the Partition, which was confined, under seal, in the National Library in Kolkata and the National Archives in Delhi for thirty years, and published only in 1988, so that he could receive a steady income? In all my correspondence, I insisted that he be offered help in a manner consistent with his dignity and self-respect. Who I wrote to didn't matter, but I wrote and spoke to people in power. They all seemed sympathetic, concerned, and full of promises. After a few weeks of waiting and follow-up phone calls, my enthusiasm tapered off. But I wrote to him and to the relatives who were taking care of him. I sent him copies of my translation of *The Rubaiyat of Sarmad* which included his uncle's essay, 'Sarmad Shaheed'. It struck me that the gleaming new volumes would be out of place among the old newspapers. I never heard back from Nuruddin Ahmed or his relatives.

Having passed the buck on to people in power, I sunk back into my inertia. It seemed that no one cared about Nuruddin, except the relatives. They looked after him in proportion with their means and the 'right' of an 86-year-old bedridden man (with no particular income or savings) over a large family of his cousins and their children. I had thought that I could be the 'saviour' by stirring public-minded people to offer their last tribute to Maulana Sahib by helping Nuruddin, but no one stirred. Nuruddin passed away quietly on September 1, 1992, in the darkness of Bright Street.

He died five months after my visit. He was buried in Maniktala, or whatever was left of it for graves after the invasion of rust and metal. When I read the news in an Urdu paper, I recalled seeing a relic in the graveyard I had since forgotten. The crumbling decrepit mosque situated at the left side of the entrance was the most exquisite piece of ruin I had seen. I wondered if Nuruddin's Namaz-e-Janaza was recited there.

Maulana Azad too at the time of his death had neither any property nor any bank account. In his closet were found some cotton achkans, a dozen khadi kurtas and pyjamas, two pairs of sandals, an old dressing gown, and an old hair brush. But there were lots of rare books which now belong to the nation's archives.

An incident which occurred much later on March 27, 2018, has left a deep scar on my psyche. It also had to do with Maulana Azad. I had never heard the name Kakinara before the day when that tehsil in 24 Parganas of West Bengal burst into front page news. I saw a video clip of a frenzied mob in a street chauraha. Most of them were in lungis. Clearly audible were the sounds of hammers pounding stone. I could make out a few slogans which were in rhythm with the pounding: *'Laga de Jai Hindu ka naara', 'laga de BJP ke raj mein', 'Randi ka bachcha'.* The hammers were shattering the bust of Maulana Azad which must have stood there for sixty years since his death in 1958. Erected in recognition of this son of Bengal who began the struggle for India's independence in 1912 in Kolkata. The man who was an active member of Jugantar and Anushilan, underground resistance movements born in Bengal before the formal struggle was launched.

The present climate of communal hatred looks for any opportunity to deepen the chasm between Hindus and Muslims. So Azad's bust is destroyed for one reason only that he was a Muslim. No one thought of what he stood for. No one in the crowd in all likelihood even knew who Azad was. They would have been most surprised to learn that he belonged to Bengal. That he lived on Ripon Street Circular Road. That his closest friend was Bidhan Chander Roy. That his wife Zuleikha was born, brought up, and buried in Kolkata along with his father Maulana Khairuddin and his one and only child Haseen. Destruction of his bust at Kakinara made me wonder when the day will come when mobs with trishuls and saffron headbands may decide to vandalise all the memorials bearing his name.

In 1994, I wrote Maulana's biography titled *Islamic Seal on India's Independence: Maulana Abul Kalam Azad.* Khushwant Singh, a staunch supporter of my work, was keen that it should be published by Penguin India and sent it to the top brass, David Davidar, then Penguin's publisher, and Zamir Ansari. But Penguin turned it down; my guess is that they saw it as bad business trying to sell a book on Azad, aka a Muslim, even if it was recommended by Khushwant. Unexpectedly within a year of completion, it was published by Oxford University Press (OUP) Karachi; unexpected because Azad was the staunchest opponent of the two-nation theory so there could be a risk for the publisher in Pakistan. Amina Saiyad, chief of OUP Karachi took the risk and it paid off. The book was reviewed by well-respected scholars in Indian and international journals. Ten years later, in 2014 the same book was published in India under the title *Maulana Azad: Islam and Indian National Movement* by OUP and was released with much fanfare in Azad's city of Kolkata, at the Victoria and Albert Museum by Maulana's grand nephew, Aamir Khan, the renowned film personality.

By 1997, I had completed my research on Azad at the Nehru Memorial Museum and Library. In my eyes, Maulana's stature had only risen. I found him one among three of the tallest leaders (Gandhi and Nehru being the other two), not only for Muslims but for all Indians.

Throughout my life, however compelling the circumstances and preoccupations were, my sustenance was writing. When I look back I have several authored books ranged on my family shelf. But more than the books are the published and unpublished pieces in journals, newspapers, magazines ,and personal memorabilia. After a lifetime of writing, books have become an anachronism. Artificial Intelligence has taken over from treatises by Kant, Ghalib, Wittgenstein, Moliere, and an endless list of authors who authored my life! So what is the fate of a bunch of old papers or bound volumes that are my entire life's sarmaya, my wealth? A glimmer of hope came a few days ago in the form of a video clip from Srinagar which I found on my phone. Fifty years after my father passed away, on his birth anniversary, Kashmir remembered his life and work. I watched a hall filled with people recalling his writings on education. His writings in both languages were evident in the presentations made in this seminar. The event which celebrated him in Kashmir was not initiated by me or anyone connected with the family. My father's books were recalled by the ordinary people of Kashmir half a century after he was gone.

I can only say in the words of my great-grandfather Maulana Altaf Husain Hali who gives me inspiration to carry on:

Bahaut jee khush hua Hali se mil kar
Abhi kuchh log baqi hain jahan mein

Meeting Hali delighted my heart
Some people are still left in this world.

In 2002, after the burning of the Sabarmati Express followed by the carnage in Gujarat which killed 1,000 Muslim men, women, and children, I led a small delegation of six women for; *chashmdeed gawahi* (eyewitness account). We wrote a small book, *How Has the Gujarat Massacre Affected Minority Women: The Survivors Speak.* In 2003, HarperCollins India published my translation of Hali's *Musaddas,* the 1879 epic of Maulana Altaf Husain Hali, consisting of 296 six-line cantos. It was a translation in verse. Hali was the first poet who used his writings to lambast Muslims for their state of inertia and inability to lift themselves from the depths into which they had sunk. Despite these towering guiding lights, what made Muslim men and women lag so far behind, I asked? I challenged myself to examine the condition of Muslim women in India. This impulse was born of a sense of guilt, in a manner, I saw myself as one who, 'despite' being Muslim, was never denied anything that really mattered in life. When I say mattered, I mean, education, and that too the very best. Wealth was never on the 'mattered' list of my family. When I looked around, I saw my co-religionists, Muslim women, as the most deprived lot in a country of 1.4 billion. The first study of Muslim women was my report 'Voice of the Voiceless' published in 2000 in my capacity as a member of the National Commission for Women. Three years later, I wrote the sequel 'My Voice Shall be Heard: Muslim Women in India'. I shall talk in more detail about this later.

9

Entering Public Life

The phone call came from the then Prime Minister I.K. Gujral, 'I want you to become a Member of the National Commission for Women.' I almost dropped the receiver. As I stammered 'Yes, Sir' my mind was racing. 'Me? Why me? What do I know?'

That was in 1997, twelve years after I returned to India. The NCW was constituted in 1990 under an Act of Parliament. It is a statutory body and has the power of a civil court. I held the position of Member, NCW, till the end of my term in 2000. Those three years were momentous, I have never spent more intense and action-filled days. The Chairperson during my tenure was Dr Mohini Giri. Daughter-in-law of former President V.V. Giri, this iconic women's rights activist had founded the Guild of Service in 1979, which was dedicated to empowering women, underprivileged children, and war widows. Under her leadership, we worked as if there was no tomorrow. We built a network of women from all over the country, women who would be the 'eyes' and 'ears' of the NCW. It was amazing how little most of us know or care to know about our country's rich, diverse, and multi-linear gender issues. At NCW, our one and only identity was gender; there was no consciousness of Hindu, Muslim, Christian, Sikh, OBC, SC, or ST. Our peregrinations across the length and breadth of India took us to places which had fallen off the map of public consciousness. We shared small and large rooms, and Indian and Western toilets with a sense of bonhomie. In the morning, using the same space, the Muslim Member (me) offered namaz, while the Hindu Member (Mohini) did her Saraswati Vandana. A third Member, Padma Seth, did neither and that too was taken in a true Sufi spirit!

As a Member of NCW, I saw and interrogated at close quarters victims of gender abuse, gang rape, honour-killing, women who had been sexually harassed, branded as witches, burnt for dowry, and abused as children. During my three-year stint in the NCW, we were able to get justice for just a handful of women. But their stories needed to be told so that they were not buried in the official records of the state and thereby erased from public memory.

My book *They Hang: Twelve Women in my Portrait Gallery* published by Women Unlimited in 2006 was about our twelve landmark cases at NCW. The book features twelve women subjected to all forms of violence; honour killing, dowry murder, and sexual abuse. I am tempted to narrate two stories that twenty-five years later haunt me even more than all my other cases. First the story of Sajoni Kisku, a Santhal woman, from the village of Bagjri, located in the Jamtara tehsil in Dumka, Bihar. I repeat her story wherever I go as a grim reminder of the 'brute' existence of many women in our society. Sajoni had a drunken lout for a husband and five children to feed. After a massive drought, the skies suddenly darkened one night and there was rain. Failing to wake up her dead drunk husband, she went into the barn, yoked the bulls to the plough, and dragged it out to her thirsty fields. Thus, she broke the most sacred rule of Bagjri village—women were strictly forbidden from touching the plough.

The entire village ran to her house. 'How dare she,' Hindus, Muslims, and Santhal Adivasis shouted in unison. 'Now there will be a famine, a drought, and an epidemic. She must immediately be made to atone for her sin.' They moved menacingly towards the woman. In a fit of fury, she shot back, 'When I lifted the plough, your pagri fell—did it?'

No one was listening. Many hands carried her towards the plough. Releasing the animals, the same hands yoked her body to the plough. She was dragged to the field. One round; second round; third round. Sticks showered blows on her to make her move. Sajoni, one woman turned into two bulls. The animal-woman collapsed in the slush. Dragged back to the shed, she was tied to the post. A basin of fodder was placed before her and her mouth was forced into it. She vomited. 'Water,' she cried. Her tormentors then dragged her to the filthy, stinking, and standing trough. More kicks, more blows of the lathi, until she fainted.

The panchayat was not satisfied. A 5,000-rupee fine was slapped on the hapless husband. The man begged them to reduce the amount. It is said that one of the panchayat members pocketed a bribe of Rs 1,000 to reduce the fine to Rs 1,100. Having collected the money, all the villagers—Hindus, Muslims, and Adivasis—retired to celebrate with tadi.

NCW received a written complaint four days later after the incident from Bitiya Murmu, coordinator of Dumka's Mahila Sabha. She wrote, 'The bestial treatment of Sajoni Kisku will be written in black letters in the history of women's empowerment.' The NCW pressed several buttons; a few worked albeit sluggishly. My tenure came to an end, and I regret to say that I do not know if Sajoni's tormentors got the punishment they deserved. I can only hope that a new NCW will have the power to deliver swifter justice to the Sajonis of India.

~

The second story took place in a hamlet buried in the village Sudaka in the Nuh district of Haryana in 1997. Nineteen-year-old Maimun and 26-year-old Idris had married against the wishes of her parents. The parents had wanted to sell her to a rich 'customer'. When they learnt of Maimun marrying a man of her choice, all hell broke loose. She was thrown to the mercy of the villagers.

'Mercy' which took the shape of a gang rape. She was raped by four men including a village pradhan. Not satisfied with teaching her a lesson by tearing her private parts, her first cousin cut open her abdomen with a butcher's knife, leaving her to bleed to death. How she was rescued by a village woman, how she reached the hospital courtesy of Umardin of Shikarpur, and how Idris found her is another story.

Our part began when the terrorised couple managed to escape from the village and reached the doorstep of the National Commission for Women. It was exactly two months since they had been married. Maimun had been raped and almost killed, Idris's face had been blackened, he had been tied up, beaten, and Rs 25,000 had been extorted from him. At times like this, all one wants to do is to give solace and protection. We could not adhere to our prescribed role as the apex body and not get involved in individual cases. But what followed was almost too bizarre for words.

News came from the village that Idris's old parents were being tied up and tortured by the villagers. This happened on the eve of the golden jubilee of India's Independence. That evening, while the country was preparing for the Beating of the Retreat at Vijay Chowk, two members of the Commission were hurtling towards the sleepy hole called Sudaka. Idris and Maimun, who was still doubled over with the abdominal wounds, were huddled in the back seat of one of our cars.

We drove straight to Idris's house. An old man and woman identified themselves as Ismail and Mauj Bi, Idris's parents. Suddenly we looked up and saw that hundreds of villagers had surrounded us. There was just one refrain: 'Give us the girl.'

'Why?' we asked. 'She is an adult and has married a boy of her choice. She has a nikahnama as well as a certificate of registration. Above all she is happy. They love each other.'

Our words fell on deaf ears. 'But we don't want the marriage.'

'Why?' we asked. 'And why are you holding the boy's parents to ransom?'

'It is a matter of Gotra,' we were told.

'What Gotra?' There is no Gotra in Islam we explained.

'We are Qureshis, they are Meos. It is not permitted,' they shot back.

'Permitted by whom?' we asked. 'Allah through His Prophet has decreed that Islam is a religion of equality; caste is forbidden in Islam. Are you not Muslim?' We were almost shouting.

The sun was going down. Suddenly the women of the village descended on us like locusts. They grabbed us and cried, wailed, and screamed, 'Give us the girl. She was abducted and kidnapped. Our families have been defiled.'

We could not breathe. Too many hands were clutching at our legs, arms, and necks. 'Listen to me,' Padma Seth (my mentor, colleague, and an ace lawyer) shouted in her powerful voice. For a moment there was silence. 'We are here for you. We understand your agony. She is equally our daughter. But no religion teaches violence. Islam has given the message of peace. These two will leave this village forever. You will never see their faces again. But what fault is it of Idris's parents? Why terrorise them?' She turned towards the young people. 'Naujawans! You need to wake up. Your religion enjoins it upon you to open the windows of your mind.'

But the windows were firmly shuttered. The few policemen present were standing around helplessly. 'These people are a law unto themselves,' they told us. As we were moving back to our vehicles, the wailing women started a cacophony. Suddenly we saw throngs of people physically lifting the car in which the girl had been sitting all along.

The car was shaken like a bag of beans. A bunch of robust village hulks tore off the handle. Our drivers and Sadiq, our lawyer, threw themselves between the girl and the mob. But the frenzied mob swept all aside. Maimun was whisked out of the vehicle like a piece of meat. Hundreds of hands dragged her away. Then there was dead silence. The storm died and hundreds of bodies that had been falling all over us disappeared into thin air. We were left with Idris sobbing in the trunk of the car and a few nervous-looking policemen.

That night as we drove back to the glitter of a capital celebrating fifty years of freedom, we let our tears flow. What have fifty years done for Sudaka or neighbouring Taodo? Two villages caught in the barbarism and ignorance of the Dens of Jahiliyyah.[21] It reminded me of the Arabian peninsula before the Prophet brought the message of Islam. Dark, dismal, and dreary, beset with the most barbaric traditions. Maimun may have been torn apart by human vultures. But they know nothing better. No one has told them that all they did to the young couple was contrary to the teachings of Islam. No Messiah has ever visited this heart of darkness.

Maimun's case received a favourable judgement by the Supreme Court. This story could have had a happy ending. But six year later, after the couple had had two children, Maimun was shot dead by her younger brother to restore the family *izzat*.

I had thought long and hard before I gave the title to my book, *They Hang: Twelve Women in My Portrait Gallery*. The pun was on the word *Hang*; portraits are hung, and these women were also hung; both strung and hung. I met them all during my trips to villages, talukas, districts, and towns, wherever atrocities occurred which triggered action and caused our small team to rush out. I thought that my book would create a storm in the country since each one of my 'stories' was based on *chashmdeed gawahi* (eyewitness accounts). I had kept newspaper clippings with photographs as proof, carefully preserved in my archives. But my book sank without a trace. Those who read it said they could not put it down for a minute and it haunted them for weeks. Chiyoka Torii, a Japanese writer and professor from the University of Tokyo, was visiting India when the book appeared. She was in Jamia learning Urdu from Sughra Mehdi at the time. Through her, she got permission and translated the book into Japanese.

Mallika Sarabhai, a classical dancer of international fame and lifelong activist, wanted to use the stories as themes for her dance presentations. Oprah Winfrey, American television personality and actor, was advised to take up the issues highlighted in the book. But none of this happened. It was just another book about Violence Against Women which at the time was on limited agendas. The Nirbhaya case would happen years later, and then VAW was spoken about only in intellectual circles and courses on gender.

When I think back about my days at NCW, I am struck by how much was packed into thirty-six months, how much pain and violence, how I swung between hope and frustration, despair and determination. Even as I write this, I realise that my tenure was strangely like a prison term. Outside the prison lay a world in which I had lived fifty carefree, oblivious years. That world receded before my eyes as I dove into this new world. I could never step into that carefree world without being tailed by Sajonis, Maimuns, and any others from my portrait gallery.

Dr Mohini Giri, NCW Chairperson from 1996 to 1999, was the first Indian to think of studying the status of Muslim women. From 1998, for eighteen months, I held public hearings across the country, listening to the voices of Muslim women. In Aligarh, Ahmedabad, Indore, Jabalpur, Mumbai, Kolhapur, Hyderabad, Bangalore, Chennai, Calicut, Thiruvanthapuram, Calcutta and Tezpur, thousands of women came and spoke on public platforms about their issues; economic, social, and political. Poverty was a universal theme which dogged their lives as the lives of all women from the deprived classes. So along with Muslim women, the hearings were open to all deprived groups, such as women of scheduled castes and scheduled tribes. Apart from poverty, the overwhelming concern of Muslim women was the tyranny of Muslim Personal Law as it was explained only in patriarchal terms.

To discuss issues raised by Muslim women in all the public hearings, our team went to Darul Uloom University in Lucknow to meet Maulana Abul Hasan Ali Nadwi—popularly known as Maulana Ali Miyan—a distinguished Islamic scholar, who was also chairperson of the All India Muslim Personal Law Board (MPLB), a leading national formation of Muslim clerics from various schools of theology. We wanted to share our findings with him. He received us with affection and warmth, probably because he had known my family, especially the writings of my great-grandfather, Khwaja Altaf Husain Hali. He spoke a language that resonated with my understanding of Islam which I had learnt from my elders, that Islam is a religion which gives the highest status to women. 'Then why is their condition across the country so different from what had been ordained?' I asked. He spoke of the 'mindset of the quom', of patriarchy, of deviation from Islamic tenets.

An important outcome of my term as Member of the NCW was my report based on these public hearings titled 'Voice of the Voiceless: Status of Muslim Women in India'. We reported that poverty was a cross-cutting theme which dogged the lives of all women from the traditionally deprived classes; Muslims plus scheduled castes, and scheduled tribes. Muslim women's overwhelming concern was the strictures placed on them by Muslim Personal Law. They were subjected to discriminatory practices such as multiple marriages, triple talaq, and abandonment. The report appeared in the year 2000 in three languages—Hindi, Urdu, and English. Its recommendations were presented to the government, Islamic bodies, and civil society for policy formulation. It was the first initiative the Government of India had taken in this regard. Nothing happened despite many Supreme Court judgments and civil society interventions. Obduracy and hegemony of Islamic bodies put pressure on governments who hesitated to take a stand for fear of losing votes. But then came 2014 and the anti-Muslim right-wing regime. In a decade of their rule 'Abolish Triple Talaq', and 'Abolish Polygamy' became slogans to gather votes and stoke communal tensions. The story is long and painful. No one, neither Muslims nor non-Muslims, has delved into the Quran to understand what is the logic behind triple talaq and polygamy. The raison d'etre of this ignorance is too complex. Regardless, there is a rational explanation. My personal view is that if rampant ignorance has persisted for centuries, it is unlikely that understanding will dawn overnight. Muslims should themselves eschew triple talaq and polygamy. Given the current regime's existing antipathy, if a law is made then blood will be spilt of the ignorant and the innocent. All great Islamic scholars—Hali, Iqbal, and Maulana Azad, have asked the quom to wake up and act.

~

In 2000, when I completed my term as a NCW Member, I started the Muslim Women's Forum. MWF was the need of the hour. Having toured the country listening to the voices of Muslim women, I felt the need to continue this work. The founding members of MWF were Dr Sughra Mehdi, Professor of Urdu, Jamia Millia Islamia, Dr Aziz Qureshi, former Member of Parliament, and later Governor of UP, Mizoram and Uttarakhand, and Begum Saeeda Khurshed, daughter of former President of India, Dr Zakir Husain. Begum Sahiba was its first President.

At MWF, we began with advocacy even without comprehending its immense need and scope! We held a few colloquiums such as 'Purdah in Islam' at a time when miscreants in Kashmir were throwing acid on the faces of girls who did not wear a burkha or hijab. We propagated the Quranic injunction extolling modesty in dress for men and women without any directive to cover one's face. We dealt with individual cases where Islam had been used by a patriarchal society to inflict violence against women. Our primary objective was to get for Muslim women the rights accorded to them in the Quran, Hadith, and Sunnah. That same year in 2000 we took a major step by bringing the Ulema and women on one stage to discuss ways whereby Quran's directive to Muslims that women be treated with utmost dignity becomes ingrained in the minds of the Ummah. We had a sense of satisfaction, when a body of Islamic scholars, the Muslim Personal Law Board (MPLB) convened a conference in New Delhi, in 2001, on the subject of 'Genuine Problems of Muslim Women and their Solution in the Light of Sharia'h'. Eminent jurists, educationists, social reformers, and religious leaders participated. We also invited women to be part of the dialogue. The President of MPLB, Qazi Mujahidul Islam Qasmi, spoke. He said that it is essential for the community to look within itself and take corrective measures. He also said that the true spirit of Sharia'h must be allowed to prevail. MWF saw in this initiative the possibility of enlisting the cooperation of this segment of Muslim men who have an influence on the Ummah.

Three years after 'Voice of the Voiceless', I held another series of public hearings under the banner of MWF. At these hearings, women deposed before our panel. They said much the same thing—men taking advantage of the distorted interpretation of the Islamic personal laws, depriving women of the dignity conferred on them by their religion. I selected an aspirational title for the report which followed the fieldwork, 'My Voice Shall be Heard'. At the time I was naive enough to think that our NCW report would yield positive results; Muslim women would get on the national agenda, hence the aspirational title of the second report.

Is it my wishful thinking or was our work one of the triggers for the Sachar Committee Report? One year after 'My Voice Shall be Heard' was published, the government decided to constitute a High-Level Committee under Justice Rajinder Sachar to study the status of Socio-Economic Communities primarily of Muslims. The committee's report presented two sets of recommendations. The first set was recommendations addressed to the central and state governments. The second set was recommendations directed at civil society, in particular, to the Muslim community.

As an organisation, our primary objective is to work for the empowerment, inclusion, and education of Muslim women. At its inception, the forum provided Muslim women a platform for expressing their opinions on matters directly affecting their lives. The distinct feature of MWF is that it derived its base from the most liberal, gendered, and compassionate understanding of the Quran, the Hadith, and Sunnah; the basic and fundamental principle of Islam which views both men and women as equal in status and worth which is the fulcrum of the Constitution of India.

In the first decade of the twenty-first century, I witnessed a slow transformation. At the time, the Muslim Personal Law Board was headed by Maulana Ali Miyan. He was open to discussion about gender in Islam and sensitive to the problems of women. Maulana Sahib opened the door for women within the organisation itself and they began to be included in board meetings. Their views expressed at MPLB meetings began to appear in media forums. Maulana Ali Miyan was succeeded by Maulana Mujahidul Islam Qasmi who continued this tradition. Maulana Khalid Saifullah Rahmani is the current head. Muslim women are represented but their voices are inaudible. Their inclusion in the MPLB doesn't make much difference to their condition because the structure remains patriarchal, and there are few who genuinely want to understand the status accorded to women in Islam. That is the harsh reality.

In the new millennium, while running MWF, I began to get more involved with peace activism especially in the context of Pakistan and India. This led to the establishment of a few organisations. For instance, a group of women, with Nirmala Deshpande, Mohini Giri, and Kamla Bhasin founded the Women's Initiative for Peace in South Asia (WIPSA). When South Asians for Human Rights (SAHR) was formed in July 2000, I was one of its founder members along with I.K. Gujral, former Prime Minister of India, Neelan Thiruchelvam (Sri Lanka), Asma Jahangir (Pakistan), Kamal Hossain (Bangladesh), and Devenendra Pandey (Nepal). In 2001, under the leadership of Rajmohan Gandhi, the Centre for Dialogue and Reconciliation (CDR), an organisation working for peace through dialogue and discourse, was formed. I was fortunate to be one of its founding members.

My struggle along with the struggle of other comrades is best expressed in this short nazm by Faiz Ahmed Faiz:

Jab dukh ki nadia mein humne jeewan ki naao dali thi
Kitna kas bal tha bahon mein lahu mein kitni laali thi
Yun lagta tha do hath lage aur naao puram paar hui

Aisa na hua
Kuch manjhi the unjaan bahut
Kuch undekhi manjdharein thein

Ab tum hi kaho kya karna hai
Ab kaisey paar utarna hai?

When we lowered our life's boat into the waters of pain
We had strength in our arms and redness throbbed in our blood
It seemed that with two strong strokes of oars
The boat will reach the shore
That did not happen

Some boatmen were novices some rip tides were unknown
Now tell us what needs doing and how to go across?

10

My Planning Commission Years

Sardars have been integral to my life at many stages. Not just in my life but in the lives of my favourite mentors and elders. Among my father's dearest friends was Dr Satnam Mahmud, a Sikh woman from Lahore who was married to a Muslim, who we met in Hawaii in 1964 and with whom we all fell in love. Another is the protagonist of my uncle K.A. Abbas's story 'Sardarji'. It is about a Sikh man who is killed by a mob (Hindu, Muslim or Sikh, does it matter?) while he is trying to save a Muslim neighbour during the Partition riots. The story was misread by both sides and slapped with sedition charges both in Pakistan and India. However, when Abbas read out the story to a Sikh regiment on Poonch border, there were tears in the eyes of the men. He was made to take a sip of rum before being declared an 'honorary Sardar' because of this very story.

My own life was deeply impacted by India's number one Sardar, Khushwant Singh, right from childhood.

One day the phone rang and someone asked me to hold on because Prime Minister Dr Manmohan Singh wanted to speak to me. That was how it began. I started my term as Member, Planning Commission, Government of India, on July 1, 2004. When I think back, I wonder, what was my qualification for planning for the entire country? Why was I selected as PC Member from thousands of women much better known and much more qualified? Was it my unflinching loyalty to the country of my birth? My Muslimness?

My work with NCW? My brief (too brief) tenure with Mrs Indira Gandhi and work-brush with Rajiv Gandhi? All I know was that first and foremost I have always been an activist and I am always willing to learn. The PM would have known this because in one of our rare meetings he asked me to go out and explore my country. 'You can write a book like Kusum Nair's *Blossoms in the Dust*,' he said. 'The book was written in 1961; it is time for an update.' He knew that I had no background in economics, development or planning. Humanities was all I had read; social sciences was not my forte. However, faith was placed in me by him and by Mrs Sonia Gandhi; I was determined to prove my worth. But it was a tough school; no teacher, no classes, no lessons. But—and that's a big but—I was under a national lens and there was no scope for making mistakes.

My boss was the Prime Minister of India. Gentle is one word which has globally been used to describe Dr Manmohan Singh. No matter what issue was on the table, he only spoke a few measured words. He and I rarely met or spoke other than at Full Planning Commission meetings. Post PC, I went to see him and Gursharan Ji a few times and he was always most courteous. One thing I knew and loved—his appreciation of my reports, probably because they were different from 'sarkari' reports. As an activist, my work was on the ground, the vast tracts of my country. Only after I had walked, felt and tested the ground did I sit down to write.

The PM enjoyed my reports because they were full of stories gathered from villages, bastis, dharnas across India. Half way through my term I wrote my book *Beautiful Country: Stories from Another India*.[22] I had toured extensively through the length and breadth of India. No part was too far, no travel was too tedious. I was fortunate in having colleagues who stood by me in learning of and planning for 'my beautiful country'—Manjulika Gautam, G.B. Panda, and Neeraj Sethi. I was also fortunate to have brilliant young people at my side who did the hard work. Gunjan Veda from Delhi, and Ruth

Zothanpuii from Mizoram. My right and my left hands, I can say Alhamdolillah for the gift of them in my life. During these journeys, lines from the poet Hyder Ali Aatish, unspoken, were on my lips:

Safar hai shart musafir nawaaz bauhtere
Hazaar ha shajar e saayadaar raah mean hain

The condition is to travel
Many hosts, much hospitality
Thousands of shady trees
Line the way forward

Some vignettes that flowed from my pen from time to time come to mind. The stories are long. If I begin you may find yourself mumbling lines of the poet Mir Mohammad Rafi Sauda:

Sauda khuda ke wastey kar qissa mukhtasir
Apni to neend ud gayi tere fasaney se

For heaven's sake Sauda shorten your tale
My sleep vanished listening to your story

I created no tables, I only had small data and no 'development' vocabulary, mostly because I did not know how to use it. It may have been a relief for the PM to read my report after going through pages of reports in bureaucratese. Two of my reports (out of a total of forty-five) are my secret pride because they brought direct policy change. One change resulted from my visit to Mewat in Haryana and the other was the consequence of my tour to Gadchiroli in Maharashtra. In a nutshell, because of my recommendation, Mewat was brought under Mahatma Gandhi National Rural Employment Guarantee Act (MGNREGA) in 2005 and the Gadchiroli experiment became a template for the National Rural Health Mission (NRHM).

In Gadchiroli, child-carers, tribal women, known as Shishu Rakshaks, were integrated in the NRHM. I have Deputy Chairman

Montek Singh Ahluwalia's handwritten note on my Gadchiroli Report 'Ordinary Women who did the Extraordinary'. The report was about the work of Abhay and Rani Bang who started SEARCH—Society for Education, Action and Research in Community Health—in 1995 in the predominantly tribal district of Vidharbha. Raised on Gandhian values and armed with an MBBS and Masters in Public Health from John Hopkins University, their idea was simple: Aarogya Samaj, a society where people's health is in their own hands. In his two-paragraph covering note to my report, Ahluwalia wrote, 'Abhay and Rani Bang... have achieved a near-miracle in reducing MMR (Maternal Mortality Rate) and IMR (Infant Mortality Rate); [there is a] 57 percent decline in infant mortality... Village health workers with training being allowed to administer gentamicin injections and life-saving drugs will not be approved by the regular medical establishment, but if doctors are not there it is surely second-best.' He concludes, 'Though long, the Report is beautifully written (as usual) and recommended for reading in toto.' Ten days later came Dr Manmohan Singh's handwritten note. 'There should be a discussion with the Health Ministry if village health workers under Rural Health Mission could be entrusted with the responsibilities of village health workers in this report.'

~

Montek Singh Ahluwalia's office in Yojana Bhavan was down the hall from mine for ten years, 2004-2014. My connection with him, however, goes back much longer; we were contemporaries at Delhi University. He was the champion debater of St Stephen's College. The duo of Montek Singh and N.K. Singh was a formidable one. The premier annual debating event was the Mukherji Memorial Debate organised by St Stephen's College. I can't recall why I, a scared and insignificant fresher, was chosen to represent my college, Miranda House, in this prestigious debate. If I close my eyes this scene from the early sixties flashes before me. The topic was 'It's better to have loved and lost than never to have loved at all'. After the debate, which featured outstanding teams from all over India, the prize was announced. The first prize went to a puny little fresher—me! And the trophy went to Miranda House. With moist eyes I looked at the three-bench jury. I suspect what got me the prize was an Allama Iqbal couplet that I had memorised on the advice of my father.

Ek bhi patti agar kam ho to woh gul hee nahin
Jo khizaan nadeeda ho bulbul woh bulbul hee nahin

The flower which lacks a single petal is not complete
The nightingale who hasn't known autumn is no nightingale

At the end of my speech I recited the above couplet with a pounding heart. As I got down from the stage, my dupatta trailing behind me, something stirred the judges' bench. Nostalgia? Regret? They announced winners. Was there a catch in their throat?

It was forty years later when I met the same team—both Montek Singh and N.K. Singh had risen to the top. Montek was Deputy Chairman of the Planning Commission; as the PM said, he was 'the first among equals'. When we came face to face in Yojana Bhawan, what I saw was the young Montek at the podium. He gave me no indication that he had known me in earlier times. It may have been deliberate, or perhaps he actually didn't remember me from college days. He was another Sardar who played a big role in my life. My ten years were spent sitting fifty metres away from him in a large office. With him and other Members, I planned for a country of 1.3 billon. My predicament was similar to what it was in NCW—being clueless about my new and onerous responsibility. I asked myself, why am I here, enjoying the perks and status of a Minister of State? A car, a driver, a house in Lutyens Delhi? My official house was relatively modest when compared to the houses of my colleagues. I chose 23 Canning Lane (now Ravi Shankar Shukla Lane) without even looking at it, for a sentimental reason. As a schoolgirl I had spent the happiest years of my life in my father's official house on Canning Lane. Modern School was walking distance from the house. My three sisters had got married from there. Four decades later, living in a house on that very lane, I confronted my inadequacies. When my father lived here he had the requisite qualifications for drawing a blueprint for education under the tutelage of one of the best minds in the country and first Education Minister of independent India, Maulana Abul Kalam Azad. I had very little.

For my entire tenure in the Planning Commission, I was the only woman in a male bastion. We sat around the large rectangular table in Room 122 for scores of meetings of the Internal Planning Commission (IPC). I usually sat next to B.N. Yugandhar, former bureaucrat. My respect for him grew as I got to know him. He was a senior bureaucrat from Andhra Pradesh who had served under three prime ministers, I.K. Gujral, P.V. Narasimha Rao and Deve Gowda. Simple, principled and straightforward. A few days after our appointment, he invited us for a Hyderabadi biryani lunch at his house. I met his litterateur wife Prabhavati who I liked instantly. Sitting next to him at PC meetings, I was always in the field of his hands and arms which he used a lot for expression and emphasis. They flashed before my face as if I was a milestone on his journey to set the world right. With my former debating adversary of college days, my relationship was mostly formal.

I was (secretly) labelled by my colleagues as 'champion of the downtrodden'. One morning I heard that there was a huge crowd at our massive iron gates. From a distance I saw many faces of friends among the protestors. Aruna Roy, Harsh Mander, Kavita Srivastava. Our apex planning body had submitted to the Supreme Court that Rs 25 per day was sufficient for nutrition. My friends on the other side of the gate were up in arms; a large contingent of police had been deployed to keep them from breaking the gates. I was told,

'Your friends are at the gate. Go meet them.' I went down with my colleague Abhijit Sen, JNU professor. We shared the same ideals. I admired him but we spoke little to each other. When we arrived at the gate, a lehar of understanding flowed across both sides. We asked the guards to stand away as we mingled with our friends. They were all holding boxes with half a banana, a handful of peanuts, one onion, one potato. If Abhijit and I had our way we would have conceded their demand on the spot. The BBC had reported India's poverty line as 52 cents a day. I felt frustrated, angry tears welled up. We returned after giving some assurances to our friends which we were determined to see through.

With one or two exceptions, my colleagues in the Planning Commission were most comfortable in the company of corporates, bureaucrats, internationals. Civil society was left to me and two like-minded members. I was able to create space for them within the formidable Yojana Bhawan. We called it the Civil Society Window. It was an open platform on which activists from all over India could present their issues directly before PC Members; they were able to go to the top instead of getting stuck in the bureaucratic stranglehold. Three of us Members were always there at these presentations—B.N. Yugandhar, Abhijit Sen and I. Others were invited depending on the sectors from which the activists came. They came sometimes, not always. The importance of civil society had not yet become central to their official lives.

My special quality, I think, was my unending interest in listening to people's voices and in recording what I had heard. My reports from several visits were factual and detailed, but being what I am, I identified myself with what I saw. Over the years, my work came to be centred around the disciplines of gender and development, and grounded in activism. I travelled with my notebook to remote corners, sparsely inhabited places, crowded urban spaces and ghettos of India. My experiences were my 'chashmdeed gawahi', eyewitness accounts of what I saw. What interested me the most were the social sectors. I was the Member responsible for Women and Children, Health, Voluntary Action Cell, Micro, Small and Medium Enterprise, and Minorities, and I was also given the responsibility of handling the states of Rajasthan, Haryana, and Himachal Pradesh. I was also the Member responsible for the Island Development Authority (IDA), a formation under the Prime Minister for the development of Andaman and Nicobar Islands and Lakshadweep. I submitted more than forty-five reports, all of which centred on ordinary people, how they lived, what they felt, and how they coped. I used the existing data but also my eyes, ears and heart, and asked many questions to understand and process all that I witnessed. Within government circles, my work was appreciated and ignored, included and excluded.

As planners we had to think big. Our responsibility was to introduce programme and policy correctives in each sector along with appropriate new initiatives in critical areas. Our mantra was to be inclusive by reaching out to all segments of society and ensure that the benefits of our schemes reach all. We had to abandon roads that led nowhere. We could not repeat the mistakes that were made in the past. Equally important for me was the human context—the human factor that sometimes goes missing in our schemes and programmes.

It was with this objective that I travelled through the nooks and corners, holding meetings and hearings across the country, investigating and reporting on issues related to ordinary women and men, regardless of caste, creed or class. From the dhanis of Udaipur to the tsunami ravaged islands of Andaman and Nicobar; from the villages nestled in the spectacular mountains of Ladakh to the verdant greens of Nagaland. I have seen young girls, stooped over dreary looms in Behrampur. In Barmer, I have seen small children travelling great distances to look for drinking water and young girls taking care of smaller children and cooking meals. In Kashmir, I met families whose young boys have been missing for years. In the tea gardens of Jalpaiguri, I met women whose husbands had been mauled to death by elephants. In the Koraput district of Orissa, I saw a lineup of old women at the District Commissioner's office. Upon enquiring, I discovered they were all widows who had been rejected by their families. The reason they appeared before the indifferent babus was to find out if perchance there was an 'empty spot' so they could become eligible for a paltry pension of a few hundred rupees. The 'empty spot' was created when a widow died and her pension could pass on to the next in the lineup. In Pochampally district of Andhra Pradesh (now Telangana) where I had gone to look at their unique handloom industry, I found an elderly couple sitting on the roadside. That moment would haunt me for months. The woman had lost one eye due to a spindle accident, the other to cataract. All the man possessed was two utensils, one for water and the other for food, blank faces craving the charity of any passers-by. Everywhere I saw despair and misery; witnessing all this was not easy. The pain that I felt was too deep to be expressed in tears.

~

Unforgettable were the stories of the people of my India. I wish I could tell all. But… Here are some that impacted me most, from Andaman and Nicobar, Varanasi, Tripura, and Malegaon in Maharashtra.

In 2005, I went to the tsunami-ravaged Andaman and Nicobar Islands. There was huge devastation everywhere. Occasionally though, there was a slight glimmer of hope. I recall with a smile, a game of volleyball in Kamorta which I saw as I was picking my way through the debris. The tsunami had devastated the island but in a manner of speaking, life was also going on.

There were two teams of strapping young boys—one team called itself Bada Enaka, the other, Chhota Enaka. They stood facing each other across the volleyball net. I was watching them while standing on the high plateau of an island in the remotest corner of the Andaman Sea. This was Kamorta Island, part of the Nancowrie group, and hardest hit by the tsunami on December 26, 2004.

Next to me sat Tang Kumar, captain of this new village. Slightly built, his face regularly lit up with a smile. He started talking about that day, the day after Christmas. All of Bada Enaka was asleep. He was the lone person standing on the shore. Then he saw it coming, a gigantic wall of water. He pulled out a boat, bundled his family—his wife, Rosaline, his three small children, and let the waves carry his tiny vessel into the open sea. The next thing he recalled was fighting the turbulence. He yelled himself hoarse, madly flailed his arms. Then it was silence. He found himself in a crumpled heap on the sands of Kamorta along with huge piles of debris. Just himself, Tang Kumar—Rosaline and the babies were nowhere to be seen.

Tang Kumar went on, 'I have found meaning in life. Having lost everything, now I have all these people. You see, madam, I became the village captain.'

The game was warming up. Their shirts were emblazoned with their names, 'Thomas', 'Deepak', 'Azar', 'Emran'. In the post-monsoon shower, their green shirts stuck to their backs. I blinked away tears as I handed out the prizes to the winning team. I had just witnessed a sun-lit drama of life and death.

Another story rises on the mindscape. UP's weavers, UP's starvation, UP's violated women; issues that often took me to that state many times during my tenure. One such visit was in 2006. It was Guria Sansthan, a non-profit organisation working with sex workers which took me there. The mohalla was called Shivdaspur. Women had collected with their children in an open courtyard of the sansthan. With tear-filled eyes they bared their arms and legs to expose their wounds. I saw where they had been beaten by the self-appointed custodians of society's morals. I was outraged, livid; I warned the police that if they touched the women again, they would have to face dire consequences. I wondered, however, how long this threat would work?

Ajeet, the founder of Guria, told us of the non-profit's plan. 'We're planning to build a night shelter where the children can sleep. We are not going to give up. Do you know, one of our children is working for WHO?'

'Do you mean the World Health Organisation?' I exclaimed.

'Yes,' he said, matter of factly. 'Most people think that the children of sex workers will either end up joining the trade or grinding masalas and making achar. But we are changing that perception.'

We move on to a nearby mohalla. A double-storied house; we climb the stairs. Suddenly we hear a voice in song:

> *Kehthey thein Bano Asghar, jaani kab tum rann se aayoge*
>
> Laments Bano, Beloved Asghar when will you return from the battlefield

It is the gentle voice of shehnai maestro Bismillah Khan. (Having visited the sex workers, next on my agenda was a visit to Bismillah Khan. No trip to Varanasi can be complete without a darshan of the maestro.)

I had heard this dirge every year of my life during the ten days of mourning in the month of Moharrum. The voice that was singing these lines was feeble and uneven but its melody gripped my heart. I looked straight into a pair of sparkling eyes set in a wrinkled face. The solace I had been seeking since we landed in this holy city of Varanasi came to me when we sat before Ustad Bismillah Khan. The Ustad had lived in his modest ancestral home in one of the innumerable gallis of the walled city. He had lived here his entire life, ninety years. His tiny room on the terrace had one charpai and one fan; he was content. 'Music is the only thing that lasts in this world,' he said. With twinkling eyes and a laughing face, he told me that in 1947, on the eve of India's independence he performed before Pandit Nehru at India Gate, welcoming the dawn of a new era. He told me he was invited to perform at the sixtieth anniversary of India's independence. 'This is my aakhri khwahish.'

Suddenly, he looked at me with great affection and said, 'Shabaash, beti.' Someone had read to him the morning newspaper report that I had blasted the police for their violence on the sex workers in Shivdaspur. 'To stand up for the rights of the weak is the deepest pilgrimage. May Allah reward you for interceding on behalf of the girls of Shivdaspur Mohalla,' he placed his hands on my bowed head. It was my great good fortune to get his blessing—he passed away the following year, in 2006.

~

My story unfolds… from Varanasi all the way to India's North East.

This memory is from Tripura in 2007. I call it the story of Sago. I was standing with some colleagues near a hut at the eastern edge of India, the southernmost tip of Tripura, a place called Sabrum. Between us and the border ran a river. Across it, we could see the bunkers of Bangladesh Rifles. Someone waved an arm, 'Chittagong'. The arm was flung towards the hills on the other side of the border. Looking through a pair of binoculars that appeared from somewhere, I saw a similar hut on the other side; there was a clothesline on which the laundry was drying. Even the print on 'that' lungi was the same as the one on 'this' lungi—blue squares on a grey background.

Sago was crouching in the far corner of the outside wall of a mud hut. Two emaciated girls stood by his side, aged six and two. 'Yes, I live here, these are mine. Yes, they go to school.'

'What do they get to eat?'

'Khichri… yes.' A hopelessly thin woman with fine features came and squatted on the dirt track. 'My mother,' he said without looking in her direction.

The words of the guide droned in the background. 'These people are Tripuris; there are altogether nineteen tribes in Tripura — Reangs, Mocs, Deb Burmans, Chakmas, Halams, Lushai. So many languages...'

In the gentle wilderness of ungentle borders and boundaries, like an angry steel apparition stood the fence, Bangladesh and India's 'hudood' demarcated with an iron finality. The black steel angles were mounted on a brash concrete platform which ran the length of the border, holding the iron firmly in place.

In between all this expensive installation, there was something that made me wonder whether to laugh or to cry. The fence had adhered to the 0-150 guideline, as agreed between BSF (Border Security Force) and BDR (Bangladesh Rifles). That meant a space of at least 150 metres from the 'zero' line. Sago had watched the concrete being poured from giant mixers, the steel girders being hauled out of trucks. Suddenly he had a stroke of luck. He was hired for a daily wage to clear the strip for concrete pouring. He had some money left over with which he planned to place a new grass roof on his hut. But hey! What was this? The fence came up as an awesome statement of steely finality. And he? He was left out. Plain and simple, left out not only from his village, his district but from India, Hindustan, Bharat. Sago Tripura's little hut could not be included on the Indian side, as it was a few metres short of 150. So there it was, bang in front of the steel angles, proudly standing on its own piece of land with its grass roof, bamboo support and mud-grass walls. Pushed out of the borders of his own country by steel and concrete, he had no neighbours, no friends, no animals, no birds. All he saw ahead was a row of bunkers. Behind them he sometimes caught a movement, a flash of metal. Perhaps the Bangladesh Rifles were cleaning and polishing their guns.

Sago was scared—he ran around in a mad frenzy. He tried to stop the workers from fixing the steel on the concrete. But they just laughed. So Sago gave up. Clutching his wage in his fist, he went with the others to the Desi Dukan for a peg or two to divert his confused mind.

At night when he returned home, he parted ways with his happily sozzled friends. He dragged himself over the half-complete steel girders to his forlorn and soulful hut standing alone in no man's land. I wrote my report, I sent it to the appropriate authorities. Then other matters took over and for me Sago was lost in time. I do not know if he ever got citizenship, but his story stays with me.

~

The journey continued…

January 2006. I was in Malegaon, a small town in Maharashtra, some 110 kms from Nasik. On the road, outside an urban ghetto, my eye caught a young boy, around twelve years old. He was standing next to some ramshackle huts, oblivious of the stench from the stagnant pool of water, the mosquitoes buzzing over his head and the constant din of power looms being operated by children his own age. He just stood there—inert frame, vacant face. Youth and listlessness—axiomatic terms that don't match, but there he was! It was the letters on his t-shirt which struck me. 'THE LOST BOYS.' Three words, on a torn black shirt summed up the story of the five lakh youth of Malegaon. 'Your name?' I asked.

'Saddam,' came the shy reply.

A communal flare up had resulted in bomb blasts. Inside the mosque I saw broken walls where the bombs had struck. I met people who had sustained injuries and shrapnel wounds.

On my way out I stopped again at the Saman Habib compound. It was close to Iftaar and the streets were bustling with people and vendors selling all kinds of food. Saddam was still standing there. 'Do you go to school?' I asked. The head went down.

'No.'

'Why not?'

'I am learning to work the looms.'

'And your friends?'

'They also work.'

The Sachar Committee Report talked about the huge development deficit in Muslim mohallas. Malegaon exemplified this. People here have seen no progress, in fact, their living conditions have plummeted far below neighbouring areas. As I left Malegaon I thought about what Mahatma Gandhi had said, 'There are many places today where a Muslim cannot live in security. There are miscreants who will kill him or throw him out of a running train for no other reason than he is a Muslim. I am ashamed of what is happening today.' Today, as a Muslim I identify with each word Gandhi spoke.

~

When I think about my field experience in the past seventeen years (from my NCW days to my PC days), it is the children, young boys and girls in tiny little village schools who have left the deepest mark on my life. Young girls in a small school in Kargil who had actually faced bullets and bombs during the Kargil war. When I met them one year later they were determined to continue studying. They wanted to be doctors, engineers, teachers in order to ensure a better future for themselves and those around them. In Leh, I remember girls sitting under the trees in the extreme cold, attending lectures for their Class 12 boards. In Malerkotla, I remember nine-year-old Parveena sitting at a bridge school with a red dupatta wrapped around her head, reciting Punjabi poems. In Jalpaiguri, I remember eight-year-old Hema Chetri in a remote tea estate who walked 4 km to get to school everyday. All these children defined two words, hope and despair.

These lines of the poet Azra Naqvi echo in my ears:

Subah hoti hai kachchi basti mein
Roz ki tarah jaag uthte hain
Nanhe mazdoor bhooke saudagar
Phool se haath waley karigar
Kaarkhanon mein shahrahon par
Tung galiyon mein chai khanon mein
Apni qismat jaganey jaate hain.

Break of morn in slum clusters
They rise each day
Small labourers hungry hawkers
Artisans with small hands
In factories on streets
Narrow gulleys wayside teashops
They arrive to waken their fate.

So far this chapter reads like we saw human misery and moved on. What did we do? What were our achievements? I will recount a few, but let the reader judge.

Struggle for inclusion of children and their rights is a challenge at every level of planning. Many doors closed in our faces, but we kept trying. I was fortunate enough to be guided by close friends who worked in this sector. They guided me in the area at a time when the word 'child' was only used in the context of education in the planning process. But my training for child rights began many decades earlier. My father, who became Education Secretary a few years after Independence, wrote, spoke and planned for children. His mentors Maulana Azad and Zakir Husain led the way. Five decades later when I wrote the chapter 'Towards Women's Agency and Child Rights', the vocabulary of the planning document had changed.

Through our consistent efforts the Integrated Child Protection Scheme became policy.

We were also able to lobby the parliament to enact the PWDVA (Protection of Women Against Domestic Violence Act). Strict directives were issued for hot cooked meals in ICDS (Integrated Child Development Scheme). I recall jumping out of the car at wayside villages to examine the quality of meals—sometimes it was a decent meal due to NGOs like Akshay Patra, sometimes it was burnt rotis and watery daal. We were able to get the Ministry of Women and Child Development to implement the conditional maternity benefits scheme. The Integrated Child Protection Scheme subsumed many existing schemes with the overall objective of preventing child abuse.

In Malegaon, Maharashtra, I saw women from different communities coming together in the aftermath of large-scale communal violence to bring back peace. Resolute women who have not only managed to build bridges between communities but also reduced the incidents of Violence Against Women by offering counselling and other services. In conflict areas like Nagaland we saw and commended women's groups like the Naga Mother's Association who were instrumental in controlling many forms of violence.

One challenge in PC was to make the bureaucracy listen to what I had to say and to take my experiences and suggestions seriously. It wasn't easy. Often, I was met with scepticism, non-compliance, even hostility. At the end of my second five year term, the bureaucracy had begun to listen. Would this become the norm for the next Planning Commission? I used to wonder.

In 2007, things underwent a churn in power centres when PC set up the Feminist Economists Group (FEG) under the inspiration of one of India's finest economists, Dr Devaki Jain. A high level committee, FEG was chaired by me. This was the first time that such a body had got official status in the Government of India. It was the first and only effort to bring together India's most accomplished economists, men and women, in gendering the planning process. Thanks to its efforts in shaping the Eleventh and Twelfth Five Year Plans, the state recognised women not just as a social group but as 'important agents of economic growth and change' and included gender as an important criteria in policy consideration across sectoral plans.

For the first time we were able to draw on paper the convergence between agriculture and poor women labouring in the field without any wages. We keenly observed whether our actions would encourage some of our progressive states to make a paradigm change. Some states did exactly that.

One achievement, if I may say so, was to identify the significant emerging trends for women in the economy and mandate policy that would integrate women into the growth agenda of the Plan. In this regard some progress was made in the Eleventh Five Year Plan and more was expected in the Twelfth Plan but in 2014 with the change of regime everything came to a grinding halt. The change in government marked the end of this breakthrough initiative.

Another milestone in the Voluntary Action Cell sector was writing the National Policy for the Voluntary Sector in consultation with the sector itself. Civil Society Window, as I mentioned earlier was to enable government and NGO interaction; it was initiated by me as the Member responsible for the sector. Since this is where I came from I wanted to bring civil society at the centre of the planning process. Implementation of schemes has been recognised as the biggest problem across the country. I gently suggested that if we enter into Public Private Partnership (PPP) with the Voluntary Sector and give them the same importance as the corporates, we can affect considerable improvement in implementation. That I could not accomplish; PPP meant only one thing—the big corporates.

Thanks to the note in the PM's handwriting (which I have

carefully preserved) the Ministry of Health and Family Welfare recognised the importance of the Gadchiroli model of child care and included it in the ASHA training. For handloom weavers, health insurance schemes were created in addition to the handicraft mega clusters. I also created a deeper focus on the Jarawas of the Andamans including schemes for the welfare of primitive tribal groups and eco-tourism. In Malegaon, I managed to secure a Special Package for development as well as the beginning of construction of the Malegaon Hospital that had been held up in red tape for a very long time.

As a Member for two terms, I have witnessed how PC became a dynamic institution with healthy tensions, checks and balances, public accountability. Planning was brought out of the cloister of Yojana Bhawan into the public domain.

Two most significant changes were made—first, taking 'people' on board from the very inception of planning and second, loosening rigidity of centrally sponsored schemes to accommodate diverse aspirations. At the start of our tenure, our Chairperson, the Prime Minister, spoke words which may be cliched, but he imbued them with new meanings: one size does not fit all.

I have been eyewitness to how the Commission tried to hold officials accountable for delivering the Plan promises. Half yearly reviews, quarterly reviews were called to determine what distance had been covered towards the defined goalposts. Given the diversity and geographic imperative, states were at different stages of development, so policies had to be tailored to address that factor as well.

On August 15, 2014, the Government of India announced the end of the Planning Commission; curtains for Yojana Aayog, enter NITI Aayog. NITI Aayog's structure was defined in the Cabinet note. Chairperson—Prime Minister, Vice Chairperson—Expert with Cabinet rank. In addition, ex officio, full-time and part-time members and the CEO. The new architecture was planned so as to ensure participation of states in the planning process and to affect 'bottoms up' instead of 'top down' planning. It was decided that all CMs will be Members of NITI Aayog. Planning will be done by the entire National Development Council, the highest decision-making body of the country.

My apprehension. The impossibility of such a large, unwieldy and excessively preoccupied body being tasked with planning for the country. How many meetings of this body will be held in the year? How many CMs given their excessive workload will attend to their duties as planners? Will the decisions then be thrown back in the lap of officials? My fear was that given the penchant of the politicians, Planning may become a paper exercise with no connect to the ground reality. Instruments like Result Framework Document were devised to keep track and enforce accountability but the actual track was kept by going to the remotest hamlets of the country to find out how people were faring. Officials were asked to move out of the Bhavans to where people were. Would that also become a relic of the past?

The word 'Planning Commission' became the verbal butt of writers and columnists ever since it was shot down by the highest authority. Words like 'Nehruvian anachronism', 'antediluvian creation', 'relic of Soviet project' have been bandied. Too smart, too soon. In time we may discover that the baby may have been thrown out with the bathwater.

Today, ten years later, how many people of my country have heard of NITI Aayog?

11

My Many Teachers

Thinking about my life, I realise how many men and women there are who left an indelible mark. Who shall I name and who shall I withhold? I don't know. What I do know is that at every phase of my life, I had someone who pulled me out of a circumstantial abyss and directed me. Among the men the first was my father, whose influence on me imbues this book. So I won't say more about him. The second one was Dr Mubashir Hasan, my father's cousin who I met as a student in 1959 when I visited Pakistan with my parents. After that we lost contact for thirty years. I met him again in 1990 and for the next twenty years he had a deep and profound influence on my life. He inspired me to continue working on Maulana Azad after I had completed my Government of India assignment of preparing four volumes to commemorate Maulana's Birth Centenary. My book *Islamic Seal on India's Independence* was written under his guidance. It was under Dr Hasan's watchful eye that OUP Pakistan published it so beautifully, after it initially failed to find a publisher in India. His understanding of Islam was in consonance with what I had picked up from my own family. It was his tutoring which firmed up these gleanings to become my personal pillars of Islam.

It was due to Dr Hasan that I became involved with Pakistan-India people-to-people initiatives. Whether it was Pakistan India Peoples' Forum for Peace and Democracy (PIPFPD), Women's Initiative for Peace in South Asia (WIPSA) or South Asians for

Human Rights (SAHR), I strove to do my bit. Year after year when I went with the iconic Kuldip Nayar and lawyer-activist and fellow Panipatwallah Ram Mohan Roy to Wagah border at midnight on August 14/15, I saw Mubashir Hasan on the other side, either in person or in spirit. Dr Hasan was an ornithologist and author of two books on the subject, it was he who taught me to love birds. Today when I scatter bird-feed on my lawn early every morning I am sure the birds know where it comes from!

At the age of ninety-eight, on March 14, 2020, he passed away in Lahore leaving behind countless peace activists in India and Pakistan who had been inspired by his tireless activities for Indo-Pakistan friendship and cooperation for three decades. A few pages here are not enough, a book needs to be written on this soldier of peace. All I want to do here is to place a poem I wrote when he passed away and left us to carry on his unfinished work. Bringing rapprochement between these two beleaguered nations through common people on both sides was his last unspoken will. On a personal note, he lived and breathed the poetry of Mirza Ghalib. Keeping that in mind, I wrote a poem:

Who was he?
Statesman poet writer ornithologist visionary?

His tall frame
Strode across South Asia
Rose to the pinnacle of power
Rose and rose
Then easily gently
Let go, let go.

Soldier for peace
I saw him in halls and streets
Of Lahore Delhi Karachi Kolkata Bangalore
Amidst women and men who

With banners and songs
Asserting the longing of masses
For a world free of concertina wires and bloodied borders.
People whose voices are usually drowned
In the cacophony of war

I saw him on Kolkata Esplanade, on Karachi stage
In Lahore Islamabad Madras Hyderabad
Dhaka Kathmandu Columbo
He gathered South Asia in his embrace
In his long arms, his hands, his eyes,
His words were carefully chosen
Before Prime Ministers, Presidents, Students, Peasants
His voice was gentle, firm
His message unequivocal
Demanding the raising
Of the banner of humanity
Above all national flags.

Soft speech, kind touch, cluttered room uncluttered life
He guided our vessel
And left this earth with markings everywhere

I see him
Somewhere in the dark depths of the unknown
Raising a salute to comrades left behind
On the parched terrain of South Asia
Knowing they will not let go
The plough and the furrow
Until the earth relents and dead land is torn by new sprouts.

~

From the many, I single out three men and three women from whom I learnt, learnt and learnt… at various stages of my life.

Faiz Ahmed Faiz

The decade of the 1970s was spent in the intense cold of the Canadian prairies, watching the snow mounting on sidewalks and driveways. I found my solace in my three children and my collections of books which I had lovingly brought from home; Urdu and Farsi, poetry and prose, became my companions through winter days when the mercury would not climb above minus 15. Those were the days when Mehdi Hasan's rendering of the poet Faiz Ahmed Faiz's poetry had gripped the heart and soul of my generation.

Growing up among litterateurs, I had learnt of the Progressive Writer's Movement very early, even before I understood their verses. I had listened to the best poets recite in my parents' drawing rooms in various official houses allotted to my father in Lutyens' Delhi. I never questioned whether they were Hindus or Muslims—all I knew was that they were Urdu poets. Sajjad Zaheer (Banney Bhai) and Faiz Sahib were at the vanguard of the movement. I had seen both of them at various literary gatherings. Banney Bhai was related to my sister Zakia by marriage, so he and his wife Razia Apa was part of the larger family circle. Faiz Sahib had become a cult figure even before I left India.

Then one day, sitting in our newly built home in Edmonton, I got the news that Faiz Sahib and Begum Alys Faiz had been invited to the city—I cannot recollect now by whom but it must have been one of the Indo-Pak diaspora—and a friend asked if they could stay with me. I was honoured and thrilled and equally humbled. My husband was away but my three small children were there to help me in welcoming these beloved guests. Much later in life I was surprised to see how much Morad, Yavar and Ayesha had silently imbibed from this visit in terms of their love for poetry and literature. We arranged their bedroom on the main floor of our house where there would be enough space for Faiz Sahib's numerous admirers, because everyone in this snow-bound city wanted to see him. My house for those four days became the centre of our diasporic universe. Invitations for dinner, lunches, poured in.

One evening, I took him and Alys to the home of an old school friend from India, Rajiv Malhotra. The poet sat by the fireplace, amongst an adoring audience of Indians and Pakistanis. Next to him was a sparkling glass of amber liquid and between his fingers the glowing tip of a cigarette; outside the world was covered with snow. The first request was for the iconic Faiz ghazal which we all had hummed for years, whether driving a car, cooking, cleaning or shovelling snow. '*Gulon mein rang bharey baad-e-naubahar chaley*'. Taking a sip of his Scotch, with his shy smile, he spoke 'Oh that one—that's Mehdi Hasan's ghazal.' He went on to explain that he had 'given' this poem to Mehdi Hasan because it was his voice which had turned it into a global favourite.

Decades later when I was in the same city recalling those Faiz days, the prairie world had changed beyond recognition. That was the evening of his life, just as this is the evening of mine; two years after the visit Faiz Sahib passed away. At the time when he and Alys came to me, he had seen it all—prison terms, privation, adulation, exile, protest, resistance. But I could not discern any mark on his face left by life's harsh dealing. He was gentle, soft, full of humour and, yes love. In my copy of his book *Zindan Nama* (Missives from Prison) he wrote these lines which I have quoted earlier:

Dil na Umeed to nahin naakaam hee to hai
Lambi hai gham ki shaam magar shaam hee to hai

Heart has lost out but hope has not
Long is this eve of sorrow but its only evening

Today these lines come to my rescue when I sense my defeat on many fronts of my life.

What shall I say about the relevance of Faiz in the world we are living in especially for the youth who are now walking the road we are leaving behind for them. Youth who will choose their branches and binaries, their compliance and protest. Faiz lived in times of military dictatorship where for him as well as for his Indian friends across the border, Ali Sardar Jafri, Sahir Ludhianvi, Kaifi Azmi, Majaz Lakhnawi, there was only one choice. Their creed in the words of my favourite Irish poet Dylan Thomas was:

> Do not go gentle into the good night
> Rage rage against the dying of the light.

So they all wrote searing lines such as these lines of Faiz:

> *Phool masley gaye farsh e gulzar par*
> *Rung chidhka gaya takhta e daar par*
> *Bazm barpa karey jisko manzoor ho*
> *Da'wat e raqs talwar ki dhaar pe*

> Flowers were crushed on garden stretches
> Colour sprinkled on the scaffold plank
> Whoever believes in it can start celebrating
> This invitation to dance on the edge of the sword.

Today in 2023 so much of Faiz's prison poetry describes our condition as if on cue, post the Citizenship Amendment Act (CAA) and National Register of Citizens (NRC) protest, and the pandemic which had us in its grip for two long years.

Faiz served several prison terms. The first and longest spell lasted four and a half years from 1951 to 1955. He was first locked up in Hyderabad (Sind) Jail for two years and then in Montgomery (Sahiwal) Jail. During this period he spent a brief time in Karachi Jail for medical treatment and two solitary spells in Lahore and Lyallpur (now Faisalabad). His second prison term was for six months from 1958 to 1959, mostly in the notorious Lahore Fort. I found his prison poetry among my books. There was an anthology of his collected works called *Waraq Waraq* (Page by Page). My generation did not know the term 'soft copies', we always read and enjoyed poetry when our fingers could feel the texture of the page and turn the paper back and forth. The anthology included five of his best collections; *Naqsh e Faryadi, Dast e Saba, Zindan Nama, Dast e Teh e Sang* and *Sar e Vadi e Sina*. There is a short article in the anthology where Faiz expresses his reluctance to speak about himself. And yet, he cannot say 'no' to his interlocutor. The first period of his life, 1920-1930, was all about love, romantic poetry. It was a period of Beauty for Beauty and Art for Art. Lines like '*Khuda woh waqt na laye ke sogwaar ho tu*' (May the time never come when you are sorrowful) or '*Meri Jaan ab bhi apna husn wapis pher de mujhko*' (My love return to me even now your beauty). Then romance gives way to despair when the evil of global capitalism casts its shadow over the country. All doors are closed for artists. As if '*Ab yahan koi nahin koi nahin aayega*' (No one, no one will ever come this way). He writes that this feeling is captured in his relatively less known poem 'Yaas' (Longing)

Ho chukka bund rahmaton ka nuzool
Bund hai muddaton se baab e qubool
Be niyaz e dua hai Rabb e Karim

The chapter of benediction is closed
The segment of concession has ended
God is indifferent to prayers

Many years later something momentous happened in my life. One nazm of Faiz said it all. It was the day the results of the General Election in 2019 were announced. I spent the morning at the adda organised by my friend and renowned media person, Seema Mustafa's online newspaper, *The Citizen*. As the results flashed before my eyes, in my mind flashed lines of Faiz. They were about a time when joy had become a distant dream, these lines kept me company all the time the tallies were being shown on the screen:

Aaj ke din na poochho mere doston
Dur kitney hain khushiyan manane ke din
Khul ke hansne ke din geet gaane ke din
Pyar karne ke din dil lagane ke din

Aaj ke din na poochho mere doston
Kab tumhare lahu ke darida alam
Farq e khurshid e mahshar pe honge raqam
Az karaan ta karaan kab tumhare qadam
Leke uthega voh bahr e khoon yam ba yam
Jis mein dhul jaega aaj ke din ka gham
Saare dard o alam saare jaur o sitam

Duur kitni hai khursheed e mahshar ki lau
Aaj ke din na poochho mere doston

Don't ask, don't ask today O friend
How far are those happy days
Full-throated laughter, trilling songs
Days of love and passion of heart

Don't ask, don't ask today O friend
When ragged insignias of your blood
Will be hoisted on the blazing sun of Judgment Day
From end to end, horizon to horizon
When with your stamping feet
The ocean of blood, wave upon wave
Will wash away torture, torment, abuse
Of this black day.
How far is that awesome Judgment Day
Don't ask, don't ask today O friend.

Salima Hashmi, Faiz Sahib's older daughter, once explained to me why her father's poetry had become so popular across continents. Poetry, by its very nature, she said, belongs to oral tradition. When it is set to music and is telecast or broadcast in manifold digital ways, it seems to take over from the recitation and the written page. When one thinks of the great Sufi poets, only a few read their poetry; originally, it used to be recited and learnt by heart, even by totally illiterate masses! Perhaps it is in the nature of poetry from this part of the world to rule over the imagination through the power of its sound. Faiz Sahib himself was a devotee of Bulhe Shah, in other words, of the oral tradition which he felt was ultimately superior to any other form.

Today in the streets of India one poem resounds. I don't know why but I have a strong sense that Faiz (from another sphere) is saying, 'I give another of my poems, this time to the rising wave of youth in 21st century South Asia. To them I give my poem "Hum Dekhenge".'

This poem has become the anthem of the movement of non-cooperation led by youth and women everywhere in this country of 1.3 billion. Beginning with its original Urdu version in my own neighbourhood, Jamia, and next door Shaheen Bagh, it resounded in Kannada, Malayalam, Oriya, Bengali, Tamil, Assamese and other languages, thereby establishing its universality in a multi-lingual land. It also marked the seamlessness of borders and boundaries in all realms of art. When sung at IIT Kanpur it created a storm. Powers across the right-wing spectrum were on the warpath against this rendering. Why? Because it was written by a Pakistani, because its language was Urdu, because it forecasted Inquilab.

I come now to the words and the context in which Faiz wrote this poem. Those were the darkest days in Pakistan; Zia-ul Haq's military rule had throttled all dissent. Many of the best and brightest were serving prison sentences for daring to speak out. Faiz himself was either in prison or in self-imposed exile. The words Faiz wrote in *Zindan Nama* were a cry for Freedom just as the song of African Americans, 'O Freedom' which, sung by Odetta in the 1960s, became a universal anthem.

The children of the 2020s stood defiant in the face of the Citizenship Amendment Act, National Population Register and National Register of Citizens, saying to the powerful, 'Hum Dekhenge'. It was this assertion which struck fear in the hearts of people who then wielded batons, tear gas and pellet guns. They dreaded and hated the youth who said that they will see the promised dawn which was struggling to break out. 'We will live to see the promised day.' The words '*Lauh-e-Azal*' create suspicion in the untutored minds of baton wielders because of their sound. Urdu? Arabic? They neither know nor care that the word '*Lauh*' means 'slate' and the word '*azal*' means 'eternity'. Freedom is written on the slate of eternity and we will live to see it. Freedom from what? Azadi from what? Hunger, unemployment, oppression, violence, anarchy, patriarchy, on and on.

The poem continues. A day will come when mountains of violence will vanish like clouds of cotton. '*Rooee ki tarah ud jaenge.*' The earth will reverberate. It will tremble beneath the feet of the oppressed. Lightning will blaze above the heads of our oppressors. Its shafts will flash, crackle. Nature will become the metaphor for revolution and in this universal chaos the slogan '*An-al-Haq*' will rise and rise. This will be your slogan, this will be my slogan—'I am Truth'.

The slogan '*An-al-Haq*' raised first by the Sufi philosopher Mansur Al Hallaj has been raised by philosophers of every faith in the world.

The lines of the poem that follow the above lines have been twisted by right-wing ideologues beyond recognition. They are declared 'anti national', 'hurting religious sentiments' et al. Ignorance of language and history is never challenged in any court of law. No bench sentences someone who deliberately creates communal hatred by distorting language. Who cares that '*arz-e-Khuda*' in the poem refers to the Kaaba, the ultimate pilgrimage for Muslims. Who cares if it is the pre-Islamic idols which are referred to in the lines '*Sab buth uthwaye jayeinge*', 'All idols will be lifted from the Kaaba'. And then the lines about the poor inheriting the earth: '*Hum ahl-e-safa mardood-e-Haram masnad pe bithae jayenge*'—'We who sat on the margins of the mosque (Masjid-e-Nabavi) will be placed on the throne'. That means power will belong to the people. Then the lines, '*Jab taj uchchaley jayeinge aur takht giraye jaiyenge*' (The tossing out of crowns and dismantling of thrones became anathema for the powerful). Finally the lines '*Aur raj karegi khalq-e-Khuda jo mein bhi hoon aur tum bhi ho*' (Power will devolve to the people of God, which is you, which is me).

Faiz wrote these lines as an anthem for the oppressed of his land, promising them the 'time' which is bound to come, sooner than later. He may have known that he was writing an anthem for the oppressed of the entire world. Poets, according to Greek philosophy, are prophets of their times. Faiz Ahmed Faiz's prophecy is now resounding through my country through the voices of the youth. It foretells a time for celebration. The harder the blows fall on the bodies of youth the greater is the dread in the heart of the perpetrator.

So Faiz's toast is raised... to Gauri Lankesh, Gobind Pansare, Kalburgi, Dhabolkar, and... yes to Sudha Bhardwaj, Gautam Navlakha, Varavara Rao, Father Stan. Hum dekhenge!

Khushwant Singh

I was nine years old when I met him for the first time. We had moved to Delhi in the early 1950s and lived in Sujan Singh Park. The Partition of India had left us children very bewildered. We heard sounds of older family members crying softly at night. In 1947, their dear ones had crossed the border and gone to Pakistan. I used to wonder, what was this Pakistan which caused us to lose 90 percent of our family? And the grief which was never really forgotten was silently passed on to the next generation.

I can close my eyes and conjure up the image of myself standing before Khushwant, tongue-tied and fidgety. This was after my story 'You Have to Learn to Make Friends' had been published in *Shankar's Weekly*. Khushwant had written me a letter complimenting me on the story, and my father insisted we go across to his flat to thank him. It was the same room which I was to visit again and again over the next forty years and more. Many years later I was to leave India to go and live in Canada. Throughout those eighteen years the memory of Khushwant remained in my mind and heart although I cannot say that I remained in his. I used to meet him every time I returned home for a visit, once when he was the editor of *The Illustrated Weekly of India* and later when he was editing *Hindustan Times*. He made it a practice to write small pieces in his columns about my 'achievements' in Canada; those yellowing news clippings have been lovingly preserved.

One day, while browsing through Indian newspapers at the library in Edmonton, I read a piece written by him. I can't recall my feelings then but today when I reread this piece I identify with each word. This was his editorial in *Hindustan Times*. Its title was 'Why I am an Indian':

> I did not have any choice; I was born one. If the good Lord had consulted me on the subject I might have chosen a country more affluent, less crowded, less censorious in matters of food and drink, unconcerned with personal equations and free of religious bigotry.
>
> Am I proud of being an Indian? I can't really answer this one. I can scarcely take credit for the achievements of my forefathers. And I have little reason to be proud of what we are doing today. On balance, I would say, 'No, I am not proud of being an Indian.'

'Why don't you get out and settle in some other country?' Once again, I have very little choice. All the countries I might like to live in have restricted quotas for immigrants; most of them are white and have prejudice against coloured people. In any case I feel more relaxed and at home in India. I dislike many things in my country—mostly the government. I know the government is never the same as the country, but it never stops trying to appear in that garb. This is where I belong, and this is where I intend to live and die. Of course, I like going abroad. Living is easier, wine and food are better, women are more forthcoming—it's more fun. However, I soon get tired of all those things and want to get back to my dung-heap and be among my loud-mouthed, sweaty, smelly countrymen. I am like my kinsmen in Africa and England and elsewhere. My head tells me it's better to live abroad, my belly tells me it is more fulfilling to be in 'phoren' but my heart tells me 'get back to Ind'. Each time I return home and drive through the stench of bare-bottomed defecators that line the road from Santa Cruz airport to the city I ask myself:

> Breathes there a man with soul so dead
> who never to himself hath said
> this is my own land, my native land?

I can scarcely breathe, but I yell, 'Yeah, this is my native land. I don't like it, but I love it!'

Are you an Indian first and a Punjabi or Sikh second? Or is it the other way round? I don't like the way those questions are framed. I am all three at the same time. If I was denied my Punjabiness or my community tradition, I would refuse to call myself Indian. I am Indian, Punjabi and Sikh. And even so I have a patriotic kinship; one who says I am 'Indian, Hindu and Haryanvi' or 'I am Indian, Moplah Muslim and Malayali' or 'I am Indian, Christian and Assamese'. I want to retain my religious and linguistic identity without in any way making them exclusive.

What then this talk about Indianising people who are already

Indian? And has anyone any right to arrogate to himself the right to decide who is and who is not a good Indian?"

Today fifty years later, I wonder if he wrote these lines for me!

~

It was when I decided to return home for good after twenty years abroad that Khushwant and I rediscovered each other. Having been away for so long I had great difficulty in settling down. Being a single mother with a young daughter meant big responsibilities. After almost two decades, how was I to begin my life? Sensing my precarious situation, Khushwant started asking from time to time for my advice on pieces of Urdu literature, mostly poetry. I used to look up poems for him, translate some verses and verify a few references for his weekly column. Slowly the trust began to build. It was then that he assigned me the thousand-page autobiography of Sher e Kashmir, Sheikh Abdullah, called *Atish e Chinar,* for translation into English. Sheikh Sahib had dictated this book to his secretary Mohammad Yusuf Taing. Penguin India published it in 1983 as *Flames of the Chinar*, but put only Khushwant's name on the cover, though we had worked on it together. The reason was obvious—he was a 'name', I was not! I was always hesitant to ask for money. But Khushwant was most insistent that I should be paid for my work and made sure that Penguin did so. 'Why should you work for free? After all this is your rozi roti!'

Among our shared experiences was that we had the same alma mater. Khushwant was one of the earliest products of Modern School. I was a student of the same school in the late 1950s. When the school celebrated its 75th year in 1995 the Trust decided to publish a commemorative volume. Khushwant was asked to take charge. But who would be his co-author? Without hesitation he said, 'Syeda, of course.' So once again we joined hands and what came out was a stunning volume called *A Dream Turns 75* containing the school's history drawn from all the archival materials I selected from the private papers, text and photographs of the families of Lala Raghubir Singh and Sardar Sobha Singh, Khushwant's father. It had been Lala Raghubir Singh's dream to found an educational institution that was truly eclectic, and this he did in 1920 together with Sobha Singh and other like-minded individuals. Once again Khushwant insisted that I be paid for my work, his work for his old school was purely gratis. So I began to move forward as a writer and slowly recognition came my way. Khushwant was visibly delighted. I often noticed the pride in his voice when he introduced me to his unending stream of visitors and admirers.

In 1999 we went together to Hyderabad where we had been invited by the Maulana Azad Institute of Oriental Studies to deliver two lectures on Maulana's interpretation of the Quran. In his inimitable style he wrote about this sombre event in a column titled 'Nawabs and Courtesans'; nothing to do with the subject, he wrote, but to induce the reader to read it! Of his own lecture he wrote that because of technical glitches it was an 'unmitigated disaster'. Then he went on to write about my presentation. 'When it came to Syeda's turn, the organisers had slipped up on one detail; there was no audience. It would have dampened anyone's spirit but not Syeda's. She is Saiyidain's daughter with his grit, learning and oratory in her genes. She had her small audience exploding in raptures of Wah! Wah! I have not heard another Indian woman speak as well as her on as esoteric a subject.' About me, he was over-generous always and I loved him for it. If similar praise was showered on me by someone today, it would run like this: 'I have not heard another Indian Muslim woman speak like this.' Khushwant intensely disliked this appellation.

In those days I was a Fellow at Teen Murti House, working on Maulana Abul Kalam Azad. It was Phase Two of the work I had begun at the ICCR when the government decided to commemorate

Maulana's birth centenary by bringing out four volumes on his work. I used to drop by to see Khushwant on my way to the library and discuss with him my chapters as they were being written. What emerged as the final outcome was my biography of Maulana Azad, *Islamic Seal on India's Independence*. Khushwant was as involved with its writing as I was. I had written a long chapter about Maulana Azad the poet, the writer, the chronicler which I derived from his exquisite epistolary collection *Ghubar e Khatir*. Khushwant with his passion for Urdu poetry enjoyed that chapter the most. As recounted earlier, he recommended the book to Penguin India, but they didn't take it up. I was hurt and Khushwant was annoyed.

Khushwant never forgot my disappointment so when the first opportunity arose he set things right in his own special way. Doordarshan asked me to suggest someone who would interview me on my book for the programme Kitabon ki Duniya. Very hesitantly I asked Khushwant, knowing that unless the show featured a 'star' no one would bother to watch any programme about Maulana Azad. To my surprise Khushwant immediately said yes. And the man who was most sought after as the subject of interviews, sat on the opposite side of the table and interviewed me! It was the most scintillating interview even if I say so myself. Kuber Dutt, the director, was thrilled. So was I at the candour and canvas within which Khushwant broached the subject.

Maulana Azad created a bond between us. We had both read Azad's *Tarjumanul Quran* over months, with great care. Almost a quarter century ago he had gifted my daughter Ayesha a copy of the Quran with Abdullah Yusuf Ali's translation and commentary. Ever since it has been used intensely by her mother but the inscription says, 'For Ayesha with love from Khushwant'.

Khushwant was my biggest cheerleader as I progressed to hold 'important' positions in government. He loved saying to his admiring evening coterie, 'Now she has a lal batti wali gadi.' But all along he prodded me to write and not get too carried away by the temporary importance these positions gave me. He inspired me to do the English translation of 296 verses of Maulana Altaf Husain Hali's poem 'Ebb and Tide in Islam' popularly known as 'Musaddas e Hali'. He insisted that I rhyme the couplets and would not relent when I said it was too difficult. Some years ago he had translated in rhyme Allama Iqbal's masterpiece poem 'Shikwa Jawab e Shikwa', which created a storm in the literary world and ran into many editions. He believed that I could do for Hali what he had done for Iqbal. It was a tough call, but by Allah's grace, it happened. Khushwant was very happy with what I had produced. He held the manuscript in his hand with great pride. Then he persuaded HarperCollins to take it on. The result was a book of Hali's landmark poem translated into English in rhyme, along with the original Urdu and 'Roman Urdu', so people would still enjoy the flavour of the language.

~

Khushwant and Kavalji, his wife, had a home in Kasauli where they would retreat a couple of times in the year. I always wanted to spend a few days with them in the sylvan surroundings of Kasauli. It was a summer in the late 1990s when I was able to tear myself away from the compulsions of work and fulfil this desire.

There were two worn-down nameplates on the gate of the house. The left one bore the letters 'Teja Singh Malik' and the right one said 'Raj Villa'. Kaval's father Sardar Teja Singh had built this sprawling summer cottage among the mountains for his children. A portrait of him as a strikingly handsome young man hangs in the front parlour. Next to it is another smaller portrait of an older Teja Singh, equally splendid, taken at the time when he was conferred the Order of the British Empire.

Sitting with Khushwant and Kaval in the evenings in their mountain home, surrounded by trees and birdsong, Ghalib's lines took on newer meanings. Ghalib wrote, 'Life just carries us along like a galloping steed. Nothing is in our control; neither the rein nor the stirrup.'

Raj Vilas has now passed on to Khushwant's son, Rahul, who continues the tradition of using it as his summer retreat. A few years before he and his partner, Niloufer Billimoria, started the Khushwant Singh Literary Festival in 2012 in Khushwant's memory, I visited Kasauli again and stayed with Rahul at Raj Vilas. The memories of my first visit came flooding back!

~

I have a dozen letters from Khushwant, written on onion paper, blue aerograms, postcards. My treasure. He wrote from Kasauli:

'The sun has gone over the hill. It is only 3.20 pm but with the long shadows comes the chill. Cicadas that chirped merrily on the pines around the villa have flown to summer hill states. I will watch Sportsview for a while then wake myself for a long walk. It is a waxing moon so coming down the moonlit path is no hazard. Then Scotch by the fireside and your visage among the leaping flame. And so to bed.'

From Glasgow (why had he gone there?) he wrote chatty letters; I could close my eyes and hear him speak:

'The *Daily Jang* [an Urdu newspaper from Pakistan] has gone for me over the Azad article in the *Indian Express* mainly on the rejection of the two-nation theory. You and I belonging to different nations! Preposterous notion! How to tell these bigots it makes no sense, much less when one strives to get close to the other person's heart. However all Paki's read *Jang*...Very idle day today. Lovely sunshine and very cool. So I will go for a stroll in Calvin Park, then pick up a samosa (very large) from a Pak grocer, a carton of milk. That's lunch. More walk after a long siesta. Then land up in some trattoria to eat pasta and wash it down with a bottle of Chianti or Barolo. Allah is in

His heaven and all is right with KS. Lots of love. If there is no letter waiting for me in London I may contemplate suicide!'

So we continued together over forty years, talking, writing, walking and most importantly, laughing. One day, I think it was in 1998, when Delhi was at its peak of flowering trees, senwal (silk cotton), tesu (Flame of the Forest), Khushwant decided that we would walk in Buddha Jayanti Park, and he would tell me about trees, their botanical names and popular names, and their blossoming seasons. That spring afternoon we walked in the park for two hours, gazing at the gulmohars in their full glory. We ambled along stone paths when suddenly we came upon thousands of salvias, hundreds of nasturtiums, two shades of yellow calendulas. We saw some exquisite bauhinias (clusters of white and pink flowers on branches). He pointed to a bird and told me its name, Teeteri and that its bird call was 'I didn't do it, I didn't do it.' He was most garrulous. Conversation with him, as always, was effortless. I also listened a lot. He liked that and I liked the feel of walking and exercising my legs. At the end of the walk we sat in the outdoor cafeteria and sipped Limcas.

Sadeqain, an artist, poet and calligrapher, was born in Amroha, UP, and died in Karachi in Pakistan. He was renowned in the Urdu speaking world for his paintings, murals and poetry. Khushwant and I collaborated (in a manner of speaking) on the translation of Sadeqain's self-illustrated erotic verses which were unknown to the world, because they were part of a private collection, never brought into the public domain. I say 'in a manner of speaking' because I was diffident and shy sitting with Khushwant and looking at the sketches and finding words to explain erotica. But Khushwant took it very matter of factly; it was work which had to be done. We sat in his drawing room and grappled with Sadeqain's sketches and poetry. I realised that when it came to translation, whether it was Iqbal's 'Shikwa Jawab e Shikwa', Altaf Hussain Hali's 'Mussadas e Hali', Faiz Ahmed Faiz's *Zindan Nama* or Sadeqain's erotica, it is nothing but hard work and sweat. Khushwant with great discipline and meticulousness ploughed through the work, ignoring my diffidence.

I was elated when Khushwant dedicated his book, *Need for a New Religion in India*, to me. In that book, written in 1991, one year before the demolition of Babri Masjid, he had with prophetic foresight quoted these lines written by Punjabi Sufi Bhulle Shah:

Masjid dha de Mandir dha de
Dha de jo kuchh dhenda
Ek kisi ka dil na dhaveeen
Rabb dilan vich rehnda

Break down the mosque, break down the temple,
Break down anything besides
But never break a human heart
That is where God resides

I wondered why he had chosen to dedicate that particular book to me. Was it because he saw me as a devout Muslim; fasting, praying, poring over the Quran and holding Majlis and observing mourning during Muharram?

In this book he explains the concept of religion which rises above individual belief to encompass all humanity. In fact what he was explaining was his own personal religious code. I think of him as one who was as close to Islam as he was to Hinduism, Sikhism and Christianity. He treated all religions with the same loveable irreverence! He owned at least six different translations of the Quran and produced two definitive volumes on the history of the Sikhs.[23] He could not stand a fanatic or a person without humour. Of 'prudes' he was most intolerant. Deep in his heart, I am afraid, he may have considered me a bit of all three. I was never able to remove that notion from his head.

The world remembers him as the scholar who wrote the two-volume *History of the Sikhs,* and his joke books. Indians remember him for that, as well as for the persona he created for himself—'Not a nice man to know', or 'With malice towards one and all' or 'Dirty old man'. All of this, so carefully cultivated! South Asia remembers him as author of *Train to Pakistan*. But for me there is one overpowering memory. I have not known anyone else who could love with equal ardour Urdu, English and Punjabi. One who had the grace, the temerity, and the warmth to recite (when I entered his house) this verse of Mirza Ghalib:

Muddat hui hai yaar ko mehmaan kiye huey
Josh e qada se bazm charaghan kiye huey

So long since my loved one was invited to my home
So long since the goblet gushed and lit up the gathering

When I sat down near him, there he was with his drink in his hand, couplet after couplet flowing from his lips, his eyes dreamy, a smile on his face. He would wander into Ghalib's Sufi musings, poetry which sounds beautiful but is difficult to fathom on account of the multiple layers of philosophy packed in each line. Who but Khushwant could recite these lines of Ghalib to a mesmerised audience, many of them barely Urdu speaking:

Kaave kaave sakht jaani hai tanhai ne pooch
Subah karna shaam ka laana hai juey e sheer ka

Don't ask me of the tortuous convolutions of loneliness
To turn nights into mornings is drawing a river of milk from
the rock

The reference here is to Farhad, the legendary lover who carved a nehr of milk through rock mountains to gain access to his beloved Shireen.

'All night it is Ghalib and only Ghalib,' he told me often. 'I think of nothing else. You know, I am never lonesome.'

The curtains in his drawing room greeted the visitors with calligraphy, a simple expression, horizontally framed, *Salam Alekum Salam Alekum Salam Alekum.* On that last day, March 20, 2014,while he lay peacefully in his bedroom, the curtains gently beckoned: 'Peace be on you, Peace be on you' to the string of visitors who filed past.

I close my eyes and there he is, sitting on his comfortably worn out chair with his old moodha as his footstool, a blanket thrown across his legs during winters, with the fire glowing merrily. In summer he is in the same chair clad in a blue kurta and white crumpled shalwar, yellow band around his head in lieu of a turban. He is lifting the phone, pouring a drink and scribbling endlessly. I think of Faiz who must have had him in his mind when he wrote:

Hum parvarish e lauh o qalam karte rahenge
Jo dil pe guzarti hai raqam karte rahenge
Maikhana salamat hai to hum surkhi e mai se
Taz'zeen e dar o baam e Haram karte rahenge

The pen and slate we will nurture and drive
What touches the heart we will always inscribe
May the tavern prosper, with its shimmering wine
We will colour, embellish the Kaaba sublime

Given his love of Urdu poetry, a love we have shared, if I had to express our friendship in one couplet of the thousands we have read separately and together I would pick this one from Faiz:

Kabhi kabhi yaad mein ubhartey hain naqsh e maazi mitey mitey se
Vo aazmaish dil o nazar ki vo qurbatein si voh faasley se

Sometimes on memory's slate appear markings of a past faint and dim
Those challenges of love and desire, that closeness, those distances.

Gagan Sethi

I met him for the first time in 2002 at my friend Kamla Bhasin's house on Bhagwan Das Road. He had arrived there four days after the burning of the Sabarmati Express had unleashed the Gujarat *qatl-e-aam* (mass killings). His question to me was direct. 'Would you be willing to lead a group of women to examine and report on this carnage? Especially what was done to Muslim women?'

I was taken aback. 'Lead? Me? Please… I can only be a member of the team.' Much later, I realised why he wanted me to lead.

Gagan began to convince me. 'Do you remember the anthem of the juggernaut which was unleashed by L.K. Advani the early 1990s when he sallied forth in his Rath Yatra exhorting innocent people to partake of his "holy" mission? "Ram Lalla hum layenge. Hum mandir wahin banayenge!" In Gujarat today this spiral of violence has spun out of control. No one knows when and how this ghoul will stop its dance of death.'

Six of us faced each other in silence. We were in Ahmedabad; all around us were devastated houses and human debris. Sheba George, Ruth Manorama, Farah Naqvi, Malini Ghosh, Mari Thekekara and I spent six agonising days in and around a city where Muslim houses, businesses, shops were selected, singled out and burnt. We fanned out in groups of two and three to other spaces around the city in which the worst stories of human depravity had happened. Gagan and his colleagues steered us through the investigation which took us to Kheda, Vadodara, Sabarkantha and Panchmahal. I recall confiding to Gagan that I had placed furniture to block the door of my hotel room at night, so palpable was the dread of what the marauders had done to Muslim women. On April 16, 2002, our report was released, 'How the Gujarat Massacre Affected Minority Women'. It was cited in the Lok Sabha by Mrs Sonia Gandhi and the Gujarat High Court. It was quoted at international fora such as the UN's (United Nations) CEDAW (Convention on the Elimination of All

Forms of Discrimination Against Women), and Human Rights panels in the USA and the UK

~

Gagan is the child of refugee parents who fled from Rawalpindi to Delhi and were forced to live a reduced existence in a resettlement colony of Delhi. 'My father talks very little of it,' he wrote in his book *Lest We Forget History*. Just before the bloodshed began they boarded trucks and reached the camps in Delhi. He saw his father struggle to support him as well as his sister and her family after her husband was killed in Rawalpindi in the communal conflagration. Characteristically, he talks very little about his personal trauma.

My own trauma runs parallel to his. We were destined to meet long before we actually met. What happened to his family happened to mine at the same time. When I was a child I heard stories that in 1947 hoodlums looted my uncle's house in Karol Bagh and came for him with naked swords. The whisper later was that this assault happened not just because he was Muslim, they also wanted his beautifully carved Kashmir furniture and brand new 'radiogram'. While the looting was going on his next-door neighbours, a Sikh family, hid him and his family in their godown. The woman sent her teenage children to join the looting mobs so they could rescue some of Azhar Uncle's precious family possessions. With tears in his eyes my uncle used to recount how they triumphantly held out his framed family photographs and a few items of clothing saying, 'Azhar Uncle, see what we brought!' Azhar Abbas, having lost everything, still opted to stay in India with his family, rejecting the idea of going to Pakistan. From here Gagan and my story diverged. Gagan's entire family, like 90 percent of my family, got into trucks and moved across the border, but in opposite directions. Ten percent of mine, remained here, the rest went to Pakistan. Gagan's family took the route from Rawalpindi to Delhi. Those of my family who stayed, did so because India was their mitti from which they refused to be parted. In this refusal was destined a meeting between Gagan and me which would turn into a lifelong friendship. In retrospect I feel that Gagan and I met because he was destined to vindicate my family's faith in choosing to stay back; is that why he chose the Indian Muslim as his life's mission?

Slowly he became my anchor no matter what problem, what issue, what disaster, he was always there for me. And for the Muslims of Gujarat, shining Gujarat, vibrant Gujarat there was always Gagan. For my lifelong work at the Muslim Women's Forum, my lodestar was always Gagan—Hindu and male, working for Muslims; such beauty in this blend of Ganga-Jamna Tehzeeb!

I had started the Muslim Women's Forum in 2000 after I had completed my term at the National Commission for Women. MWF was born out of my desire to continue my work with and for Muslim women which I had begun at NCW. But then in 2004 until 2014 came my two terms in the Planning Commission, which meant my absence from MWF. When I rejoined the organisation in 2014, it had become very different from its original vision. There was no money; in 2006 MWF was refused tax relief under Sec. 80G on a very flimsy pretext. I was then Member, Planning Commission, and had the wherewithal to appeal against this irrational decision. In the vortex of sarkari life, however, I forgot to rescue my own organisation. We began in 2014 with no money and an inactive board but the spirit was still strong there. This is when Gagan entered MWF.

In 2018, MWF initiated the project 'Leadership and Capacity Building for Muslim Women' with the support it received from another lifelong friend of Gagan, Martin Macwan, who also became my steadfast hamasafar. Martin is a Dalit human rights activist and founder of Navsarjan Trust. In 2000, he was awarded the Robert F. Kennedy Human Rights Award and in the same year, Human Rights Watch named him one of the year's five 'outstanding human rights defenders'. As an aside, Gagan and Martin named me the chairperson of Dalit Foundation. A Muslim woman chairing a Dalit Foundation! That was Gagan and Martin's kaarnaama. Today how many will believe that such a thing happened in Gujarat of all places?

Under the Leadership project, we sent out MWF teams to identify potential Fellows who could become grassroots community leaders and carry on community activities in their own areas. MWF identified fifteen women from five locations—Delhi, Koraon (UP), Chhatarpur (MP), Tezpur and Barpeta (Assam). The two months training was conducted at Dalit Shakti Kendra in Sanand (50 kilometres from Ahmedabad). It was the first time that most of them had left their homes.

Ruth, Sahla and I accompanied the girls to Sanand, and dropped them off at the Kendra, after which I returned to Delhi. When I left, the girls looked so sad, so forlorn. I felt a mix of relief and guilt. Should I have stayed back to hold their hand for a few more hours? Like two sentinels, my young colleagues, Ruth and Sahla, were standing with them, as my taxi, driven by 'Driver Ben' Samina, came out of the gates of DSK.

It was two months later that Gagan and I reached DSK for a commencement function arranged by Martin Macwan and Indu Rohit. As the evening cooled the burning ground in front of the Admin block, a line of young girls began emerging from the buildings. Were these the same girls I had seen standing in silent resignation on these grounds barely eight weeks ago?

Two months ago, they had sat with us in a quiet circle in a room at Dalit Shakti Kendra. Unsmiling, tense, anxious. Each of us spoke gentle words of encouragement as we tried to draw a smile from their grim faces, a word from their pursed lips. My eye caught a small girl who was almost in tears. Stunted, malnourished, skin and bones. Would she survive two months in these hard conditions in rural Gujarat?

I was about to witness a miracle that evening. First it was their appearance. Razia from Chhattarpur was draped in a glowing red sari with a gold border draped around her shoulders. Ambreen was in a blue flowing kurta, her gold earrings like moons on both sides of her face. Najma, the tiny frail Najma, was dressed in a smart churidar with a flush in her cheeks. And Jahana, the stone-faced mazdoor child from Koraon, looked confident, well-groomed; her high cheekbones a model's dream. I could go on and on.

This was their transformed appearance. But it was their internal transformation which was DSK's miracle. Hameeda Parvin from Assam, who since childhood had never been permitted to go out to run or to play games, was declared this batch's most outstanding sportsperson. Tall and slim, she walked away with the best sportsperson award. Afsana Khatoon, who had never spoken a word in any forum anywhere, was orator number one. And Afsana Bano was the best essay writer of the batch. She spoke with passion about social justice and violence against women. She spoke of Asifa, the eight-year-old Bakerwal child from Jammu & Kashmir. Where was God when she was raped and mutilated in a temple, she asked? Ambreen Bano spoke about how DSK expanded the horizons of her mind. 'Before coming here, when we looked at the mirror, we saw our own faces. But the mirror DSK held up for us was "Mirror of Truth". We saw the world in its reflection.'

It was a defining moment in the history of DSK and MWF. My two friends, who had sowed the seed of DSK twenty years ago, sat on my right and left. Gagan Sethi and Martin Macwan. Their journey began with a seventeen-year-old girl in a village in Saurashtra. They both had gone on a mission to create awareness about the scourge of manual scavenging. After hearing them, people who had gathered around them made a resolution. They would never ever carry shit loads again. 'What will you do?' Martin asked. 'I will sell brooms,' said one. 'I will buy a cycle, tie brooms on the carrier and sell them,' said another. The inexorable curse of 'broom' refused to go away. Then from the back row one girl spoke up, 'I will buy material and sell pieces for blouses.' Thus DSK was born.

'At DSK, you learn to grab your azadi. Physical and emotional azadi. Go empowered from here and then get involved in the big Ladai called life'. Gagan was addressing the students. Then it was Martin speaking. 'There is no one who comes to DSK and returns empty. We all carry something away from here. If you had not come, our lives would have been empty, dull. When you go tomorrow, we will feel sad, but we will also be happy because a new batch will arrive to follow your footsteps. Now we will wait. We will look eagerly for your names to appear in newspapers and TV to mark the work you will do in your communities.' Over the years, DSK has trained 9,930 youth for community work, 51 per cent of them women.

~

In 2021, I invited Gagan to join the governing body of MWF. He watched our penurious state quietly for a few months. Then he suggested a roadmap. 'Why don't you start explaining the spirit of Islam to people of India? Isn't that what the world needs desperately?' His initial idea was that Kamla Bhasin and I criss-cross through rural India explaining the spirit of Hinduism and Islam. That could not happen. Then on his suggestion we began workshops on Understanding Islam: Theology, Sociology and Legality. The idea was to help women to increase their understanding on issues related to Islam, to provide the participants an opportunity to increase their understanding, awareness and sensitivity on a range of issues related to Islam. It was open to all. Today we have men and women participants from all communities. Our first workshop was held in a training centre which Gagan and Martin had built in Sanand. Four of us—Sheba George, Reyaz Ahmed, Sarover Zaidi and I held the workshop there for Sangram, a voluntary organisation for sex workers in Sangli, Maharashtra. It was founded by an old friend of mine, Meena Seshu. That was the start. Our workshops were then held in Lucknow, Bangalore, Patna, Bongaigaon, and Delhi. Everywhere we had superb partners, quietly nudged by Gagan.

Then Covid struck so we went online, holding workshops with participants from all over India. It was a successful experiment over eight months. Then we noticed fatigue since attendance grew thin as the country gradually opened up. Gagan, once again, bailed me out. 'Make a film and use it as a pedagogical tool.' So we began. A film on Understanding Islam in fourteen parts with the most important voice in films, Naseeruddin Shah, as its anchor. Dhananjai Sinha was the director. A Hindu, making a film on Understanding Islam—this is my India!

~

The year 2022 marked two decades since the Gujarat carnage. The name of that beautiful state has become synonymous with Muslim killings. Bilkis Bano and Kausar Bano have become its iconic martyrs. When I think of Gagan's role in getting Bilkis justice, I define it as the work of a momin, a true believer in God, though he is an agnostic, yes, a momin.

The story of Bilkis Bano has gone down in the anals of contemporary history. It happened on February 28, 2002. Five months pregnant, the twenty-one year old Bilkis was gang raped, her young daughter Saleha was smashed to death, and several members of her family were killed before her eyes. She named the eleven assassins: Sailesh Bhatt, Mithesh Bhatt, Vijay Maurya, Pradeep Maurya, Lala Vakil, Lala Doctor, Naresh Maurya, Jaswant Nai and Govind Nai (the last three gang-raped her). An FIR was filed and a medical examination done on the insistence of the District Collector, Jayanti Ravi. Rape was confirmed.

Gagan along with Farah Naqvi, a woman with amazing grit and

determination, were at the helm of the 'Justice for Bilkis' movement along with Subhashini Ali, Brinda Karat, Vrinda Grover and others. An FIR was filed via the National Human Rights Commission and the case transferred from Gujarat to Mumbai. Shobha Gupta, Bilkis' lawyer, was a woman on a mission. For twenty-one years, she fought to take the case to its conclusion. In 2019, in a landmark judgement, the Supreme Court directed the Gujarat government to give Rs 50 lakh, a job and accommodation to Bilkis Bano. Her eleven assailants were sentenced to life imprisonment in January 2008, only to walk out free on bail to a heroes' welcome on 15 August, 2022. It was Gagan who took Bilkis and her family to an unknown place for their safety, once the killers were on the loose.

Finally, on January 8, 2024, the Supreme Court's landmark judgement was out. The eleven convicts of the Bilkis Yakub Rasool vs Union of India case were to return to jail, by January 22. The seizure of their freedom, sixteen months after their release, became inevitable thanks to the tireless effort of Shobha Gupta, Gagan and his colleagues.

Gagan continues to be my inspiration. Thus I, a Muslim woman was directed by a Hindu man towards what would become my mission for the rest of my life; telling whoever stopped to listen what Islam stood for when it was first revealed in 7th Century AD in the Arabian peninsula. The man is unswerving, steadfast, gentle; Allama Iqbal's lines were written for him:

Khuda ke bande to hain hazaron
Banon mein phirte hain marey marey
Mein uska banda banoonga jisko
Khuda ke bandon se pyar hoga

Thousands there are, Allah's servants
Wandering in wildernesses
I will be servant of him
Who loves the servants of Allah.

Some relationships cannot be described. The unspoken bond between us defies description. Need I say more?

~

Three women have been responsible for what I am today. The first one was my mother, Aziz Jahan Begum or Ammi as I called her. The second was my father's younger sister, Saliha Abid Husain. During their lifetime I never considered them my role models; it was later that I saw myself, inadvertently, walking in their footsteps. The third is the woman who brought me into public life, Mohini Giri.

Aziz Jahan Begum

I was twenty years old when my Ammi died. I was too self-absorbed to understand her as more than 'just my mother'. She was always there first during school, college, and then higher studies in the US. Always there.

Two of my sisters, Zohra and Bilquis, had graduated First Class, attaining first and second positions at the Bombay University. A third sister, Zakia, had started by studying medicine but then fell ill and changed to home science. Zohra, the eldest, had gone to Cambridge on a Government of India scholarship. As for me, I never achieved a First Class at school or college so I had no chance of a scholarship. But I was lucky to have got the chance, being the youngest, to go with my parents for higher studies in the US. Lucky also because I enjoyed the comfort of a home along with the challenge of graduate school. Mother lavished endless love on me and since I was the youngest, endless indulgence. I knew about her longing for a male child but that did not give me the slightest complex mostly because of her love for me, her baby daughter. It was much later, after she died, that I began to understand my mother, Aziz Jahan Begum.

She came from the Rampur royal family, steeped in the nawabi tradition. Her father Shabbir Ali Khan was the younger son of the best-known and most erudite ruler of Rampur, Nawab Kalbe Ali Khan. Nawab Sahib had two sons by his two wives. The older son, Mushtaq Ali Khan, was the *wali-ehad* (heir). But there was an impediment to his succession. Being physically disabled, he was not eligible for the *gaddi* (throne) according to orders of the British Empire. Nawab Sahib's great love for his disabled son led to a massive court intrigue whereby he was propped up by two bodyguards during the coronation ceremony in the presence of a British agent. He had just been married into another feudal family, so the royal seed had been planted, but he died before the child was born.

The posthumous child was crowned and became the next ruler. Thus, Nawab Hamid Ali Khan ascended the throne, and his uncle's (my grandfather) fate was sealed as a Sahibzada, which was the title given to uncles and siblings of nawabs. He never got his due never became Nawab Shabbir Ali Khan. His disabled brother's posthumous son, Nawab Hamid Ali Khan, ruled Rampur State for many years. Hamid Ali Khan's son was Nawab Raza Ali Khan, and his grandson was Nawab Murtuza Ali Khan, popularly called Bachchan Sahib. Murtuza Sahib became very close to my mother's family, specially to her brother Sajid Ali Khan's children. My family was close to him because his father, Nawab Raza Ali Khan, had invited my father as Educational Advisor to Rampur State. All his life, Bachchan Sahib was conscious that the rightful heir was not his great-grandfather Mushtaq but our grandfather Shabbir. He always used an expression 'khoon chakan ho gaya ab koon baha hona chahiye' meaning blood has been spilt, now blood money must be settled. No one living today is an eyewitness to what he used to say. Only my Mamujaan's daughter, Hamida, who has since passed away, used to tell me, 'This expression was Bachchan Sahib's *takia kalaam.*' *Takia kalaam* can be broadly translated as 'signature tune'. This saga has been told in a book I co-authored with my sister Zakia Zaheer: 'Gold Dust of

Begum Sultans'. The book is my Ammi's story set in Rampur. One of the wealthiest states in pre-colonial India, the Nawabs of Rampur were revered for donating a gold dome to Ajmer Sharif Dargah. They saw their wealth dwindle over the years until it became a heap of dust hence, the title of our book, Gold Dust.

Ammi was raised in her maternal grandfather's palatial houses, first in Rampur and then in Nainital. The patriarch died, allegedly poisoned by a palace directive from the highest authority. Ammi and her only sibling, an elder brother whom she adored, were brought up under the eagle eye of the grand matriarch, her grandmother Qaisar Zamani Begum. Second-in-command was her mother, Sultan Jahan Begum, who married Shabbir Ali Khan on her father's condition that he became a 'ghar damaad', that is to say, he would reside with his in-laws. After a few years he left his wife, her family, and the grand Mustafa Lodge. My mother was six months old, her brother, Sajid Ali Khan, was six. It was a segregated household—the mardana, or men's quarters, and zenana, or women's quarters, were strictly demarcated. Ammi's brother had very little say, and she had no say at all. Her grandmother's writ ran the household. For Ammi, going to school was out of the question. She was taught at home by English governesses and *mullanis* (women maulvis), who taught her the Quran and Urdu. Nannies and mullanis catered for her and taught her the fine arts and crafts in which nawabzadis were supposed to be proficient. Purdah was strictly observed, as were all religious practices, especially all practices of the Shia sect. One pastime loved by women across generations was to play with dolls. So, my Ammi and her young companions created a fairy world of dolls. Whatever was observed and commemorated in the house was replicated in the doll world. Doll birthdays, doll marriages, doll ramadan, and doll muharram. Clothes for the dolls were stitched with the same finesse and care as the Begums' garments.

Hamida Apa had carefully preserved these precious relics that were invaluable in recreating this forgotten chapter of history. We recreated Ammi's world a few years ago in the form of an exhibition curated by renowned artist, friend, and exhibition designer Ranesh Ray and filmmaker Iffat Fatima. It was held at the Indira Gandhi National Centre for the Arts, Delhi, and the Centre for Creativity, Kolkata. Dolls with their silver utensils, jewels, farshi ghararas and karchob dupattas (embroidered in gold and silver for weddings), and furniture were on display.

Ammi was married to a man, who by Nawabi definition, was a commoner, picked for her by her brother, Sajid Ali Khan. Unlike his peer nawabzadas, Sajid Ali Khan was deeply immersed in his studies. For higher education, he, like most elite Muslim youth, chose the Aligarh Muslim University. His best friends were studious, serious, and mostly from middle-class families. My father and he were class-fellows at the AMU. My Mamu was very impressed by this earnest young man, Khwaja Ghulam Saiyidain, who was very bright and very principled. At home, he saw dashing young nawabzaadas, mostly as hedonists. The fact that my father was a Shia would have played a significant role. However, for his sister, nothing could have been more different from her palatial home than the household she was married into. It was a Panipat family of modest means; without exception, all were highly educated, well-versed in religious teachings and literature. They not only shunned but looked down upon ostentation of all kinds. Their most renowned family elder was Maulana Altaf Husain Hali, an Islamic scholar and social reformer, besides being India's first feminist poet. Thinking about that match today, I marvel at the polarities they represented. I can't even guess why Qaisar Zamani Begum, my great-grandmother, agreed to her son's suggested groom for his sister. One sentence she spoke when she heard about my father's salary has gone down in the annals of our family history. She said, 'A monthly salary of four hundred! That is not enough to bear the expenses of my child's paandaan!'

I don't know how Ammi adjusted to her life with a husband who shared nothing with her, neither upbringing nor education—a man whose sisters were writers and poets who were proud of their poverty and high moral values. Simplicity, according to the Sunnah of the Prophet of Islam, was their creed. One minor example is the difference between their tables—Rampur's elaborate cuisine versus Panipat's frugal meals. Another example is their respective styles of commemorating Moharrum. Rampur's dazzling silver and gold emblems and brocade banners against Panipat's few small silver or brass alams and plain banners. She was the proverbial princess who landed in ashes. How she endeared herself to her husband's family and blended into their life without compromising her love and duty to her own family is beyond my comprehension.

My father began with a Qasba school, then rose and rose. From academia to state service, he superseded IAS officers and reached the top position of Secretary in the Government of India. Mother simultaneously became more modest and retiring. She shunned elite sarkari gatherings and banquets, preferring to stay home with her children and staff. Her personality shone when she could serve someone in need. I remember how she avoided invitations to elite weddings and preferred to attend small weddings such as one in Kandhla, Shamli district. This was the marriage of the daughter of a barber, 'Bhai Kale', and 'Phupi (aunt) Shireen'. They were a dearly beloved part of Ammi's marital home.

In retrospect, this dichotomy may have been the reason why she suffered from 'dauras' which literally means fits. There were days that were shrouded in secrecy; we children were kept away because she was 'unwell'. Words like hysteria were spoken by elders in hushed tones but all we knew was that it would pass and things would return to normal.

She was fifty-two years old when she, who had always been surrounded by family and innumerable retainers, died in an alien land with only my father and me at her side. She was deeply mourned and written about in prose and poetry. On her grave was inscribed a quatrain written by a man who was her relative, her ardent admirer, and one of the founders of Jamia, Dr Abid Hussain. The last two lines were a Tarikh or Chronogram:

Tumhare pyaaron ko hai ye shikwa
Isi se rehlat ka saal nikla
Dilon ki balti ujaad daali
Aziz tumney basaii jannat

Your loved ones complain
The year of your death is enumerated thereby
You have devastated the realm of our hearts
Aziz! And embellished the realm of Paradise

I remember her love for me was constant but not overly demonstrative. She must have inherited this trait from the nawabi norms of her mother and grandmother, who, from what I recall from childhood days, were always restrained and reserved. It was later that I saw her love gush forth when she adopted a small girl, Munna, and then another one, Bobby. Munna was her husband's cousin Abbasi's daughter. Bobby was Naseem Makhmoori's daughter. Abbasi had three daughters so she left one under Ammi's care. Bobby's mother was constrained to leave her child alone when she went to work to support her family. Ammi's overwhelming love for children made the respective mothers happily leave them with her. Later, when her third daughter Zakia gave birth to her third boy, Shahid, she finally had the male child she longed for. All three children were eventually returned to their parents but for a time they were only hers. I witnessed her unrestrained love break through her customary reserve. That was the final moment of her fulfilment; a few months and she had gone forever. I don't resemble her, I am not her imprint, but she is inside me—my lifelong adherence to namaz, observance of Moharrum, and my increasing inclination towards universalising the true spirit of Islam, are because of my Ammi.

Saliha Abid Husain

Another great influence in my life was Saliha Abid Husain, born in the fertile land of Panipat, the fifth and youngest child in her family. Her father, whom she barely knew, was an eminent lawyer and Member of the UP Legislative Council. While his work took him for long spells to Meerut, Saliha's mother stayed with the extended family and looked after the children. 'I was the dark, sickly sibling of two brothers and two sisters, all fair and beautiful,' Saliha would say. 'People wondered how I would survive. "She has nothing of her father and mother," they said. She is like dregs of the womb! They shook their heads, predicting my early demise.'

But Saliha lived to be a grand old woman of seventy-four, an author of fifty books which included novels, short story collections, biographies, plays, children's literature, translations, religious treatises, and collections of articles. She was a Sahitya Akademi and Padma Bhushan awardee. Her hopes, sorrows, loves, and trials form the substance of her autobiography, *Silsila-e-Roz-o-Shab* (Sequence of Days and Nights). As a child, I used to read her novels with intense fascination. It was my interest in her books that made me fluent in Urdu before I started my English education. They also taught me about family structures among Muslim ashraf in pre-Independence India. Dignity and status accorded by Islam to women became entrenched in my life thanks to her writings and her practice.

At the end of her life, I saw her pain and hurt at the stance taken by Muslim hardliners especially in the Shah Bano case. Though her voice had become weak, her spirit and pen were still strong in defending the rights of the 74-year-old Shah Bano. She wrote articles explaining the status and rights of women in the Quran and used the plea that it was contrary to the spirit of Islam. Advancing age and declining health prevented her from joining the youth who hit the streets protesting against the Muslim Women Act 1986. Until the end she propagated before the world the true face of Islam—liberal, enlightened, and gendered.

Saliha was the second wife of Dr Abid Husain, who, together with Dr Zakir Husain and Professor Mujeeb, was one of the founding pillars of Jamia Millia Islamia in 1920. Abid Sahib had been married in his teens to his first cousin (without consultation with either side). The two had lived apart since then, he in Germany for further studies and she in their ancestral village, Daipur, in the district of Kannauj in UP. They had no children, but he took great care of maintenance and other needs of his wife, who continued to live in their joint family for most of her life. After seventeen years of living alone, Abid Sahib married Saliha. He was a close friend of my father, her older brother Saiyidain, the sibling she loved and admired intensely. His advocacy of Abid Sahib impressed her, and despite being much younger than him, she agreed to the marriage. Today, I say with confidence that they had one of those happy marriages one rarely saw then and hardly sees now. It was her delicate relationship with Shafa'at Fatima, first wife of her beloved husband, that forms a beautiful and fascinating part of her autobiography.

Saliha prided in calling herself a profoundly religious person, but very early on, she had learnt from her elders the lesson that Islam was not just a collection of practices; it was a well-defined and articulated way of life. In one of her articles, she writes in detail about her uncle, Khwaja Ghulamul Hasnain, who made a great contribution to her understanding of religion. He taught her that Islam was free of narrow-minded prejudices. He expanded the horizons of her faith. She used to hold Miladun Nabi gatherings in which she encouraged young girls to write small articles about the Prophet and read their pieces on his Seerat (character) before large gatherings. In the same spirit, she used to hold Moharrum majlis in her home, that were attended by women in Jamia, both Shias and Sunnis. She gave up *matam* (chest beating) in deference to the Sunni mourners of Husain who did not follow this practice. In all matters of religion, she referred to Maulana Abul Kalam Azad's Tarjuman-ul-Quran. That, plus his explication and commentary, remained her guiding light throughout her life.

In 1947, she remotely witnessed the communal riots following Partition as she was visiting her brother in Pune. Panipat, was emptied of its original dwellers, which included her entire family who were then forced to migrate to the newly created Pakistan. She wrote her second collection of short stories, *Niraas Mein Aas* (Hope in Hopelessness), as an expression of her anguish at the bloodbath, especially in Punjab. Hope for her was in the form of Gandhi; he would steer the ship to safety, she firmly believed. She finally removed her burqa in 1947. She wrote, 'I have removed my burqa, but cherish my modesty.'

I have referred to two of her works regularly for the past forty years. The first is her edited two-volume compilation of the Marsias of Mir Anis, the greatest chronicler and poet of the colossal Karbala tragedy. The second is her collection of essays Silk-e-Gohar about Imam Husain's martyrdom in Karbala, a slim book which people read every year during the ten days of Moharrum. In her flowing style, she writes about the tragedy of the Prophet's family, a lyrical dirge which draws tears from the listeners while providing them with role models to be emulated in life.

Being a practising Muslim was precisely why she was free of prejudice and bigotry. In my work with Muslim women and understanding Islam, I have derived a wealth of knowledge from her articles on women in Islam. Her prose, simply and elegantly, methodically removes all the bigoted and recalcitrant understandings of Islam. She writes that Islam categorically forbids instant triple talaq. She explains polygamy in the proper context, arguing that Islam was revealed at a time when men indulged in scores of marriages and had multiple mistresses. By curtailing them to four, in one stroke, Islam showed the way forward, but the self-anointed custodians and gatekeepers closed forever the gates of Ijtihad (forward interpretation), so four remained four! She draws attention to the Quranic injunction of meting out the exact same treatment to all four wives, along with the qualifying statement that it is humanly impossible to do that, so it is better to adhere to monogamy.

In her book *Rah-e-Amal* (The Practical Path), she says that Islam is not just about sitting in a corner reciting and reading the Quran and observing namaz; ask yourself, 'How do I help my fellow human beings?' She engaged in dialogue with the ulemas and maulvis on issues concerning women. She was never afraid to speak her mind. My experience is that the Quran and Islam have been seen from a male lens; men have been its explicators and commentators. Women have worked less in this field, but there have been some women, like Saliha who, imbibed the Quran from a gender lens.

In 2008, I was asked to perform a nikah by Naish Hasan in Lucknow. I thought about Saliha. What would she have done? She was no longer with us for me to consult. I asked my uncle, Dr Shubbar Hasan, what I should do. He said six words, 'Syeda, you go ahead, say yes.' I knew no recent precedent of a woman qazi though I knew women had attained the position of qazi and mufti during the time of the Prophet. So far, I have solemnised sixteen marriages, the latest being the nikah of the great-grandson of former President Dr Zakir Hussain, Gibran Rehan Rahman, with Ursila Ali in March 2022. A video of the marriage ceremony surfaced on social media, and I was informed that it had gone viral online with over 57,000 views, with many claiming that I have broken the patriarchal ceiling. Maybe I did, but I continue to believe that a pathbreaking is not an exception, but a norm in Islam. Many Muslim women have guided Islam when its practitioners have erred. The tradition of Muslim women voicing movements for human rights and the dignity of women has continued over the centuries. The twentieth century witnessed many outstanding women leaders in Islam. Those who challenged the rigid structures of society, structures towards which we keep regressing, and those who helped to create a more human and progressive society, a society which is mindful of the rights and dignity of those who have historically and structurally been oppressed. Saliha is at the top of that list.

Saliha wrote seminal books that expounded her belief in social justice inherited from her great-grandfather Maulana Hali. In her book *Yaadgaar-e-Hali*, she recalls an incident when Hali, walking in a gulley in Panipat, saw that a small child had fallen in a drain while people stood around, invoking the help of Bhagwan Ram. No one was willing to rescue the child since she was from the untouchable caste. 'Shame on you all, invoking Ram while his very image is struggling for life,' he said as he stepped into the filth and lifted the child in his arms. That Saliha had inherited the same DNA was my own experience. All the women who came to clean toilets in her Jamia neighbourhood used to be called 'Bahu'. As a child, I imbibed the idea of untouchability from my Lutyens Delhi surroundings. One day, Saliha noticed my reluctance to accept something from the hand of the woman who used to clean the toilets in her home. After a few quiet moments, she said, 'Bahu, give this little girl Syeda a katora of water.' I was stunned but had no choice but to accept and drink it under her watchful eye. After Bahu, left she explained to me the basic tenet of Islam, the abhorrence of caste hierarchy. Very early in life, she and my father had taught me Allama Iqbal's immortal couplet:

Ek hi saf mein kharey ho gaye Mahmud-o-Ayaz
Na koi bunda raha aur na koi bunda nawaz.

Mahmud (the Emperor) and Ayaz (the Slave) stood in one row
Then there was no Master no Slave.

In an unexpected way I was instrumental in featuring Saliha as a playwright on the national and international stage. I had carefully preserved an old notebook in which Saliha had written her play Jhoot Sach, inspired by Oscar Wilde's *Importance of Being Ernest.* In 1966, after completing my Master's degree, I joined Lady Shri Ram College (LSR) as a lecturer. My love for theatre was akin to that of my colleague, Uma Kapoor, who also taught in the English Department. Uma and I decided to start a dramatic society and stage an inaugural play. Necessary permissions were obtained, and for the first time, LSR invited boys from Delhi University to act with the girls. The play we chose was Begum Saliha's delightful comedy, Jhoot Sach. But with her permission, we changed its name; she suggested one which was derived from a couplet of the last Mughal Emperor Bahadur Shah Zafar II. The Emperor wrote his famous dirge when he was exiled to Rangoon. The last line was: 'Kitna hai Badnaseeb Zafar' (How unfortunate is Zafar). This she changed to 'Kitna hai Khush Naseeb Zafar'. From Delhi University, we invited two boys to play, Algernon and Ernest. Later, they became bright stars of Bollywood—Kulbhushan Kharbanda and Dinesh Thakur. The former has made scores of landmark films, and the latter made one memorable one, Basu Chatterjee's *Rajnigandha*, but very sadly died young. Our LSR play became a grand success. Thus, Saliha 'moved' out of Jamia into the Delhi theatre scene.

It was a few years later, in 1975, when the same spirit moved me to begin an Urdu Drama Club, SEAL (Society for Eastern Art & Literature) in Canada. To make a long story short, Saliha Abid Husain's *Kitna Hai Khush Naseeb Zafar* and Qudsia Zaidi's *Aazar ka Khwaab* (inspired by Shaw's play *Pygmalion*) was performed in Edmonton, Alberta. It played to a packed house in the Thrust

Theatre of the University of Alberta. The role of Henry Higgins (Aazar) played by my husband, and that of Colonel Pickering by our lifelong friend, librarian, and tabla maestro, Masood Ahmed. Masood Sahib was the son of Shahid Ahmed Dehlavi, the iconic editor of the Urdu journal Saqi. The event was supported by businesses owned by South Asians, Hindus and Sikhs (Pritpal of Asia Import House, Sunita Kumar of India Imports). In the arctic winter chill of Canada, Quasi Zaidi and Saliha Abid Husain's plays made a spectacular debut on the international stage, where her name was taken with reverence and awe.

Saliha Abid Husain, unsung, unknown, and unheard outside the Urdu circle, was a chronicler of her times. She was a commentator par excellence, a natural storyteller, and above all, a woman who believed, practised, and propagated her religion in its most liberal and humanitarian spirit, which she learnt from her buzurgs, her personal study, and from Maulana Azad's translation and commentary on the Quran. I imbibed all these traits from her.

Mohini Giri

The third woman who had a deep influence on me was Mohini Giri. I met her for the first time when I stepped inside the National Commission for Women as a member. She took one look at me as I sat across the desk, feeling very nervous. She asked me what was my experience in this field. I had very little to offer, so I mumbled some vague answers. Then she said something which I will never forget, 'I am not running a gender training school here.' That was in 1997. What began on that sour note was a friendship and camaraderie that spans a quarter century. We travelled together across the length and breadth of the country, rushing like a rescue engine wherever women were subjected to violence. Whether it was the cry of a victim or a newspaper report, Mohini propelled us to action. Wherever we went, we mostly stayed at circuit houses. We would rise early each morning, with me offering my namaz and her offering puja. There was no clash between a Muslim praying to her Allah and a Hindu praying to her Bhagwan. I often think of us as Ganga and Jamuna, rivers beloved by Hindus and Muslims. I am reminded of a poet from Pakistan, Jaun Elia, who was born and brought up in Amroha. After many years in Pakistan, which he termed 'exile', when he landed at Delhi airport from Karachi, he placed his forehead on the tarmac and kissed the earth of his *watan* (country). Mohini and I understood the impulse which propelled him. He wrote lines which exemplify us both; it was as if he was writing about our bond:

Mein jo bagoola ban kar bikhra waqt ki pagal aandhi mein
Kya mein tumhari lehar nahin hoon Ganga ji aur Jamuna Ji
Baan nadi ke paas Amrohey mein jo ladka rehta ttha
Ab vo kahan hai mein to yehin hoon Ganga Ji aur Jamna Ji

I who rose like a bagoola in the hurricane of time
Am I not your wave, Ganga ji and Jamuna ji?
On the banks of river Baan there used to live a boy
Where is he now? I never left you… Ganga ji and Jamuna ji

Looking stunning in her kanjivaram saris, her jewellery, her bindi, and her tightly knotted grey hair, as Chairperson of NCW, she took central and state governments to task on behalf of women. She deserves to be written about in all languages because she was present in all parts of the country. Padma Seth, a lawyer and daughter of Ananthasayanam Iyengar (the first Lok Sabha Speaker), and I were her left and right hands. I saw her myriad moods during the two years we were together in the Commission. Disgusted with the Ministry of Women and Child Development, which was trying to override a statutory Commission, she created a furore at a Vigyan Bhavan meeting chaired by the then PM Deve Gowda, 'If this treatment endures, Mr Prime Minister, here is my resignation.' The audience was stunned, and the PM refused to accept the piece of paper she had held out. Later, the then Minister of State, B.S. Ramoowalia, apologised and assured her that the NCW would be given its due dignity as a statutory body.

Mohini taught me to rush to wherever there was a crisis. Padma and I, on her directive, drove to Sudaka village, in the Nuh district in Haryana, to rescue a couple, both Muslims, who were being threatened by the entire village. They had married within their 'gotra' which was against their customary law. When I told the villagers that there was nothing like 'gotra' in Islam, they lashed out, 'Don't teach us our Islam.' Honour killing, revenge rape, gang rape, paedophilia, and sexual harassment, we were fire engines whirling through the toughest terrains across India. I did not understand the nuances of feminist pedagogy, but I was a willing foot soldier because she was my captain. I watched her with wonder when, with several bales of hand-spun cotton in her hands, she rode a train from one end of the country to the other, stopping at each station to address hordes of women who had come to sign the cotton cloth as a directive to the Central Government, for the Women's Reservation Bill to be passed in parliament.

2014 was a historic year. The Congress-led UPA (United Progressive Alliance) was replaced in the centre by the BJP-led NDA (National Democratic Alliance). I had demitted office along with my colleagues at the Planning Commission. Mohini was returning home from her office when she saw a girl being beaten by a group of men on the road near Vasant Kunj. Characteristically, she jumped out of the car to help the girl. In the scuffle, she also received injuries. A PCR van passed by, but no one came to their help. A beat constable told Mohini that she should not have intervened. It was an ominous indication of times to come.

A few years ago, Mohini took all her staff out for a treat. She was stopped by from entering the Chinese Room by the Delhi Gymkhana Club staff who told her that her maids and drivers were not allowed inside. After a lot of verbal lashing her staff was allowed inside. Mohini Giri, daughter-in-law of former President of India, V.V. Giri, gave me another lesson in caste and class. I had learnt it earlier from my Ammi, who showered her love on the humblest retainer of the family, from Saliha when she taught me to respect Bahu, and from Mohini in her own dramatic manner. One is never too old to learn.

The Delhi Gymkhana Club management imposed a fine on her for this altercation; she refused to pay. In her resignation letter, she wrote, 'It shocks me to know that the club is still suffering from a hangover of a colonial rule and carrying forward the unfortunate legacy of class distinction in a democratic country. In the seventy-eighth year of my life, I am learning that in India, to speak out against class bias and injustice invites punitive action. I am resigning from a club where I have been a member for the last fifty years. Life is always a learning experience. Now I know that we have to still walk a long path for true democracy.' Her final sentence is a scathing indictment. 'I am afraid most Indians may not be able to meet the criteria of the club. Clothes and general demeanour cannot be used as indicative of status. Had Mahatma Gandhi entered the club in his famous dhoti, he perhaps would have been thrown out too.'

More recently, in 2020, Mohini and her two comrades, Padma Seth and I, spoke from our hearts at the death of institutions, in this case, the National Commission for Women. The tipping point was the Hathras gang rape case of a Dalit girl child. With us standing on either side, Mohini spoke: 'Today what we are seeing is the slow death of Women's Commissions, bodies which were created by the hard work of mentors like Pramila Dandavate, Vimla Farooqui, Susheela Gopalan, Geeta Mukherjee, and Margaret Alva... Recent role or non-role of NCW and SCW in the heinous Hathras incident proves the point.' This was in reference to the response of the NCW Chairperson Rekha Sharma about Amit Malviya from the BJP IT

Cell sharing a video of the victim. She dismissed it as 'unfortunate and illegal'. The State Women's Commission Chairperson called the incident 'definitely objectionable'. People from political parties and civil society groups went to condole and offer solidarity to the bereaved family, but these apex bodies for women with statutory powers spoke measured words from the comfort of their official houses. From Mohini, I learnt to see through their hypocrisy. They spoke words like 'unfortunate' and 'illegal' and 'definitely objectionable', but no one went to comfort the broken Dalit family. Ironically and tragically, the police picked up a New Delhi-based Kerala journalist, Siddique Kappan, who dared to report the truth. He languished in jail for more than two years, with no access to the chargesheet filed against him by the UP police.

I remember that in 1997, when I joined the NCW, Mohini promptly acted on a complaint filed by the then UP Chief Minister and BSP General Secretary Mayawati against the Union Defence Minister and Samajwadi Party supremo Mulayam Singh Yadav. Mayawati wrote to the NCW chairperson Mohini Giri, 'Yadav has used vituperative and offensive language against me in public.' The letter said that being the UP Chief Minister, it would not be proper for her even to repeat the language used by the defence minister at a meeting in Bareilly on June 6. Mohini was deeply disturbed by Yadav's foul language. Asserting that this was not an isolated incident, she said, 'Abusing women in public or private is a gross violation of their rights. We will enact a law which bars ministers and politicians holding public offices who make such degrading, sexist remarks about women.' Assuring Mayawati that NCW will investigate the complaint, Mohini collected evidence and found five persons who corroborated the allegations.

Mulayam Singh Yadav sent his aide Amar Singh to depose before the Commission, who apologised on behalf of the Minister. I, a novice in the NCW, was wonderstruck at how she used the power to which its statutory status entitled the Commission.

In 1998, the Commission heard depositions from Shabana Azmi and Nandita Das on Hindutva brigades vandalising the set and stopping the shooting of Deepa Mehta's film Fire. She summoned the attackers who vandalised and violated the three women.

Another incident was the summoning of the then Prasar Bharati chairperson following complaints from women newsreaders in Doordarshan that they were discriminated against on account of their 'looks and age'. Mohini's interventions, numerous as they are, are recorded for anyone to examine.

A few months ago, I saw her lying in a resplendent sari as if waiting impatiently for the last rites—Mohini, always in a hurry, urging us all to get on.

My words for my Mohini have been spoken best by Mirza Ghalib:

Aisa kahan se laaoon ke tujh sa kahein jisey

Wherefrom shall I bring someone who can be like you

Many other women have left a deep mark on me, global women, global citizens. Kamla Bhasin, who taught me feminism and courage; my mentor Satnam Mahmud in Hawaii, who planted the seeds of India-Pakistan Dosti. Sister Marion Norman of the Loretto order was my thesis advisor and later became my daughter Ayesha's godmother. The list is long, but let me stop here.

12

My Pillars of Islam

There are five pillars of Islam which form the basis of the faith—Kalima (Tauheed), Namaz (Prayers), Ramadan (Rosa), Zakat (Charity), and Haj. My own strongest pillars are Namaz and Ramadan. My namaz is threaded throughout this book. So this part is about Ramadan. I have added my personal pillar, Moharrum which is where I draw strength to accept life as it deals its winning and losing hands.

In the second Surah of the Quran, Surah-al-Baqarah verse 185, there is a clear injunction.

> Ramadan is the month
> In which was sent down
> The Quran as a guide
> To mankind

The instructions about the beginning and end of the fast are clearly stated:

> And eat and drink
> Until the white thread
> Of dawn appear to you
> Distinct from its black thread
> Then begin your fast

The fine line of dawn and dusk, thus described, means that the fast is to be observed for the duration of daylight. Pre-Islamic rules about fasting and abstinence were stringent. With the revelation of Islam, the injunction was softened.

Ramadan is all about patience, holding back the craving for food and water, and thereby understanding the meaning of hunger. It is also about perseverance in continuing the practice daily for a whole month as a test of will.

As a child, I watched my parents observe Ramadan. I could hardly wait until I turned nine for my roza kushai, meaning roza commencement. From then on, I fasted off and on, but was never forced to fast. My parents strictly observed the Quranic injunction, La Ikra Fiddin (there is no compulsion in religion). For many years now, I have fasted primarily because my religion enjoins it but also because it gives me a sense of self-control and strength. Since we follow the lunar calendar, sometimes Ramadan falls during the hottest month of the year; the challenge becomes greater; it is fifteen-and-a-half-hour fast, the longest for countries of South Asia.

Ramadan touches every aspect of life. One month of fasting is a prescribed way of cleansing the entire system, physical, spiritual and mental. In a word, it is observing *eitedaal* or balance in every aspect of life. The word eitedaal is the key to good life, which is taught not only by Islam but by all religions. Eating and drinking is permissible between sunset and sunrise, but never in excess. At the time of Iftar, when hunger and thirst are at their peak there is a need to pull back both in food and drink. The injunction is to drink limited water, eat high energy items such as dates and fruit, and refrain from fried items like pakoras and samosas. The beauty of Ramadan is the rhythm it creates by following this as a daily routine. It also means experiencing the joy of sitting down to a meal after abstaining the whole day.

Another fact about Ramadan is the Quranic instruction that it should be integrated with daily life. It is strictly forbidden to use fasting as an excuse to reduce or lighten the work routine. Islam is categorical that all normal functions should be carried on as usual during the fast. The most precious aspect of Ramadan is that it is the month of revelation of the Quran. It is believed that Lailat-ul-Qadr (Night of Blessing) occurs in the last quarter of Ramadan when Prophet Mohammad received through the Angel Gabriel the first verse of the Quran.

Among the many benedictions of Ramadan is the empathy it creates in the hearts of those who fast towards those whose fate is to 'fast', meaning suffer from chronic hunger. It is within these contexts that this month is not the month of privation but the month of glory. When I was growing up, the enmity between Hindus and Muslims was narrated in stories of the mass killings of 1947. In the following decades, through the work of leaders like Gandhi, Nehru and Azad, who inspired the masses of both communities, the hatred seemed to melt away, and this bonhomie filtered down to us children; we became friends without consciousness of religion. The month of Ramadan was jointly commemorated, and Eid was jointly celebrated.

I think of three people who were an integral part of my Ramadan and without whom this month will never be complete for me.

One was Khushwant Singh, who became deeply interested in my observance of Islam. In particular, he was intrigued by my adherence to Ramadan. Sometimes, I got a feeling that he looked at religion through my prism. Perhaps that was the reason why he dedicated one of his books, *Need for A New Religion in India*, to me. Come Ramadan, and he always asked, 'When will you come to me for Iftar?' A date was set and I would arrive on time. His timing was as inviolable as the timing of Iftar. I insisted on a simple Iftar of one khajoor, some fruit, one small sandwich, a cup of tea, and lots of water. So Chandan, his cook brought out my tray at the first sound of the Iftar siren. I would begin with khajoor while my host would watch me eat. We spoke very little. When I had finished I moved to the study to offer prayers on a special mat which he reserved for me. I stayed for a short while, being too tired to linger for a chat, an exit which suited him, being a stickler for his own precious time.

The other integral part of my Ramadan began when I returned to India in 1984. Professor Bimal Prasad was among India's best-known historians; his three-volume *Pathway to India's Partition* is the best analysis of Hindu-Muslim relations in the context of the politics of Partition. He was Dean of International Studies at JNU and was also sent as India's ambassador to Nepal. His deep respect for Ramadan was part of his boyhood in Bihar, where he learned about the pillars of Islam from his beloved Muslim teachers. As a child, he recalls how his mother dressed him in a new dhoti, tied bells around his waist, and asked him to run on the village road where Moharrum taziyas were displayed. So, one Iftar, I dedicated to him. I usually opened my fast at his home in Rabindra Nagar, sometimes at the India International Centre. But I loved his home best, where Bruno, his dog, watched us, and Ashok ji, his Man Friday, served the Iftar, which consisted of several dishes and Earl Grey tea, served beautifully in exquisite china, a hallmark of his home.

The third and last link in this Ramadan chain was a man who had a deep love for the spirit of all religions. My Planning Commission colleague Ramesh Jhamtani, who was my 'Jhamtani Sahib'. His faith was rooted in his Pir and mentor from Larkana Sahib in Sind, from whom he drew his spiritual guidance. For the last ten years, one Iftar was held at his home. His Iftar was elaborate, despite my insistence on keeping it frugal. Sometimes, the table was laden with delectable food only for me; at other times, he called friends and neighbours to whom he proudly showed me off as someone who exercises balance and restraint. On his invitation, I offered prayers in his special puja room where he spread the prayer mat before a blank wall, since praying in front of pictorial representations is forbidden in Islam.

Years have gone by, I still observe Ramadan every year, but now without them. I still feel their presence everywhere. Perhaps they are watching me from some meta space.

The essence of this month, which my three friends imbibed and practiced, is encapsulated in these lines from Surah Al-e-Imran of the Quran:

> O ye who believe
> Persevere in patience
> And constancy; vie
> In such perseverance
> Strengthen each other
> And fear Allah
> That ye may prosper

~

The most poignant memory of my childhood is mourning for the martyred family of the Prophet during Moharrum. For as long as I can remember, the first ten days of Moharrum, also known as 'Azadari', were times of great sobriety. My mother was the moving spirit behind those ten crucial days. Certain setting-up rituals were observed by her, and we copied her practice without question; we removed all ornaments and dressed only in black or green. Women who came especially for the occasion from her hometown, Rampur, set up the imambara in our house. The women bathed in rosewater all the silver alams, which are replicas of the emblems of Imam Husain's 'army'. Then, they tied the most beautifully sewn banners to the base of the Alams and lovingly propped them on wooden spikes lined up inside the imambara. After every Majlis, all those who attended were given packets of sweets or savouries to take home called tabarruk. We children sat through the Majlises, and the words of the recitation seeped into us, even though we did not understand much of the language or poetry. Sometimes it was my father, my mother, an aunt or an uncle who read the main marsia or poetic rendering of the event. Mir Anis, the iconic chronicler/poet of Moharrum, was recited with reverence and love. All my life, his lines have rung in my ears—in all months not only the month of Moharrum. We children were asked to join in the chorus of voices which preceded and followed the main recitation and sang/recited poems called soz, salaam, and nauhas.

It was my mother's faith in this event which has had a profound impact on me. Today, when I observe the decorum around the tragedy of Karbala, it is her image which rises before my eyes. For sixty years, I have listened to the same narrations in prose and poetry. In each one of these years, ten days in a row, I have recited and heard the verses of the immortal poet. For sixty years, I have seen tears flowing profusely as a tribute to this unparalleled human tragedy. What is it that even after fourteen hundred and fifty years the pain of Karbala does not abate? As the poet Najam Afendi has said:

Sab gham hain do roza gham-e-Shabbir wohi hai
Chaudah sau baras baad bhi taseer wohi hai

All grief is momentary except Shabbir's grief
Fourteen hundred years! And still the same pain

The story of Karbala can be folded into a simple narration. Husain, grandson of Prophet Mohammad, refused to place the leadership of Islam in the hands of Yazid, son of Mu'awiya, the ruler of the day. Father and son wanted temporal and spiritual fused in one person. Husain knew that the stewardship of Yazid would mean the end of Islam. Yazid could remain the temporal head of the Islamic world but not the spiritual head. On his part, Yazid knew that unless Husain gave him the mandate, no one would recognise his authority. All attempts to influence Husain failed. The only way for Yazid was to kill Husain by finding some pretext and cornering him in a remote place. This he saw as the only way he could become Khalifa of the Islamic world. He therefore, plotted to waylay Husain as he was on his way to Kufa where he had been repeatedly invited by the people of the city. Husain sent his cousin Muslim Bin Aqeel as his advance emissary to Kufa where he was killed along with his two small sons.

Even as he left his home in Medina, Husain knew what might happen. He knew Yazid's moves and intent. But instead of an army, Husain gathered his family and friends and set out on the arduous journey. Just before entering the desolate desert, Karbala, a spot which is the site of the world's bloodiest massacre, he called together his small band and made the most unforgettable offer in human history, 'You all know what awaits us in Karbala. I am extinguishing this candle which lights up our tent. In the cover of darkness, I offer you, my beloved friends, a chance to leave quietly and escape certain death.' The Imam extinguished the candle. When he lit it again, he saw that none of his followers had moved.

Finally, dawned the day when Husain would show the world by, personal example, the meaning of qurbani (sacrifice). He had a band of seventy-two in his 'army', which included youths and seniors. Yazid's army consisted of thousands of mercenaries. They forced the Imam to move his tents away from the only water source in the desert, Nehr-e-Alqama. This 'nehr' had been given as mehr to his mother, Hazrat Fatima. Yazid's forces stopped him from drawing water, so thirst became synonymous with Karbala.

On the tenth day of Moharrum, known as the Day of Ashura, the battle started. Husain's small band included eighty-year-old elder Habib Ibn Muzahir, young boys like his brother, Imam Hasan's thirteen-year-old son Qasim and his child Ali Asghar, who was six months old. One by one, these men and boys, Husain's followers, would go to the battlefield, recite rijz and perform Jehad. One single *mujahid* (a word, which over the years, has lost its original pristine meaning) fought with thousands of archers, swordsmen, lancers and foot soldiers! As they fell from their horses with severed limbs and hundreds of gashes, the drums of victory were sounded. Husain would go to the battlefield to bring home the dead. After the friends, it was the turn of family members. Finally, even the six-month-old baby Ali Asghar was martyred when an arrow from the ace archer Hurmula pierced his tiny neck. Only Husain was left to perform the last *hujjat* (argument), the last rite of sacrifice. It is said that when Shimr, one of Yazid's mercenaries, placed the sword on his neck, Husain had put his bloodied forehead on the burning sands of Karbala for the last sijdah. When someone asked Shimr what the Imam was murmuring as his last words, even the executioner shed tears and said, 'He was praying for the redemption of his Ummah saying, they do not know what they are doing.'

Although most of those who commemorate Moharrum in every corner of the world are Shias, Sunni Muslims also hold it in great esteem. Tazia processions all over the world are taken out by all, not only Shias and Sunnis but by Hindus and Sikhs. Professor Bimal Prasad once told me that in his village of Kudra in the district of Shamabad in Bihar, it was a tradition to set up sabeels for offering water and sherbet to the mourners.

I remember, as a child, listening to the poet Gopi Nath Aman reciting his own poignant marsias before large gatherings. There were many other Hindu marsiya writers and reciters. For the last twenty years, I have listened to the best rendering of soz and salaams by my dear friend Jyoti Pande, who was an Indian Ambassador to Kyrgyzstan. During this entire period of mourning, his voice rings in my ears, like Hazrat Bano's lament for her six-month-old son. 'Kehtien tthein Bano Asghar jaani kab tum rann se aagoge' (Laments Bano, Beloved Asghar when will you return from the battlefield?)

The night before the penultimate day of Ashura, there are usually 100 women in my house attending the last Majlis. One shab-e-ashur Majlis, my friend Vidya Rao, who is a renowned classical singer, began the Majlis by rendering soz in Awadhi, one about Hazrat

Bano, wife of Imam Husain, who was lamenting the killing of her husband. 'Kahein Bano mein sees navaoon kahan mera siayyan to maiko bisaar gaya' (Says Bano, where shall I bow my head, my beloved has left me forlorn). I have never seen such outpouring of grief as I saw that night. Simple, ordinary women cried openly at Hazrat Bano's tragedy, as rendered by Vidya. It was a dirge unparalleled. At the end of the Majlis, a young Hindu woman came in quietly to pray for her children and touched her forehead to the ground before the glowing imambara. Vidya's soz has become an annual feature of our majlis, on the night of Ashura. I pray that her voice rings before my imambara long after I am gone. This for me is the real power of Moharrum, cutting across caste, class, and even religion to touch every heart, elevate every soul.

The most heart-wrenching Majlis was Shaam-e-Ghariban (Evening of the Desolate). The killings were over, the Imam's family witnessed the burning and looting of their tents. Their loved ones lay dead in the desert, no kafan, no burial. We the mourners sat in the dark and listened to the devastated state of the ahl-e-bait. My mother's voice, firm and gentle rose in the dark; the entire marsia was recited by memory. It was the same year after year, while even we children wept uncontrollably:

Jab ke khamosh hui sham-e-imamat rann mein
Din ko paida hui zulmat ki alamat rann mein
Aur tadapne laga who sarv sa qamat rann mein
Saaf zahir huey aasaar-e-Qayamat rann mein
Charkh hilta ttha zameen khauf se tharrati thi
Nala-e-Fatima Zehra ki sada aati thi

When the lamp of Imamat was extinguished in the battlefield
Darkness threatened the light of the day
And that lofty form was writhing in pain
Skies shook, earth trembled
Fatima Zehra's dirges resounded in the desert

13

Kashmir

The Desolate Paradise

I have no recollection of the events of 1947 when the marauders attacked Kashmir, and the instrument of accession was signed by the Maharaja. But the subliminal consciousness of my birth has taken me back again and again to the Valley, my birthplace.

My father was invited to Kashmir by Maharaja Hari Singh as Director of Education in 1937. He was urged by his closest friend and mentor, Dr Zakir Husain to accept the offer. It was not an easy decision for my parents who were happily settled in Aligarh where he was Head of Department (Dean of Education) at Aligarh Muslim University.

For the next seven years, my family lived in Srinagar. I have photographs of my father riding on horseback and visiting schools in far-flung areas with dirt tracks for roads. His autobiography has more about these seven years than the forty years of his career as an educationist and service in the Ministry of Education in the government.

My return to my watan in 1984 began my tryst with Kashmir, a tryst which will end with my death—I will choose which one of my two homes—Delhi or Kashmir—will give space to my bones. Raj Bagh in Srinagar, the home of Maulvi Mohammad Jan and Safia Jan, has been my home for the last twenty years. Two beloved people with whom I spent my summers in Srinagar and who spent their winters in my humble home in Delhi. Safia Baji, a devout Sunni, used to sit with equal devotion in my Moharrum majlises. She used to recite these lines; I always think of her in poetic terms:

Hujoom-e-bulbul hua chaman mein kiya jo gul ne kamaal paida
Kami nahin qadrdaan ki Akbar kare to koi jamaal paida.

Nightingales crowded the garden when the rose came in full bloom
There's no dearth of admirers O Akbar if only one creates beauty.

One instance of my past-present connection in Kashmir arises in my mind. In 2017, I was invited by a friend, Syed Farooq, to Kupwara to inaugurate the new block of Dolphin School, an educational institution he had set up for children of this troubled district. At the inauguration, there was a surprise awaiting me. Almost fifty years after my father's passing, the speakers spoke in glowing terms of the work he did in bringing education to the remotest parts of the Valley. I could not hold back my tears.

Since childhood, I had been told by my father, through his recitation of Allama Iqbal's poetry, that Kashmir was the bedrock of harmony between different religions, classes, creeds and castes. I remember listening to the stories of the great Sufi, Shaikh Nuruddin Wali, or Nund Reshi, as he is called in Kashmir. I had read the Vaakhs (poetry) of the Sufi saint Lal Ded or Lalla. But now, whenever I visited the Valley, I winced at the unending suffering inflicted by the state and centre on the people of my beloved janmabhoomi, the land of my birth. Paradoxically, when I returned, I felt healed. The slow poison of metropolitan living was drained out of me by the alchemy of the Valley.

Although I was born in the state and I have a birth certificate, I have always regretted that I do not qualify as a state subject since my parents were not born in Kashmir. However, no one can challenge my Kashmiriyat. It goes further and deeper than anything that is signed and sealed on stamp paper.

After returning to India in 1984, I was part of several women's groups in both official and unofficial capacities, for which I travelled to Kashmir. This continued during my term as a Member of the Planning Commission. I tried to understand district-specific issues and review the overall health scenario especially, the adverse and steeply declining child sex ratio in the state. After the earthquake in 2005, I visited Kashmir and witnessed how different voluntary organisations from across the country travelled to the remotest villages, taking with them whatever was needed.

I cannot write all that I have witnessed. But I will try to write some of it because I need to speak about being witness to two decades of turmoil in the land of my birth.

~

In the summer of 1999, when guns boomed on the Kargil front, war rhetoric was at its highest pitch. Many of us women, in our separate spaces, found ourselves increasingly disturbed. That brought a few of us together with our shared and yet unspoken grief at the escalating war-like situation, bloodshed and animosity. The WIPSA (Women's Initiative for Peace in South Asia) was then born.

We travelled to Pakistan, Bangladesh and most importantly, Kashmir. My companions, who went with me to the Valley, said it was their Karmabhoomi. For me, all my visits were 'homecoming'. The WIPSA had three demands. No war or bloodshed, peace at the borders, and commitment by both governments that the nuclear button would never be pressed. We demanded assurance by all governments that South Asia would become nuclear free.

When we set up WIPSA, the catalysing force was a poem written in Punjabi by eminent writer Rami Chhabra, which expressed unspoken feelings about us women. It was titled 'Asmaan Hai Sadi Saanjhi Seema', that is, sky is our common boundary.

Asmaan Hai Sadi Saanjhi Seema
Charka-chand-sitara vich nigh bhariye
Bhook gharibi pichhrapan duur dariye
Agli shadabti vich daat ke wasiye

And it goes on:

The sky's the limit for our shared ambitions,
The sky's horizon is the true limit that need bound our borders-visions,
If only, if only, we would work together, make the charkha-chand-sitara come closer,
We could banish hunger, poverty, backwardness wide and afield
And live in the next century sheltered by dignity's shield.

When ahead lies the tantalising horizon of the sky
Tell me, why on ink-lines we need to die?
Why from togetherness we should shy?
The sky is our common reach,
If togetherness we understand and seek.

The year 2000 saw the culmination of three programmes on peace by WIPSA. All of them exemplified women's initiatives in creating peace. The first was a bus journey for peace undertaken by forty-three Indian women to Pakistan. It was followed a month later by the return journey of sixty-three Pakistani women to India (more about this later). The third was Kashmir. Our plan was that Indian and Pakistani women would visit their respective Kashmiris. Sadly, that could not happen.

On June 24, 2000, I found myself on a train with a five-member delegation under the banner of the WIPSA to visit Jammu and

Kashmir. Our group consisted of our leaders Nirmala Deshpande and Mohini Giri, media persons Suman Gupta and Kumkum Chadha, and fellow home-towner from Panipat, Ram Mohan Rai. We remembered the words of friends who had cautioned us against trying to undertake a journey for peace in this 'troubled' land. But the peace imperative was such that a journey had to be undertaken.

Muralia Village is in a Tehsil in Ranbir Singh Pora, near Jammu. This village of forty households consists of Gujjars and Bakarwals (nomadic tribes). We sat on charpais and listened. They told us that landmines often killed people, in the nearby Jora Farm. Sometimes, the bullets grazed women and children—the dusty fields of Muralia are open targets. Firing from across the border also killed their animals.

In Nagrota, the tragedy of Kashmiri Pandits numbed us. Many families had to leave the land of their birth, their property and their homes. When they left Kashmir in 1990, they broke away from their past and lost their future; but their Muslim brothers and sisters, they said, always stood with them. They had to leave due to the threats from the militants. In the refugee camps in Nagrota, they were huddled together and living in subhuman conditions. Inside their dwellings there was hardly any ventilation. Bhushanlal Dhar was one of several Pandits who lived in a suffocating, one-room windowless quarter, but dreamt of the saffron fields they left behind in Pampore.

We left for Srinagar but were warned by friends in Jammu. A total strike at Srinagar had been called by the Dukhtaran-e-Millat (Women's Wing of the Jama'at) against custodial killings of the Kashmiris. We went regardless, singing the song our leader, Nirmala Deshpande, had taught us. It was written by a poet from Sind, Hunduraj Dukhayal, a companion of Vinoba Bhave, who created the Bhoodan (Land Gift) Movement. Padyatris of Vinoba's 'army' used to sing this song as they walked from village to village:

Bhed bhav torne, dil ko dil se jodne
Kaam ko sanwarne, jaan apni warne
Shanti ke sipahi chale, chale'

To eliminate communal disharmony, to bring hearts closer,
To fulfil their duty, to lay down our lives,
The soldiers of peace march on…

These lines echoed in our hearts; we knew that the cynics and hawks would mock us for this 'romantic nonsense'.

At a seminar organised by the Kashmir Welfare Centre, we were asked why Kashmiris should not be allowed to place their case in an International Court of Justice. 'Both India and Pakistan have contributed to the mess in Kashmir. Visit the graveyards, which can be seen everywhere in the Valley. Kashmir, the land of rishis and saints, has now become a land of graves. From the First Bridge to Yusmarg, there are only sixteen shrines of saints but fifty-six qabristans.'

A nineteen-year-old boy, Aijaz, had been killed in custody the previous week. We reached his house after traversing narrow gullies, which were choked with drains and garbage heaps. From the gate onwards, the place was filled with wailing women. Aijaz was the only son; there was a younger sibling, a daughter.

Family members, amid the laments of wailing women, narrated the facts of the case to us. Aijaz had completed high school and had just been granted admission to an engineering college in Bangalore. One day, he left the house to visit relatives in the city. Next, the family learnt that he was picked up by the security forces. The parents had been asked to pay a ransom of Rs 20,000 for his release. They scrambled to collect the money, but when they went to get him, they were turned away and asked to return later. Their daily ordeal of visiting the police station began. A few days passed, Aijaz's dead body was thrown near the police station. 'Killed in an encounter,' claimed the authorities. His fingernails had been removed and there were gashes on his neck and waist. Hundreds of people gathered for his funeral. Tempers were high. The police swung into action. We were shown many newspaper clippings of the janaza and the police wielding their weapons.

Everyone wanted to speak. Above the din, I could barely hear the voice of the people translating for us from Kashmiri. Suddenly, one woman proclaimed the 'Nara-e-Takbeer', and a chorus was raised—the calls to Allah resounded through the room as we left. At the neck of the gulley, we saw a bunch of angry boys. Neighbours and friends of Aijaz. They shouted, 'Hum kya chahte hain?' (What do we want?) 'Azadi' (freedom) was the deafening rejoinder.

Nearby lived Rafiq Ahmed Baqal, a young man in his thirties. Rafiq, along with a few friends, had gone to a wedding. That night, he was returning with four friends when they were all stopped at the Amira Kadal Bridge. The security officer questioned the four and let them go, but he retained Rafiq, who he said would be released after a few questions. Many versions exist of what happened next. People who visited the nearby Hanuman temple that morning remember hearing agonised screams. A few hours later, Rafiq's body was thrown on the road. 'Killed in encounter,' was the official version. Sitting inside the room was a woman with her small children—a four-year-old girl and one-year-old twin boys. The woman did not move or blink. She sat there, pale and inert, while the family and friends poured out their hearts. Rafiq had a small provisions shop. Anyone who dared to ask military men to pay for their purchases was asking for trouble. Young men, friends of Rafiq, were full of rage. 'Why have you come?' someone asked. 'You too will go back and forget.' With one look at the woman's pale stone face, we understood the hopelessness underlying the statement.

The office of Shabbir Shah, leader of the Jammu and Kashmir Democratic Freedom Party, is lined with the most graphic photographs of torture.

Syed Ali Shah Geelani, leader of the All Parties Hurriyat Conference (APHC), met us at his home. Geelani Sahib spoke to us from his heart about the expansionism, imperialism, and arrogance of the Government of India. 'Go to the rural areas if you wish to see the atrocities inflicted on innocents. In Daragam, villagers were detained by the security forces for eighty-six hours without food, water, and even permission to defecate. Is this a humanitarian protocol? In the Nandgaon Basti near Banihal, a mother and her daughters were raped in front of each other. The Special Task Force (STF) was a "qatilon ka giroh" (band of murderers). About these heinous excesses, the state has nothing to say.' He said that they were willing to talk to the Government of India but without any preconditions, not even 'within the Four Corners of the Constitution.'

'Sir, could you sustain yourself as an independent nation?' I asked hesitantly.

'Azadi is such a huge blessing that everything can be done.' I can never forget his last words as we were leaving. 'Agar Hindustan sarkon par sona bichhaye to bhi hum Azadi hi chahenge' (Even if India covers roads with gold we still want Azadi).

Mirwaiz Umar Farooq, Chairman of the All Parties Hurriyat Conference, sat in front of us. I was mesmerised by his personality. A man who had witnessed his father Maulvi Farooq's assassination and the firing by CRPF on his funeral procession where seventy-two people were killed. He spoke softly. The APHC was formed in 1993 as a forum for expressing the will of Kashmiris. He told us that Hurriyat always stood for the return of the displaced Kashmiri Pandits to the Valley. The Hurriyat office has thousands of registered families who have lost members and not received compensation because of the suspicion that they may have harboured militants at some point in time. He continued, 'Then, we hear the Minister of Information and Broadcasting announcing, "No action will be taken against the forces because it affects their morale."' We wonder. What about the killing of innocent villagers as a fallout of the Chittisinghpura massacre? He said that militants may have been trained in POK, but if the Government of India has honest intentions, Hurriyat should be given permission to talk to the people on the other side. 'We are prepared to find a solution but only through dialogue.'

Abdul Ghani Lone, the veteran politician, enumerated the killings, the arrests, and the custodial deaths. He told us that youth were forced to lift their guns because of oppression and torture by the state. 'Go to Handwara and see for yourselves. At the chowk, they have a bunker next to which they have dug a ditch in which innocents are hung upside down.' Going through the details of Chattisinghpora he said, 'SP, Anantnag, announced the names of the terrorists they had killed and the security forces were given an award of six lakhs for their "karkardagi" (resourcefulness). When the villagers discovered their missing family members, their cries reached worldwide. Three hundred Bakarwals took out a protest march. When they reached Barakpora, they were ordered to disperse. Having lost their kin, they refused. The army's consequential firing killed eight innocents.'

Then came his words, which are etched in my heart, 'It is the people's money that supports the army. It is for the people to reject this carnage. In fifty-three years, we have never considered ourselves a part of India. For this, you Indians are responsible. Government murda jismon par raaj kar ley magar jazbaati taur sey hum alag hain. (Government can rule over dead bodies, but emotionally, we are separate). The Indian State is a brute state, but we have no means of telling the world what they have done to us. Did we fight for independence from the British to annihilate our own people thus?'

Many political activists talked to us with relative ease. Our belief that in any peace process women have to play a major role was vindicated by the confidence that the common people reposed in us. We promised them we would carry their message to the rest of the country with candour and clarity. Peace will come through dialogue, and not through the barrel of the gun.

In Anantnag, a large gathering collected by an NGO, Friends of Kashmir, met our delegation. Most of the speakers referred to Kashmir as a Jahannum (hell) rather than the popular epithet Jannat (paradise) used in world literature. The unrest of unemployed youth was a cause for Kashmir's trauma. 'Why does one side refer to Kashmir as "atoot ang" (integral limb) and the other as "shehrug" (jugular vein)? No one bothers to ask: "What do people think?"'

After this tense and draining session, we drove to Beerwah, a tehsil in the district of Budgam to participate in the Annual Day of a school run by the Syed Mazharul Haq Society. A special feature of the day was the dowry-less marriage between Syeda Fareeda and Syed Farooq which exemplified the simplicity enjoined in Islam. The moment of respite from endless sorrow came when older residents of Beerwah spoke with great reverence about the work my father did in taking education to the most far-flung areas of the Valley.

On our way back from Gulmarg, we saw slogans on signposts. 'India is a bouquet, Kashmir a rose in it.'

During private conversations, we were told that in Baramulla, a new order was being implemented. People in certain villages were being forced to submit coloured photographs for police registration including women and girls. Parents were sending their young daughters away for fear of being identified by the forces for sexual exploitation.

Doda, a district with an area equal to the rest of the Valley, is a world in itself. Inhospitable terrain, dense forests, and an almost equally divided population of Hindus and Muslims living together in amity—that is, Doda. Even though the area is militancy affected, the mutual amity between Hindus and Muslims is remarkable. We reached Doda around midnight. A large number of people were waiting for us. In the town of Bhadarwah, Akhil Bharat Rachnatmak

Samaj youth had worked to rebuild the forty-three houses burnt in communal clashes. This had a deep impact in rebuilding interfaith amity, which has never been disturbed since then.

We then proceeded to Kishtawar, where we met groups at Thathari and Sarthal. Sarthal is a Hindu pilgrimage point facilitated by Muslims. We were warmly received, particularly by the women who reaffirmed that if people came together, they could thwart all nefarious designs to divide on communal lines. The District Commissioner received us and promised to look into the complaints we presented. This young, dynamic officer was called 'farishta' (angel) by the local population due to his responsive and friendly approach.

People resented being treated as a territory to be fought over by two belligerent neighbours. They want the Pandits to return and take up life again. Young girls and boys carry on their faces the raw wounds of their losses. They long for peace, to be allowed to live and bring up their families with safety and dignity. They resent having to prove themselves in their land by presenting their identity card everywhere. They hate the epithet 'ghaddar' (traitor) being flung at them.

~

Another defining moment was my visit to Pahalgam in 2018. 'On the face of the earth if there be Firdaus (Paradise), it is this, it is this, it is this,' wrote the poet Amir Khusro. These lines exemplify Pahalgam. Its beauty is breathtaking. My eyes and ears wrapped the sight and sound of River Lidder around my heart. The trees were bluish-green, silent against the backdrop of majestic mountains. It was almost 8 pm; there were still some streaks of silver in the sky. The hills stood before me as if in patient disdain. There were deep vertical black gashes where the trees had been cut.

The last time I came to Pahalgam was when Professor Mushirul

Haq was Vice Chancellor of the Kashmir University. My daughter Ayesha and I played badminton on the lawns of the Vice Chancellor Lodge. He had sent the three of us, my cousin Sughra, my daughter Ayesha and me, to Pahalgam for the day. Fourteen years later, I sat on the same spot and thought of my host, Mushirul Sahib, who was abducted while he was going to Hazratbal mosque for Friday prayers and killed on the spot during the month of Ramadan. I think of his wife, who grieved all through the next few years she lived after him.

Many years ago, in the Forties, we used to live in Srinagar, where there were waterways in the city. I was told Srinagar was our Venice. Shikaras were the common means of local travel. Now, the smell of diesel hangs like a poison cloud over the city. But Pahalgam sits ensconced in the silence of the surrounding mountains, detached from that mayhem.

On the way up, my friend Sushobha Barve and I had to stop at a few military checkposts. Two jawans peeped inside the Sumo and said: 'Two women going "alone" on this route. Don't you have any husbands or children? How can we allow you to stir out alone?'

'You are our children,' we said. 'We are not afraid.' They look surprised but let us go.

In the reception area of the sprawling building of the Pahalgam Club hangs a sign 'Temporary Membership Rs 5'. Membership tagged at Rs 5! Even back then, it was ludicrous! Days and hours in Pahalgam cannot be price-tagged. The lawns of the club showed signs of the handful of people who came earlier in the day—plastic wrappers, half-eaten sandwiches, and mango peels. In the rain and light breeze, the magnificent chinars stood as silent spectators of this human degradation. Our waiter was my husband's namesake, Abdul Hameed. We chatted with him; he had no other guests to look after. We asked him about the killings of the Amarnath pilgrims in 2017. What he narrated made us wince with pain. We realised that in this morass and quagmire, no one can tell where truth disappears.

At the Pahalgam Club we learnt that we were the only occupants of the entire building. The sweeping wooden staircase was dark, books in the library untouched. For a long time, no one had played ping-pong or billiards on the empty tables. The hallways were silent. The only sound was of the River Lidder and the droning of the generator. The smell of kerosene hung above the fragrance of the flowering trees.

Abdul Hameed served us dinner on a long table with twenty-four chairs. As I sat at the head of the empty table, I imagined this room being filled with the laughter of men and women, some music, some revelry, and a cool breeze from outside fanning their warm faces. The waiter graciously insisted that I eat a little more. I wondered if he had eaten? He had told us that he had served at the club for twenty years. 'Do you think the good times will return?' I asked.

'What can I say?' he answered. 'They may….' Stock words spoken without hope. I blinked back my tears and went up a dark staircase to my dark room. Lines from Sahir came to mind:

Guzishta jang mein ghar hi jale, magar is baar
Ajab nahin, ke ye parchhaiyaaan bhi jal jaayen

In the previous war, only homes were burnt, but this time
Nothing strange, if shadows also get burnt down

A year later, in 2019, I found myself walking on the Abdullah Bridge, which ran parallel to the now-defunct Zero Bridge. Below me was the Jhelum with houseboats lined on each side. To the left was the Jammu and Kashmir Arts Emporium. Once a beautiful wooden building, it had burned down during the early days of the insurgency. Suddenly, I felt something brushing my head, quite hard. I looked up to see a large bird flying away from me. That impact, though not harsh, was quite startling. I covered my head to avoid more bird brushes and wondered what the ominous message of the bird was?

I had been reading Arabian Nights over the previous few days. During his seven voyages, Sindbad often encountered the mega-giant bird, Rukh. This mythical bird symbolised only one thing to me—immense power. My bird was powerful, too. I thought I was a little like Sindbad. He had an insatiable yearning for the sea, and I have an insatiable desire to return to Kashmir again and again. I had also been reading the poetry of Allama Iqbal, which often features the mythical bird, Shaheen symbolising ultimate freedom. Azadi is the ultimate dream of the people of this beleaguered land.

I had come back to my janmabhoomi to be healed. I had come to Kashmir Valley hoping for a balm. One always returns home to be healed. And I wanted the Valley, which has been torn and hurt beyond description for so many years, to make me whole again. Why? What had I done for the Valley?

The first sight of Dal Lake is as if one has glimpsed a sliver of divine glory. Closer to the Sher-i-Kashmir Conference Centre, the lake became a still mirror. there were hardly any shikaras in the water and very few cars on the road. I saw the thinnest slice of a crescent moon announcing the first day of the new month, Rabbi-us-Sani. A deceptive calm hung over the Valley.

Just beneath the still surface lay the human tragedy to which I bore witness—hundreds of youth who fell to bullets. A young auto driver is hauled up by two security officers. I don't know what fate awaits him. A five-year-old child asked, 'Why have they caught an auto-uncle?' No one answered and false assurances were on my lips. Military bunkers dot the route that I carefully picked for my walk, thinking it would be a quiet stretch.

The splendid views of the Valley from the various vantage points of Chashma Shahi and Pari Mahal are out of the reach of ordinary Kashmiris. Women and men whose generations sowed, planted and nurtured the Valley are deprived. Golf courses are built at astronomical costs, while the environment of the Valley has been raped and pillaged by various state and non-state actors with rapacious appetites.

Newspapers, much subdued in present times, used to print raging headlines against the unjust regime. The day before I left, the front page story in Kashmiri Times was of Abdul Salaam Bhat of Kulgam, who was killed in custody by the BSF. The story broke because the Kashmir State Human Rights Commission (SHRC) held the BSF personnel responsible and ordered an ex-gratia payment of five lakhs. According to the complaint, Bhat was picked up by the D Company of the 78 Battalion of BSF deployed in Qazigund in Anantnag. His body was chopped into pieces and dumped into a nearby stream. Police got wind of it and quietly buried the remains. The family had it exhumed, and the case was given to the SHRC.

There are many Abdul Salaams whose chopped bodies lie buried all over the Valley. Who knows how many pieces of human flesh have been dumped in overflow channels? The bird that hit my head may have been a vulture that does the scavenger's work for humans but is loathed by most of us. It is the human vultures who should be loathed, those who are steadily pecking away at all of Allah's bounty with which Kashmir was endowed. Or maybe the bird was Allama Iqbal's Shaheen, promising a new dawn. Who can tell?

An unknown poet wrote:

> *Ghair mumkin hai ke Kashmir ki guththi suljhe*
> *Ahl-e-danish ne bahut soch ke uljhaee hai*
>
> Impossible that the skein of Kashmir will ever be unravelled
> Experts have entangled it with great care

~

On August 5, 2019, India scrapped the law that grants special status to Indian-administered Kashmir. The President had signed a decree abolishing Article 370 of the Constitution, stripping Kashmir of the significant autonomy it had enjoyed for seven decades amid an indefinite lockdown and massive troop deployment in the disputed region.

In the first few days of August, tens of thousands of additional Indian troops were deployed to Kashmir, a major Hindu pilgrimage was cancelled, schools and colleges were shut, tourists were ordered to return to their home, telephone and internet services were suspended, and regional political leaders were placed under house arrest. It had been speculated that Article 35A of the Indian Constitution, which gave some special privileges to the state's people, would be scrapped. But the Indian government then stunned everyone by saying it was revoking all of Article 370, which has been the basis of Kashmir's complex relationship with India for seventy years.

Article 370 allowed the state a certain amount of autonomy—its own constitution, a separate flag, and the freedom to make laws. Foreign affairs, defence, and communications remained the preserve of the central government. As per the Article, Jammu and Kashmir could make its own rules relating to permanent residency, ownership of property, and fundamental rights. It could bar Indians from outside the state from purchasing property or settling there.

After having watched from the distance of Delhi, the land of my birth, in agony for weeks, I visited again.

The Valley withstood the lockdown in silence until the first landlines were restored. Everywhere, I saw photographs and opinion pieces about Kashmir. For the real news, I joined the dots from whatever bits I found, and a fuller picture emerged.

Empty roads, lanes and pathways. Closed shops and closed businesses and minds numb with fear and waiting. It was neither the first nor last time in history that people have been held hostage in their own land. When it happened elsewhere, we protested but with the fake comfort that it was happening elsewhere. But this time, it was happening right here, in my homeland, to my people.

I read 'Kashmir Caged', a citizens' report published on August 13, 2019. It was written in the immediate aftermath of the abolishment of the Article by four people who spent five days in the most militarised region of the world. This small band of brave people kept moving from house to house, gully to gully, asking questions, avoiding security, keeping peoples' confidence, and daring to speak the truth to the world. 'When Nitish Kumar imposed prohibition, he did not ask the alcoholics. The situation is the same here.' These were words spoken to the group by Ashwini Kumar Chrungo, BJP spokesman from Jammu. In the same vein were lines written by a former foreign secretary, who wrote while referring to a Kashmiri girl, 'In terms of economic development, Kashmir is in the Stone Age.'

Politicians and officials in high places barely understand Kashmir and are contemptuous in their view of Kashmiris. Their refinement in arts, literature, crafts, and cuisine is unique and comparable with the best anywhere in the world. Ten thousand women and men protested in Soura on August 9. There were scores of victims of pellet injuries in hospitals, hundreds of political leaders, and civil activists were under arrest. Women gave birth in hostile spaces en route to hospitals. And the sharpest cut—hundreds of young boys and teens picked up without a warrant.

Parents were terrified of telling their names for fear that their beloved sons would become one of the thousands of 'disappeared'. Terrified that the army would deny, the state would condone, and their child would be dumped in one of the mass graves. In a word, Kashmir was silent—'Bandook ki khamoshi'(The silence of the bullet), 'Qabristan ki khamoshi' (The silence of the graveyard) says the report. Girls in Nagbal told us, 'How can we celebrate Eid? Our brothers are in police custody.'

Then, there was the taxi driver who was out to buy an inhaler for his father. He was hauled up by a security man, his inhaler snatched, and stamped upon. 'Their hatred for us came out of the boot which crushed the inhaler,' the cab driver said.

There were many voices: 'Parties which batted for the Indian State, look at them, they are being humiliated now,' said one man.

'Article 35A means land will be sold cheap to Adani and Patanjali.'

'Congress ne hamari peeth mein chhura bhonka, inhone samne se.'

'If they have broken 370, our relationship is broken. Leave us alone.'

A film was made in 2022, *Kashmir Files*, which was purportedly on the plight of the Kashmiri Pandits. The film was widely criticised for being communal and one-sided. The following year, Prabhash Chandra made *I Am Not the River Jhelum*, in response, giving the other side of the picture. A voice in this film rang out, 'I am a Kashmiri Pandit. Where is my Kashmiriyat? We used to celebrate all our festivals together. Eid, Diwali, Holi.' In the background was a chorus. 'We want freedom. Article 370 wapas karo' (Restore Article 370).

Kashmir was smouldering. Conditions have never been *samanya* (inclusive) as claimed by all major news media. Lies have been spoken unabashedly. 'Normalcy' is a word that needs to be expunged because the anger is raging below the surface.

To me these lines of an unknown poet say it all:

Barf girti hai barf girne do
Barf girne do rehguzaron par
Barf girne do kohsaron par
Aag Ka Aag Kashmir ke chinaron ki
Hai ameen atisheen baharon ki
Barf isko daba nahin sakti
Jo lagi hai bujha nahin sakti
Phir ye grami jumood tode gi
Saare mahaul ko jhinjhorey gi
Barf girti hai barf girne do

Let the snows fall
Let it fall on boulevards
Let it fall on mountains
Fires of Kashmir's chinars
Are witness to the smouldering spring
Snow cannot cover it
Snow cannot extinguish it
This heat will melt the stillness
It will convulse the atmosphere
Let snows fall

Yawar Ahmed Bhat from Chandgam in Pulwama died in Srinagar's SMHS hospital on September 20, 2019. It was forty-five days after the state was locked down on August 5. He was fifteen years old. He allegedly died by suicide after consuming rat poison. The following circumstances were reported.

On September 17, Yawar told his sister that he had been detained and beaten up by some soldiers from a local army camp. They took away his identity card and asked him to report to the camp the next day.

Yawar's father said the boy seemed upset that night. 'He usually slept in my room. That night, he did not. My wife found him at the window, vomiting,' Abdul said.

He was terrified of being tortured by the Army. He knew it would happen, whether he went to the camp or stayed home. His family rushed him to the district hospital and then, somehow, to Srinagar. At SMHS hospital, he could not be saved. That was the end of Yawar Abdul Hameed.

The Army has denied having had any part in this incident. SSP Chandan Kohli started inquest proceedings, and when asked by the media, DC Pulwama Syed Abid refused to comment.

I was one of five women who had visited Srinagar from

September 17 to 21, forty-three days since the lockdown. In our report 'Women's Voice', we had recounted this tragedy.

Yawar died the day after we left Srinagar, but there are many more Yawars whose testimonies we heard and recorded. My urge to write these lines emanates from a very personal experience that I have never shared. I feel that this is the time to speak from the heart.

My son's name is Yavar, and my late husband's name is Abdul Hameed. The only difference is in the spelling, Yawar and Yavar. Everything else is the same. This death in Pulwama seems like a death in my own family. I feel like I am one with this unknown Pulwama family. Until yesterday, they and many like them were strangers whose voices we were carrying to the world through our report. Today they are family.

When my son Yavar was four or five years old, I lost him at a crowded mall in a foreign country. I went mad. I screamed out his name in all directions. In heart-stopping moments, I felt I would never see him again. Tears and cries in the midst of swirling crowds of tourists while escalators constantly moved up and down. All this is etched in my mind even after forty years. It may have been some ten minutes later when I saw a little boy with a tear-streaked face coming down the escalator. It was decidedly my life's happiest moment.

But what about the mothers of Kashmir? When their sons walk out of the door, whether to play, run errands, or go to school, mothers must die a little each time they see the back of a shirt or a school bag. Will he? Won't he? Torture? Death?

We wrote in our September 2019 report that the sight of young, even very young boys, raises hackles, and stokes anger in the minds of the 'masters'. For them, every child has 'stone pelter' written on his forehead. Snatching cell phones, demanding identity cards, and hauling them off to secret chambers is the new normal in Kashmir.

Everyone knows of the infamous torture chambers, known as Papa One and Papa Two, during the 1990s and 2000s, but today their whereabouts are largely unknown. Parents who have no means of knowing, no money to bribe, no public transport to use, have no option but to live every inch of their pain.

There was a petition in the Supreme Court about disappeared children after the Kashmir lockdown. The disappearance of youths in Kashmir has been going on for a long time, but suddenly there is a deluge. Two distinguished child rights activists, Shanta Sinha and Enakshi Ganguly, have petitioned before the Supreme Court bench headed by the Chief Justice of India.

The CJI asked for a report from the Jammu and Kashmir Juvenile Justice Committee headed by Justice Ali Mohammad Magrey. The CJI, then occupied by the Ayodhya case, subsequently transferred the case to a colleague. The Committee report was submitted to the Supreme Court via the Jammu and Kashmir High Court. After obtaining the views of several state agencies, the Committee concluded that 'averments made in the petition are totally baseless, fallacious, and offer only a biased version based on media reports that have no evidentiary value…'

What will be the fate of these innocents, these Yawars and others who are being held somewhere, away from the loving arms of their mothers and fathers? What will be the result of this struggle to save children who are in the first spring of their lives? At both ends, children at one, parents at another—there is pinning and longing, but there is nothing that connects them to one another, not even a lowly telephone line.

Postscript

2023. Tomorrow, I am going to my birthplace. Spread before me are newspaper articles with Kashmir news. Yesterday, May 21, was the anniversary of the assassination of Mirwaiz Maulvi Mohammad Farooq. Today, May 22, the G20 tourism working group meets in

Srinagar. There are multi-tiered security arrangements everywhere since it is the first international event since the abrogation of Article 370 four years ago. Sher-i-Kashmir Centre is the venue; 180 delegates, including sixty from G20 countries, are expected to attend.

It plays out like a theatre of the absurd. Yesterday, world leaders were in Hiroshima for the G7 where India's PM Modi met Britain's Rishi Sunak and Brazil's Lula da Silva. He talked of dialogue and diplomacy in the context of Ukraine. These words ring hollow given the killing fields at home, especially in Kashmir, in the North-East and many parts of this beleaguered land. From there, Modi dashed to Papua New Guinea, where its PM, James Marape, got his photo on the front page of Indian newspapers by almost prostrating himself before Modi. Another person who made it on the front page is the US President Joe Biden, who asked for the autograph of star Modi. Australian PM Anthony Albanese recalled an audience of 90,000 people at Narendra Modi Stadium, where the two stood hand-in-hand in Gujarat earlier in the year.

I identify with the family of Mirwaiz Maulvi Farooq, who was gunned down in his office by two assailants. Who sent them? We will never know. Bullets rained on the dead body as it was taken from Soura hospital; bullets on the youthful carriers. Kashmir burnt then, and Kashmir burns now.

Today, a G20 subgroup meeting is being held to 'show off' to world visitors India's crown jewel. In his poem 'Ai Wadi-e-Kashmir', the great poet and our dear family friend, Jagan Nath Azad, described Kashmir:

> *Tu Hind ke maatthe pe hai ek taaj-e-drakhshaan*
>
> You are the radiant crown on Hind's forehead

From 1940 to 1947, while my father toured the terrain on horseback, our home became the hub of culture, frequented by poets, writers, and artists from all over the country. Kashmiri Pandits from many parts of India were in our home reciting exquisite Urdu poetry including Brij Narayan Chakbast, Gopi Nath Aman, Anand Narayan Mulla, and many others. One manuscript survives in my library. Jagan Nath Azad's handwritten poem was embargoed until 1959. It is falling apart at the folds.

Taasir wo ek teri hawaon ko mili hai
Jo khaak ko tiryaq karey zehr ko akseer

Your breeze has the efficacy
To make dust … to make poison elixir

Kashmir was universally beloved by writers from everywhere. Its present state was predicted by two of its many lovers, Allama Iqbal and Faiz Ahmed Faiz.

Iqbal wrote:

Aaj woh Kashmir hai mahkoom-o-majboor-o-faqeer
Kal jisey ahl-e-nazar kehtey the Iran-e-Sagheer

Today that Kashmir is crushed, helpless, beggared
Who people of vision called 'smaller Iran'.

And Faiz Sahib:

Nisar mein teri galiyon pe ai want ke Jahan
Chali hai rasm ke koi na sar utttha ke chale

O my country I sacrifice myself on your roadways
Where the diktat is that no one can walk with his head held high

Today, on his death anniversary, I think of Maulvi Farooq, the 45-year-old spiritual leader who was gunned down for bringing enlightenment to our community. Other images rise to my mind. A Vice Chancellor deeply respected and loved, Prof Mushirul Haq, who had invited me to visit Srinagar with my daughter in 1990, weeks before he was brutally killed. I think of Moo-e-Mubarak, the Prophet's relic stolen from the precincts of Hazratbal and the Mirwaiz's effort for its restoration. I think of thousands of disappearances of boys and men and the torture and brutalising in detention cells, Papa One and Papa Two. In my mind are played scenes from my beloved friend, Iffat Fatima's film *Khoon diy Baarav* (On a Trail of Vanished Blood), about these children, their parents and the woman who tried to bring the issue to the international stage. Parveena Ahangar is the protagonist of Iffat's film; the title speaks volumes.

My daughter in London is reading the Kashmiri poet Agha Shahid Ali, who wrote *The Country Without a Post Office*.

> Everything is finished nothing remains
> I must force silence to be a mirror
> It's raining as I write this I have no prayer
> It's just a shout held in.

14

India-Pakistan

Dooriyan Nazdeekiyan

Since 1947, Pakistan and India have fought four wars—1947, 1965, 1972, and 1999. Hostile statements and cross-border skirmishes make headlines daily and are debated at global forums, including the United Nations. With such a history of hostility, it is no surprise that a political solution to the wide range of issues between India and Pakistan has remained elusive. Three generations of constant conflict akin to ongoing low-intensity war have built a hate wall which is harder than tempered steel. This structure, forced and reinforced by two belligerent states, has prevented repeated attempts at solutions from meeting with success.

At the Nuremberg Trials, just before he was sentenced to death, leading Nazi leader Hermann Goering said, 'Why, of course, the people don't want war. Why should some poor slob on a farm want to risk his life in a war when the best he can get out of it is to come back to his farm in one piece? Naturally, the common people don't want war—neither in Russia nor in England, nor for that matter in Germany. That is understood. But after all, it is the leaders of the country who determine the policy, and it is always a simple matter to drag the people along, whether it is a democracy, or a fascist dictatorship, or a parliament, or a communist dictatorship… Voice or no voice, the people can always be brought to the bidding of the leaders. That is easy. All you have to do is to tell them they are being attacked and denounce the pacifists for lack of patriotism and exposing the country to danger.' This, he explained, was how the Jews were exterminated. And this is how, even today, thousands of young men and women are killed on the battlefield and millions in their own homes.

The animosity that exists between our two countries is propagated by the states as inexorable; external pressures are created, propaganda is ubiquitous, truth is twisted, and facts distorted. The 'other' is always blamed for everything that goes wrong; in all this, the media is centre stage.

Political leaders and biased history textbooks may have created boundaries and cleavages on lands and minds. But I still believe that deep down, people on both sides are united in their heart. My reason for believing in this is from my own personal experience, As I am writing this I learned that my niece, Zeba is in ICU in Karachi. How could I go to comfort her mother? I have been at the receiving end of calls like this for sixty-seven years. Have I rushed to my loved ones? Visa obstacles are insurmountable, there are no flights, no trains, and no buses. Loved ones have grown apart. This is the everlasting *zakhm* (wound) of the Partition. And yet, the ties remain.

The mid-1990s saw the start of a people-to-people wave between India and Pakistan. Its first trickle occurred in 1993 when a delegation of four Pakistani peace activists, Dr Mubashir Hasan, Asma Jahangir, Nisar Usmani and Nasim Zehra came to India. They were concerned citizens who had come at their own expense to tell the people that war offered no solution to any problem between India and Pakistan including the intense upsurge in Kashmir. They were ready to talk to anyone ready to listen.

Dr Mubashir Hasan, an engineer by training, was Zulfikar Ali Bhutto's Finance Minister before he became what warmongers call a 'peacenik'. Since 1990, he started his crusade for peace between the two countries. During this visit, the group met several political leaders, including Rajiv Gandhi. Four years later, in 1994, a few people from both sides of the border met at Lahore and thus began the Pakistan India Peoples Forum for Peace and Democracy (PIPFPD). In the next few years, six large Conventions were held in Delhi, Lahore, Karachi, Calcutta, Peshawar, and Bangalore. I recall walking with Pakistani delegates in a magnificent procession on the Esplanade in Kolkata and being joined by ordinary residents of the city. It was a stirring moment for the people of both countries.

Several years later, a 7th Convention was held at Allahabad in 2016. Political manoeuvres, overt and covert, were made to thwart and throttle the ties thus created by women and men across the divide. But ordinary peace activists of these two beleaguered nations kept the movement alive.

I believe there is a peace activist in each one of us: the mother who teaches her child tolerance, the doctor who treats patients in remote villages, the engineer who builds roads and bridges that connect people, the student who stands up against violence, and the journalist who steers away from propaganda. We simply need to identify and recognise this activist.

The first small steps taken in the 1990s culminated in another initiative on March 25, 2000, when thirty-five Indian women on a peace mission rode the bus to Lahore. This was under the Women's Initiative For Peace in South Asia (WIPSA), of which I was one of the five founder members. The hosts of this peace mission in Pakistan were the Human Rights Commission of Pakistan, the Pakistan Chapter of PIPFPD, and several other women's organisations.

With the irrepressible Nirmala Deshpande and indefatigable Mohini Giri, we headed for Lahore while the Kargil war was at its peak. A few odd lumpen voices on both sides decried our effort. But the majority cheered us on. We had pooled our money to pay the bus fare. From the other side, Pakistani women had turned out in hundreds to greet us on the lawns of the Faletti's Hotel in Lahore. On the bus, we rehearsed a song written by our beloved leader Kamla Bhasin, the song became an anthem for Indian women and later has become an anthem for women's movements all over South Asia. As we pulled up on the grounds of Faleltti's Hotel, the same song was on Pakistani lips! 'Tor tor ke bandhanon ko dekho behney aati hain' (Sisters, come, breaking the shackles). Carrying blue silk scarves and blue bangles for peace and sisterhood and candles for hope, they were there to greet us. Their eclectic appearance; women with short-cropped hair, fashionably attired, and women in hijab, but all with the same sentiment, struck us. Among myriad colours, the black veils of the hijab stood out, and Urdu journalists were generally veiled.

Other than visas, we had sought no permission from either government. Yet within three days of our arrival, we were invited for a meeting with President Musharraf. We met him in a small delegation of seven. Among us was a student from Lady Shri Ram College, who was then the President of the Students Union. She looked the President of Pakistan in the eye and spoke words I will never forget, 'Youth from both countries don't want to haul the baggage of the past; that is your baggage. We want to move on to enjoy each other's music, art, and lifestyles.' He smiled, 'I agree.'

As we moved through the gullies, mohallas, bastis, and kuchchi abadis we saw the *mehnatkash* (hard-working) women of Punjab, toiling in fields or in their homes. 'Tum India se ho?' (Are you from India?) asked Husain Bi during one such jaunt through Mughalpura. Sitting on a charpai in the dalaan outside her house, she called the neighbours to meet women from 'Bharat'. Punjabi women of all ages came out, some with their babies. There was some initial shyness, which was soon overcome by healthy curiosity. Hindi films were the greatest bonding factor. Amir Khan, Shahrukh, Salman but, above all, Hrithik were spoken about. Little boys, looking out the corners of their eyes, broke into a dance only to be reprimanded by their mothers. We gave them the few packets of bindis we were carrying in our purses. The little girls looked at their mothers before taking them from our hands. 'You are just like us,' Husain Bi said, 'then why the *zulm* (ill-treatment) in Kashmir? Why do you mistreat the Muslims?' No, we don't; I wanted to explain, now look at me, I am a Muslim... Even as the words came to my lips, I realised that this was a mohalla and not a conference room.

That was twenty-one years ago when I could not have imagined being in the vortex of Muslim hatred, especially post-2014. So I said, 'Yes, we have many problems but we can solve them together?'

'Yes, yes', they said at once. In a chorus, they spoke, 'Aana jaana to hona chahiye; tum ne achha kiya aa gayeen.' (Travel should be allowed, good of you to come.) Husain Bi, Masoom Bi, and Sakina were very keen to come to 'Bharat'. Unlike the initial sadness of the older generation, when we parted from the women of Mughalpura, it was on a note of hope.

During the next few days, we sat at roundtables discussing nuclearisation, militarisation, globalisation, and its impact on women. They were concerned, as were we, with the omnipresence of multinationals, patenting our traditional knowledge. We spoke on identical concerns: human rights violations in both countries, atrocities against women, lack of political will, and the rise of fundamentalist forces. They spoke without fear, lashing out against repressive policies. For six days, we spent all our time together. When we were leaving, the oldest woman on our side, Tirpat Kaur, a war-widow of the 1965 India-Pakistan war, said, 'I feel I am leaving my mother's home and going to my sasural.'

'One has been told India is the enemy, but finally, when we look back at the face of the enemy, it smiles back at us,' said Rubina Shakeel, who worked for a crisis centre in Lahore. Women at the Indo-Pakistan Women's Solidarity Conference held on the third day of our visit echoed these sentiments. Scores of women spoke about their desire to build solidarity with Indian women. Everyone spoke of resolving the Kashmir dispute in consultation with and according to the will of the Kashmiri people. Jugnu Mohsin, editor of Friday Times, spoke about recent times when tension had peaked. Her friend took her 11-year-old son to a dried-up well in her neighbour's house. 'In case of an emergency,' she warned, 'go right to the bottom of the well and lie face down until help comes.' She had been reading the memoirs of a survivor of Hiroshima. Bone-chilling.

Asma, Hina, Nighat, Nusrat, Bina, Bela, Nigar, Shahtaj, Najji, and Saleema are women with the same hopes, fears, dreams, and aspirations. Whether they belonged to the far left or Jama'at-e-Islami, whether they were the pioneers of the women's movement in Pakistan or youth wanting to break free from the legacy of a beleaguered past, they loved the same food, enjoyed the same music, watched the same films, fought against the same patriarchal order. They were 'we' and we were 'they'—much to share, and if the present stand-off remains unresolved, much to lose.

Many of us members of the delegation fanned out to the mohalla bazaars and bastis. Talking to the common people, we encountered incidents of courtesy, friendship and a certain level of curiosity bordering on suspicion about India. There were heartening incidents of shopkeepers not charging for STD calls made and offering the best bargains because 'You are our guest'. Early the next morning, we left on the bus for Delhi, which was operated by Pakistan Tourism. We received the best treatment all the way to the Wagah border. We arrived in Delhi after a thirteen-hour drive and were greeted by friends, well-wishers and members of the visual and print media.

A month later, on May 5, 2000, two busloads of women, a sixty-women delegation from Pakistan led by Asma Jahangir, arrived in Delhi to an overwhelming welcome. Photographs of the two busloads have remained etched in the minds and hearts of an entire generation of people from both countries. Issuing a statement on behalf of the women, Asma said, 'People have been hurt, and there has been an environment of hostility for many years. All those who have been grieved, on both sides, need solace.' The statement was released at a lunch hosted by the former PM, I.K. Gujral. From the Indian side, Nirmala said, 'We need to apply balm on the wounds rather than replay the mistakes of the past.' Mr Gujral said no two nations could remain locked in the past. They have to look towards the future.

The first words Asma spoke as she stepped on Indian soil were, 'From here, let a message go to the politicians of India and Pakistan that the people want to live in peace and with dignity.' She then challenged the governments of the two countries to throw open the Wagah border and see the response of the common people. 'I am confident there will be traffic jams.' Many from both sides picked up Asma's statement as a refrain. 'For one day and one night, gates on both sides of the Wagah border should open.' This was the dream of many who had struggled for three decades against strong contrary currents. Kuldip Nayar and Asma Jahangir were among the 'first dreamers' who gave their lives for Pakistan-India bonding.

~

Despite every effort to throttle them, people-to-people movements are alive and well today. I recall my favourite moments.

It was August 14, 2001. At the Wagah border, thousands of people collected to celebrate the friendship between India and Pakistan from a platform called the Hind-Pak Dosti Manch, an initiative of the common people of Punjab. Kuldip Nayar was at the vanguard of this movement. He, along with his brother-in-law and fellow traveller Justice Rajinder Sachar, was among the last of the breed who had experienced 1947. In fact, it was they and contemporaries on both sides of the border who inspired the poet Raees Amrohvi (himself one of them) to write lines, which are the anthem of displaced people. Mani Shankar Aiyer translated the poem during his days as Counsel General in Karachi. Here is one poignant stanza and its translation.

Kya hum bhula sakeinge
Ajdaad key watan ko
Bhooli hui fiza ko bisrey huey chaman ko
Ganga ki dilkashi ko Jumna ke bankpan ko
Maazi ki suhbaton ko yaaron ki anjuman ko
O Hind ke musafir soz-e-kalaam leja
O Hind jane waley mera salaam leja

Can we ever forget so
The earth of our ancestors?
The wind which wafts in memories
Of brothers and of sisters,
The gurgling waters of the Ganga
The Yamuna swirling fast,
The friendships of our younger days,
Dalliances of the past.
Oh! You who go to India
Affection fills our yearnings,
Oh! You who go to India
Carry to them our greetings.

For twenty-three years, on the night of August 14/15, Kuldip would go to the border at the stroke of midnight to light candles to mark the Independence Day of each country and promote love and friendship between the two neighbours. He had a few comrades, especially two young men from Amritsar, Satnam Manik and Ramesh Yadav, who stood by him for a quarter century of his struggle to bring these two beleaguered countries on the Aman Dosti Path. Slowly, the caravan grew. People came with him from Delhi, and gradually the people of Amritsar took charge and ownership of the campaign. Kuldip had transformed it into a locally tethered national initiative, attended by people from the country, city and many villages around Attari, plus people from all walks of life from the bustling, burgeoning Amritsar.

I had gone there with the very first group. At the stroke of midnight, we walked on the strip called 'no man's land' with stalwarts Nikhil Chakravarty, Justice Sachar, Bharati Nayar, and Kuldip ji leading the way. At a distance, we could see the gate on which was inscribed 'Islamic Republic of Pakistan'. We craned our necks to see if the Pakistan Rangers would permit any of our friends to come up to their side of the strip. We learnt later that they had been refused permission to come to the check-post. The respective Home Ministries of India and Pakistan had denied permission to both sides. Thanks to both governments, when midnight struck, there was no one on either side of no man's land to light candles of friendship. Regardless, thousands of candles were lit at the stroke of midnight, albeit 800 yards from the border. As torch-bearers, we epitomised these lines of the poet Majrooh Sultanpuri:

Jala ke mishal-jaan hum junoon sifaat chaley
Jo ghar mein aag lagaye hamare saath chaley

Having lit the taper of life we, mad people, set forth
Whoever's ready to torch the easy life should come along

From start to finish, it was a peoples' show, which accounted for its vibrancy and vitality. Right from the time we Dilliwalas were received at the Amritsar station and taken to the campus of the Guru Nanak Dev University, we experienced the warmth and hospitality of Punjab. We reached the border just before the retreat ceremony was to begin. On both sides of the gate, there were the usual throngs of Indians and Pakistanis, primarily youth, both women and men. It was an exuberant, elated crowd. On the Indian side, a smart military band was playing popular Daler Mehndi and Mohammed Rafi songs like 'Bolo Tara-ra-rara' and 'Ye desh hai veer jawanon ka' (It is the country of brave young men), while Pakistan was playing songs of the chart-busting group, 'Junoon, Dil hai mera mulk, meri jan, janan-e-jan.' We walked very close to an enclosure where we saw hordes of Pakistani women; they were clapping, waving flags and hands, shouting slogans. On the other end, thousands of young men and boys were dancing, singing, and doing *nara-bazi* (sloganeering). On our side, the crowd returned song for song and nara for nara. Our hosts from Amritsar told us that this 'tamasha' happens every year. Since August 14 is their celebration, the Pakistanis come out in much larger numbers. At the end of the event, they will become uncontrollable, they said, and the police have to apply the baton! They told us that in 1993, there was a Punjabi mushaira on the Indian side. On the other side, people had crept as close to the border as they could. So, while poems were recited from this side, the 'Wah! Wah!' emanated from the other!

The actual retreat ceremony consisted of the lowering of the two flags, the BSF and the Pakistan Rangers marching down their respective strips, and one officer from each side stepping on no man's land. Belligerent posturing, flailing of arms and legs and aggressive strides characterised it. The young soldiers' faces were contorted with hate-filled expressions. Their body language was strident; the stamping of feet, the facial distortion and overall aggression was identical.

At Jallianwala Bagh, earlier that night, Kuldip lit the torch of friendship, which was to light thousands of candles later. It was pitch dark when we walked through the narrow gulley, at the end of which Colonel Dyer had stood and showered bullets on ordinary Indians—Sikhs, Hindus, Muslims, and Christians, innocent people of Amritsar. A slight breeze arose, but even as the taper was lit, a nearby mosque called the azan for the Isha prayer. Kuldip said, 'This is real India. And it is this sound, rising in the vicinity of the Golden Temple, which gives us the hope, which keeps us going.'

It was past nine when we reached the pandal erected outside the

Wagah check-post. On the way, we saw hundreds of people, on cycles, on foot, in bullock carts, and some in cars, going to the venue of the concert. Hans Raj Hans was going to perform. I had never attended his concert but knew him as the star whose songs topped the charts on both sides. That night, he sang and danced, and his audience, consisting of people from twenty-odd villages around Attari, from Amritsar and Delhi, sang and danced with him. Among his audience were fifty-five girls and boys who had taken the bus from Delhi to show solidarity with the cause. Most of them were students, and some artists who had taken up peace and nuclear disarmament as their life's mission. They pooled money to travel twelve hours on the bus from Delhi to Wagah and managed to reach the border when the concert began. We saw them swaying and dancing to the music, oblivious to the fatigue of the non-stop journey.

Hans Raj Hans began with a message from his 'Badi Behan', Abida Parveen. He had spoken to her before coming here. 'She said, "You go and perform and I will sit here in Sind at the shrines of the Pirs and Faqirs and pray for India Pakistan friendship and peace."'The man who usually charges a hefty sum for his concerts had donated his performance and also brought along his entire band free of cost.

What was immensely important was that throughout the excitement of a rock concert by Punjab's most popular star, the message of peace between Pakistan and India remained central. First, the Joint Declaration prepared on July 12, 2001, by 450 Pakistanis and Indians (endorsed by over 200 organisations) at the 'Peoples' Solidarity Conference' held in Delhi was read. Then, members of the Hind Pak Dosti Manch read, one by one, the resolutions they had drafted about peace between the two countries. They were careful to stress that they fully respected the separate identities of the two neighbours but desired that their similarities should bring them close as friends and well-wishers. One could see how hard they had worked to prepare the documents. At the end, they asked the crowd to raise their hands in support. Thousands of hands went up at once. Kuldip's face was glowing. He had said to me earlier, 'Long after we are gone, they will remember us as people who tried to build peace.'

Hind Pak Dosti Manch had arranged a langar for 700 people. The food, the service, the hall, and everything else was donated by people from the city. In the large hall next to the venue, the food was simple, hot, delicious, and plentiful. I could not help thinking of the five-star meals in air-conditioned halls where 'Peace' Conferences are usually held and compare its desolateness with this vibrancy. Students from Delhi were directed to the langar well past midnight. They had already lit the candles and placed them at the outer gate of the check-post as thousands of little reminders that as far as India and Pakistan are concerned it is the people and not the governments who will make the difference. 'That time has come,' said the Peoples Solidarity Conference, the Hind Pak Dosti Manch and many others across India and Pakistan.

From my personal archive, I found two newspaper clippings, both from the *The Hindu*, dated August 16, 1996, and May 3, 2000. The first was a photograph of Kuldip Nayar and Nikhil Chakravorty (who was one of the most respected names in Indian journalism, a courageous and independent columnist whose uncluttered style and great integrity won him an audience much more significant than that generally associated with a Left-wing writer) at the Wagah border holding candles. I was seated next to Nikhil. The second photo was of Asma at the door of the bus 'Paigham-e-Aman', poised to release a 'Pakistani' pigeon to the Indian skies. The bus had just driven inside the Ambedkar Bus Terminal. A second women's bus from Lahore was to arrive the next day. All three buses had one slogan, Goli Nahin Boli, Yudh Nahin Budh (no bullets, only dialogue, no war, only wisdom).

In my own humble manner, through newspaper articles, I asked that for twenty-four hours, ordinary people, Indians and Pakistanis (not ones with SAARC stickers and diplomatic passports) should freely walk across, mingle with one another as a tribute to Kuldip and Asma, these two Safiraan-e-Aman or Emissaries of Peace. I floated this idea again in a piece I wrote from Amritsar on August 22, 2018, while holding back tears the day Kuldip died. At the airport, on my return to Delhi, I saw a man who I had always associated with Kuldip; it was Hans Raj Hans. 'Hans Raj Ji, will you come to Wagah border if we hold an open-gate meeting to honour Kuldipji and Asmaji?' I asked this man who I had seen in 2000 at midnight performing at Wagah before an audience of 10,000 fans on this side and hundreds on the other side, who were glued to the border posts. Hans placed his hand on his heart and spoke just three words. 'Taa umr haazir' (So long as I am alive, I will be there).

I write these lines in 2024. One hundred and fifty people arrived at Wagah border on the night of August 15/16, Hind-Pak Dosti Manch and Aghaz e Dosti. On the other side were the same number of people with identical sentiments. What greater proof do we need?

On October 24, 2007, I visited Pakistan again, this time with my young colleague from the Planning Commission, Gunjan Veda. It was a 'no agenda trip'. I had no meeting, no conference, no shopping, and no sightseeing in view. My family in Delhi had warned me against going on 'that' side during such dangerous times. Regardless, I went ahead with Gunjan, who had always dreamt of going to Pakistan. She told me that no one from her family had expressed any reservations about this trip; excessive caution about Pakistan has nothing to do with being Muslim or Hindu. It is more of a mindset than religion. Generational attitudes play their part; elders carry the baggage of the past, and the youth thankfully leave it behind.

But what I am recalling now is twenty-four years after the candle lighting began. The year 2019 marked the worst mahaul ever between the two countries. Post abrogation of Article 370 in Kashmir, Pakistan had taken strident measures against India. India had retaliated, blow for blow. In Gandhi's words, two belligerent countries were blinding the whole world. We were filled with apprehensions since the abrogation on August 5. Would our journey to the border be stopped in its tracks? Peace activists on the other side who were planning to light candles at their Baab-e-Azadi to coincide with Indians on the Attari-Wagah border, had received a red alert from their respective government. Even as we flagged off the Yatra from our mentor Mohini Giri's home, there was more bravado than hope, at least in my heart.

Our anthem was the same, taught to us by Nirmala Deshpande, a song that she sang during her pad yatras:

Shanti ke sipahi chale, kranti ke sipahi chale
Le ke khairkhwahi chale rokne tabahi chale
Shanti ke sipahi chale
Bhed bhav chhod ke dil ko dil se jod ke
Desh ko sanwarney jaan apni warney
Shanti ke sipahi chale

This was the song of Acharya Vinoba Bhave when he set out on his 80,000 km yatra across India to find land for the landless.

The youngest yatri was the five-year-old child of Deepak Kathuria, and the oldest was 93-year-old Haru Tai, freedom's child from Satara in Maharashtra; all under the watchful eye of Ram Mohan Rai from Panipat and Ravi Nitesh from Delhi. The yatra began with Kundli in Haryana and ended with Jalandhar. They made fifteen stops on the way, holding roadside meetings. The travellers from Karnataka, Telangana, Kerala, UP, MP, Rajasthan, and Maharashtra spent over twenty hours, stopping to hold corner meetings and *nukkad-nataks* (street plays). Their overwhelming peace constituency were roadside labourers, auto rickshaw drivers, farm labourers, and schoolchildren.

Their initial apprehension disappeared when they saw the response of the common people. Students, housewives, farmers, labourers, wayfarers, and people from all walks greeted them with garlands, sweets, food, chai, and warmest bonhomie. Overwhelming public response meant delay at every *padao* (step). They had to honour the hospitality that awaited them at every stop. To a group of students at the Karnal stop, they asked the question. 'Give one reason for wanting friendship.' The answer came in a single phrase. 'Insaniyat ke naatey' (In the name of humanity). 'Goli nahin boli, Yudh nahin Budh, Jang nahin Aman', people on the road chanted along with the yatris.

At Wagah border, these lines from the poet Ali Sardar Jafri were on everyone's lips:

Tum aao gulshan-e-Lahore se chaman bar dosh
Hum aayein subh Benaras ki raushni le kar
Himalaya ki hawaon ki taazgi le kar
Phir use baad ye poochhein ke kaun dushman hai?

From gardens of Lahore you came carrying blossoms
We come carrying the dawn of Benaras
Carrying freshness of Himalayan breezes
And we ask each other who is the enemy?

Never were these lines more poignant than the night when sixty people stood at the Swarna Jayanti Dwar at the Wagah border. Sixty pairs of hands held candles to dispel the darkness that shrouds the relationship between Pakistan and India. Several eyes welled with tears thinking of Asma Jahangir, Justice Rajinder Sachar, Madeeha Gauhar, and other beloved comrades, now gone from our midst. The leader of this gang, Kuldip Nayar, was watching this scene from his hospital bed in Delhi.

Preceding the border event was an elaborate symposium organised over two days by Hind Pak Dosti Manch, Folklore Research Academy

Amritsar, Punjab Jagriti Manch Jalandhar, and Pakistan India Peoples Forum for Peace and Democracy. It was dedicated to the world's greatest symbol of peace whose 550th birth anniversary was being globally commemorated that year: Hind Pak Friendship Festival dedicated to Guru Nanak Dev Ji. At the elegant Punjab Natshala, a packed hall of young and old listened to some scintillating speeches. There were academics, artists, activists, students, and people from all over Punjab. Some had come all the way from Maharashtra, Andhra, Telangana, Delhi, Haryana, and Tamil Nadu. They had travelled the distance to join their Punjabi comrades in this mission for Aman Dosti.

Everyone recalled that the seed of people-to-people contact had been placed in the fertile soil of Punjab by Kuldip Nayar in 1996. He was an eyewitness to Partition and wanted to pass on its lesson to future generations. A few young men joined him including Ramesh Yadav and Satnam Manak. On the Pakistani side, the flag bearer was Imtiaz Ahmed who founded SAFMA (South Asia Free Media Association) around the same time twenty-three years ago. This period witnessed the forging of deep bonds across the border. There were frequent journeys back and forth. For Asma Jahangir and Madeeha Gauhar, Amritsar had become a second home. Pak India Theatre flourished on both sides with the partnership of Ajoka in Pakistan and Kewal Dhaliwal in India. Even during the darkest of times, these two women kept the link alive.

Satnam Manak and Ramesh Yadav, Kuldip Nayar's peace shagirds, who have held the candles with a steady hand despite many adverse winds, steered the morning. Speakers like Kumar Ketkar, then Member Parliament; Siddarth Varadarajan, Editor, The Wire; Jatin Desai, crusader for fish workers on both sides of the border and others spoke on 'Indo Pak Relations and Guru Nanak Dev Ji's 'Philosophy of Coexistence'. Professor Gogwani referred to Guru Nanak as Hindu ka Guru or Muslim ka Pir. Kashmir came up during every intervention. Through this platform, Satnam Manak appealed to the nation to keep democracy alive, adding that Punjab, the land of sacrifice, will fight the good fight. Kamla Bhasin spoke from the gender perspective saying that in the walls that divide hearts and separate people, women are 'deewar mein daraar' (a crack in the wall).

There were seven organisations whose names were inscribed on the banner. From this platform, speaker after speaker spoke from the heart and the audience listened in rapt attention for four hours without a break. When Satnam Manak read the resolution, it was the audience who added a line condemning commodification of Kashmiri women by top leaders of the ruling party.

The evening melted into Sufi music, mostly Punjabi, which began with Nusrat Fateh Ali Khan's Allah Hu and ended with 'Tu uthh ke jalade mombatiyan' both sung by Sunny Saleem and his brothers. Kuldip's spirit hovered over the mehfil. Many eyes were moist. Then, a beautiful young boy made his debut singing Punjabi nazms about Jallianwala Bagh; 100 years of unmitigated grief was reflected in his singing. Who is he? I asked. 'Yakoob Gill, a boy from our Pind,' I was told. I suddenly thought he was the namesake of Hazrat Yaqub, one of the prophets mentioned in the Quran, this boy was my living symbol of Ganga-Jamni tehzeeb.

Om Thanvi, editor of the newspaper with the largest circulation, Jansatta of the Indian Express Group, spoke of the symbiotic relation between Urdu and Hindi and the present effort to give them a religious identity. Kewal Dhaliwal, a theatrical stalwart, spoke about Indo-Pak theatre as a binding force. Dr Charanjit from Jalandhar spoke about the geo politics of the region.

'I am from an RSS family,' said a man from the audience during the question hour. PM Vajpayee, after his historic bus journey, had said about Pakistan, 'You must win their hearts.' So I went there, but when I returned this is what I felt:

Unhon ne kaha tha dil Jeet ke aana
Hum lut gaye wahan!
Dil haar ke aa gaye

They said 'win hearts when you go'
But I returned having lost
My heart to them!

Students from Khalsa College, DAV College, Doaba Arya College, Millennium School, and Springdales School listened to each word in pin-drop silence. Standing at a distance from zero line, a hundred people held up candles to peace and to the comrades across the gates and beyond, who were trapped in the imperatives of the state machinery. I was standing on my side on the land of five rivers. All the people around me were of my very own pind, my watan, Panipat, in the heart of the undivided Punjab!

Buses stood ready for the 25-minute journey to the border; its creation in 1947 took the lives of one lakh Hindus and Muslims. The monument erected to this by Folklore Research Academy located right in front of the 'no man's land' bears testimony to that.

As the candles were raised in the hope that love will be victorious, a melodious voice rose, singing the song of the South Asian icon Nusrat Fateh Ali Khan.

Aaja tainu ankhiyan udiktiyan

Away from Delhi, during these two days in this heart of Punjab, we all felt that peace was possible. In Delhi's vitiated atmosphere, we are often blinded by strident television discussions and deafened by the rhetoric of leaders. The real India remains hidden from our eyes because we never bother to leave our comfort zone. Here in Punjab each one of us felt a surge of hope. It was the youth who demanded that the colossal waste of resources in the name of enmity between two closest neighbours be turned towards human development on both sides of the border. Children on both sides are still dying of starvation. The small flames that were lit rekindled the hope that leaders of India and Pakistan would, for once, listen to the voice of their own people.

The bus, was called Aghaz-e-Dosti and Ravi Nitesh and Devika Mittal, creators of Aghaz-e-Dosti, led the youth component. I was present when this group launched a calendar in 2017. The idea was born in the minds of youth in India and Pakistan and began in 2012. To build peace between these two beleaguered countries. So they approached schoolchildren on both sides who were asked to paint their idea of friendship. They discovered teachers who encouraged the kids to express this idea in their art. Schools from Karachi, Lahore, Swat, Toba Tek Singh, Gwadar, and Khyber Pakhtukhwa took part from the Pakistan side. In India, the schools were from Dehradun, Delhi, Cuttack, Mumbai, Kolkata, Surat, Vadodra, Bulandshehr, and Lucknow.

When children talk peace, it is a head wind, which propels the Ship of Hope. That was my feeling when I entered the packed hall where the calendar would be launched. A quarter-century of struggle for peace in South Asia had exhausted many of us, but what I saw there renewed my flagging spirits. It was joie de vivre bubbling at the brim.

The calendar has twelve paintings. Each painting tells a story, a few young artists spoke about why they painted what they painted. For example, there was Tanvi, who painted the Indo-Pak border. She knew that the border is famous for its hate-spewing drill every evening, watched by hundreds of Pakistanis and Indians on either side, jeering and cheering. So she painted little girls and boys with naughty smiles, who were armed with knives and scissors with which they were cutting the barbed wire. The words inscribed on their mutual sky were: 'Breaking the knots/Our young tots'. All twelve paintings were outstanding works of art. The response to their call for paintings was so overwhelming that this year they started a runners up category. One painting in this category struck me. The artist was Johar from Gwadar in Balochistan, it showed Mohammad Ali Jinnah and Mahatma Gandhi on either side with the two flags and two clasped hands in the centre.

Scores of organisations have been working for three decades on both sides to bring sanity to Indo-Pak relations. I have been associated with PIPFPD since 1994 when it was formed. The best public minds on both sides were part of this initiative including Nirmal Mukerjee; former Cabinet Secretary, Amit Mitra; former Finance Minister of West Bengal from India; Justice Dorab Patel, former Chief Justice of Pakistan; and Mubashir Hasan former Finance Minister, to name a few. In 1998, at a Kolkata Joint Convention, when 100 Pakistanis were granted visas, thousands of local women and men joined them in a walk for peace in the city streets. Almost nineteen years, later the visa regime is so harsh that four years in a row, the Joint Convention had to be cancelled on account of visa refusal from both sides. Instead of opening up, the knot or shall I say, the noose, has tightened. Regardless, between the night of August 14 and 15, we continue to light candles at the border.

The overwhelming desire for peace between the common people of the two countries can succeed only if the new generation of Indians and Pakistanis view each other as comrades, despite political rhetoric and fraudulent appeals to patriotism and nationalism, if they remember the highs and lows of our three-decade struggle for Hind-Pak Dosti. Civil society on both sides of the border will have to continue to assert their right to mingle with their fellows and, yes, their loved ones on the other side.

As Helen Keller, who I sat with when she visited my house, said: 'Strike against war, for without you, no battles can be fought! Strike against manufacturing shrapnel and gas bombs and all other tools of murder! Strike against "preparedness" that means death and misery to millions of human beings! Be not dumb, obedient slaves in an army of destruction! Be heroes in an army of construction!'

15

Inteha: Conclusion

I once asked Khushwant, 'Have you ever thought of an obituary?'

'Yes' came the answer. I quickly wrote while he spoke.

> Here lies one who spared neither man nor God;
> Waste not your tears on him; he was a sod;
> Writing nasty things he regarded as great fun;
> Thank the Lord he is dead, that son of a gun.

Khushwant could make fun of himself; that was one reason so many loved him. And me? I take myself far too seriously, probably secretly referred to as a prig and a prude! So what will my obit be? I will leave it to others.

The spectrum of my life, which I have lived myself and 'lived' through my ancestors, begins in 1911 when my paternal grandfather K.G. Saqlain embarked on his travels to Iran, Iraq, Turkey, Syria, Egypt, and Medina. His travelogue was published in 1912 in Urdu; today, the only copy is in the archives of Khuda Baksh Library in Patna. A hundred and ten years later, in 2022, it was translated in Farsi by Laila Abdi Khojeste, a scholar from Tehran. Recently, while arranging my father's archives, I came across a yellow parchment, which was an old official report of his official visit to Iran. At the end of the report (perhaps an afterthought), he appended a personal experience which was linked to his father's visit to Tehran fifty years ago. He, too, like me, was archiving his father's papers when he came across a reference to the visit. His father had written that his reformist spirit led him to contact a few Iranian youth who were struggling to gain freedom from British and Russian domination and the autocratic rule of the Cachar kings. Lo and behold! K.G. Saqlain, a foreigner, dared to criticise the existing regime in a series of powerful speeches made from the rostrum of Masjid-e-Shah. At the time, free speech was a huge risk that few dared to take. As a consequence, he was compelled to leave Tehran. He left behind two friends he had made during his stay—Agha Mutarjim Nizam and Agha Taqi Zade who had responded with great courage to his message delivered from Masjid-e-Shah.

Fifty years later my father writes that, in deference to his father, he visited Agha Mutarjim's house, where he met his son. He wrote, 'As soon as his son learnt that I was the son of Khwaja Ghulamus Saqlain, he called out to his brothers and sisters and their children. This meeting with an utter stranger was a thrilling experience for all of us. Out of gratitude for what he had done almost fifty years ago, my father had become a legend in the family, and he was held in such affection and reverence by three generations as falls to the lot of very few. They told me moving stories of what his leadership meant to the movement at that time. And in what affection and esteem, his memory was held by those who had seen him. They treated me as a long-lost brother and showered all possible kindness on me. I value the experience not merely because of its familial significance but also because it shows how sincere work pays in wonderful ways and how good men can cherish its memory across the divide of race, geography and time. The Quran says that he who will strive for the values of the spirit and put his best efforts into it is a man of faith. Verily will the labour of such person bear fruit before Allah.'

Today, as I conclude the story of my life, I think of Iran as I mourn for the 22-year-old Kurd girl Mehsa Amini, who was killed by Iran's moral police. The spirits of my ancestors, Altaf Husain Hali, Saqlain, Saiyidain, and Saliha mourn with me. I, who am the child of Ganga-Jamni Tehzeeb today, find its debris scattered everywhere I go. Devi Prasad Mishra, Hindi poet born in 1958 in Pratapgarh, UP, wrote his classic piece 'Woh Musalmaan the' (They were Muslims). The lines unravel our story and I quote a few of them here:

Woh Faras se aaaye
Turan se aaye
Samarkand Farzana Sistan se aye
Woh bahut dur se aye
Phir bhi Prithvi ke kuchh hisson se aye
Woh aye tthe kyonki woh aa sakte tthe
Woh Musalman the
Ya Khuda unki shaklen
Admiyon se milti thein hu ba hu
Woh na hote to Lucknow na hota adha Allahabad na hota
Mehrabein na hotiein gumbad na hota adab na hota
Mir Makhdum Momin na hote Shabana na hoti
Woh na hote upmahadweep ke sangeet ko sunane wala Khusro na hota
Woh na hote to purey des ke ghussey se bechain hone wala Kabir na hota
Woh na hote to Bhartiye upmahadweep ke dukh ko kahne wala Ghalib na hota
Woh Musalman the lekin Damishq unka shahr nahi ttha
Woh Musalman tthe magar Arab ka petrol unka nahi ttha
Woh Dajle ka nahi Yamuna ka pani peete tthe

They came from Persia
They came from Turan
They came from Samarkand, Farhana, Sistan
They came from afar but still came from this very earth.
O Khuda!
Their features were exactly the same as other humans
If they hadn't come,

There would be no Lucknow nor half of Allahabad
No arches, no domes, no adaab
No Mir, no Makhdum, no Momin, no Shabana
If they hadn't come there would be no Khusro
To play music of our subcontinent
No Kabir to ventilate the anger of our subcontinent
No Ghalib to express the angst of our subcontinent
They were Musalmans, but Damascus was not theirs
Arabs petrol was not theirs
They did not drink the water of Dajla
They drank from the Yamuna River.

There was a time when India was known for its wealth, for its gold, silver and gems. We were known equally for our culture and intellectual wealth. Today, times have changed. Cauldrons of animosity, distrust, and hatred have drowned the celebration of diversity. Our once humane society is breaking down, fissured across so many lines. Our region, our South Asia, is burning, our bonds of community are dissipating, and people-to-people relations are under strain. We are witnessing increasing intolerance, dwindling respect and suspicion for other communities. Our children today are growing up as spectators of a divided society where terrorism has been given the garb of religion. Often, to secure ourselves, we blame the other, the innocent. Many people are framed for believing in a certain religion, for their name and identity. If we don't stop this spiral of hate, we will be known as a nation that kills in the name of religion, caste and gender, where human life is trite and dispensable.

Strength comes from diversity; the danger of painting everyone in the same colour looms overhead. We are mesmerised by the ideas of diversity that come to us from other agencies. But in our own mitti, our own land, we have the ingredients of diversity, which has made this country what it is. The richness of the fabric of diversity we read about is in our literature. Although we are sometimes mindful of diversity, yet we have heinous incidents of communalism. I think it is because in a country of 1.4, billion how many know that it is our individual responsibility to safeguard this sacred diversity? It is what Prophet Mohammed, and prophets of all religions, all philosophers have enjoined: to open the windows of our mind, not to allow obscurantist ideas to fog our windows, to open, to accept the winds of change.

One of the great influences in my life has been my father, who taught me humanism, to love my neighbours, whether they are just across the street or across the world. I learned about the human family and the global village when I was very young. Even before the Canadian communications theorist Marshall McLuhan talked about the global village, it was talked about in my house. I want to quote three lines from my father's letter. The letter is dated December 19, 1969, and I read it three years later, on the very he passed away. People say, 'Yeh to har jagah hota hai,' (this happens everywhere) but my father wrote: 'And it is no consolation for me to know that such things (war, communal riots and so on) have been happening in other countries, sometimes even more blatantly. This makes the tragedy even deeper, for in such matters, "my country" and "your country" has no meaning for me whatsoever. Whatsoever degrades a man or woman, whatsoever degrades one human being, degrades a whole people, and whatsoever degrades one country degrades the whole world.'

This resonates with my own philosophy that borders and boundaries melt away. Humanism holds us all together. I started off by sharing with you, my reader, that most of my family, 90 per cent of my family, just disappeared—I have lost track of most of them. Borders and boundaries determine our lives, but when borders and boundaries melt away, then whatever happens anywhere affects me as it affects many of my beloved friends. Palestine, Gaza, Manipur, Churahandpur, Kashmir, and Kupwara. If people are butchered and killed anywhere in the world, it kills me. What degrades any section of humanity anywhere in the world equally degrades me.

As I draw close to life's end, I know I will die believing and practising a religion that has given me wealth unbounded—a religion that encompasses all faiths as equally true, equally universal. Hinduism, Christianity, Sikhism, and Judaism are one at their core, says the Quran. Amir Khusro in the thirteenth century and Mir Taqi Mir in the nineteenth century, expressed the same thought.

Khusro:

Ashiq ham az Islam Kharab ast hama az kufr
Parwana chiragh-e-haram-o-dair na danad

The intoxicated lover knows no distinction between Islam and kufr
A moth does not choose between the burning candle whether it is in the mosque or the temple.

Mir:

Uske farogh-e-husn se chhalke hai sab mein noor
Sham-e-Haram ya ho diya Somnath ka

It is the extension of His beauty that illuminates all.
Whether the candle of Kaaba or the lamp of Somnath

The point is to keep going. As the saying goes, it is the journey that counts not what lies at the end. Writers in all languages have expressed this thought. For the last word in this book of my life, I chose a few lines from the Greek poet, Constantin P. Cavafy, born in Alexandria in 1863. The poem 'Ithaka' reminds me that the journey which is more important than the destination.

As you set out for Ithaka
Hope your road is a long one,
Full of adventure and discovery…
And may you visit many Egyptian cities
To learn and go on learning from their scholars

Notes

1. *Sita's Kitchen: A Testimony of Faith and Inquiry* by Ramchandra Gandhi, published by State University of New York Press, 1992.
2. The events of September 11, 2001, are commonly known as 9/11. On the morning of September 11, 19 Islamic suicide terrorists belonging to the al-Qaeda, hijacked four commercial airliners and crashed two into the twin towers of the World Trade Center in New York City, one into the Pentagon headquarters in Arlington, Virgina, while the fourth crashed in Pennsylvania. An estimated 2,977 people were killed on 9/11.
3. The clash between the Jat and Muslim communities in Muzaffarnagar district in UP in August 2013 are regarded as one of the worst incidences of violence in the state in the last 20 years. The original cause of the rioting is disputed according to bipartisan claims largely concerning the affected communities. According to one version, the cause was a minor traffic accident involving some youths which then spiralled out of control when it eventually took on religious overtones. In the second version, a girl from the Hindu Jat community was allegedly harassed in an eve-teasing incident by one Muslim youth in Kawal village. In retaliation, Jat relatives of the girl in question, Sachin Singh and Gaurav Singh, killed the youth named Shahnawaz Qureshi. The two brothers were lynched by a Muslim mob when they tried to escape. In all, 93 people were injured and more than 50,000 displaced.
4. *Need for a New Religion in India and Other Essays* by Khushwant Singh, published by UBS Publishers and Distributors, 1991.
5. The Kandhamal incident refers to widespread violence against Christians, allegedly incited by the Bajrang Dal, Rashtriya

Swayamsevak Sangh and the VHP, in August 2008 after the murder of the Hindu monk Lakshmanananda Saraswati. According to government reports the violence resulted in the deaths of at least 39 Christians while 395 churches and 3906 Christian houses were completely destroyed. Many Christian families were burnt alive. Thousands of Christians were forced to convert to Hinduism under threat of violence.

6. Graham Stuart Staines (18 January 1941 – 23 January 1999) was an Australian missionary who along with his two sons, Philip (aged 10) and Timothy (aged 6), was burnt to death in Mayurbhanj in Odisha by members of the Hindu nationalist group, Bajrang Dal. In 2003, Bajrang Dal activist Dara Singh was convicted of leading the murderers and was sentenced to life imprisonment.
   Right wing Hindu groups alleged that Staines had tricked, lured or forcibly converted tribals to Christianity. The Wadhwa Commission claims that although some tribals had been baptised at the camps, there was no evidence of forced conversions. Staines's widow Gladys has also denied forced conversions ever happened. She continued to live and work in India until 2004. In 2005, she was awarded the Padma Shri in recognition of her work in Odisha. In 2016, she received the Mother Teresa Memorial International Award for Social Justice.
7. The CAA protests occurred after the Citizenship Amendment Act was enacted by the Government of India on 12 December 2019. The CAA amends the Indian citizenship act to provide accelerated pathway to citizenship for illegal migrants who are Hindu, Sikh, Jain, Parsi, Buddhist, and Christian, from Afghanistan, Bangladesh, and Pakistan, who entered India before 2014 following religious persecution. The bill does not mention Muslims and other communities who fled from the same or other countries. The CAA sparked widespread national and overseas protests against the act, and its associated proposal of the National Register of Citizens (NRC), specifically against the exclusion of Muslims.
8. *The First Muslim: The Story of Muhammad* by Lesley Hazelton, published by Riverhead Books, US, 2014.

9. *Invocation and Prayers of Khwaja Abdullah Ansari*, translated by Sardar Sir Jogendra Singh and Arthur John Arberry, published by Speaking Tiger, 2022.
10. Hājar, known as Hagar in the Hebrew Bible, was the wife of the patriarch and Islamic Prophet Ibrahim, and the mother of Isma'il (Ishmael). She is a revered woman in the Islamic faith. According to Muslim belief, she was the daughter of the king of Egypt who gifted her to Ibrahim's wife Sarah. Although not mentioned by name in the Qur'an, she is referenced and alluded to via the story of her husband.
11. On August 5, 2019, the Government of India abrogated Article 370 of the Constitution, taking away the special status accorded to Jammu and Kashmir at the time of Partition. This special status granted autonomy to the state and allowed it to formulate certain laws in respect of its permanent residents. The constitution of Jammu and Kashmir was abrogated, and a single Constitution now applies to all states which also allows non-Kashmiris to buy and own property in Kashmir.
12. *A History of the Sikhs, Vol. 1 (1469-1839)* by Khushwant Singh, first published by Oxford University Press, 1963.
13. The Sarvodaya movement was started by Mahatma Gandhi. Based on the principles of equality and liberty, the main objective of this movement was to establish a new India based on non-violence and love.
14. *The Golden Treasury of English Songs and Lyrics* is a popular anthology of English poetry, originally selected for publication by Francis Turner Palgrave in 1861. It was later revised with inputs from Tennyson. The book continues to be published in regular new editions, still under Palgrave's name, and includes his selections and notes, but usually includes a supplement of more recent poems.
15. Padinjarethalakal Cherian Alexander was an Indian Administrative Service officer of the 1948 batch who served as the Governor of Tamil Nadu from 1988 to 1990 and as the Governor of Maharashtra from 1993 to 2002. He was considered as a candidate for the post of the President of India in 2002. He passed away in August 2011.

16. An IAS officer, Gopi Arora grew to be one of the most influential, and controversial, bureaucrats during the Rajiv Gandhi premiership, Before being handpicked for the PMO, he was Secretary, Information and Broadcasting. He passed away in 2024.
17. H.Y. Sharada Prasad was an Indian civil servant, journalist, and writer, best known as the media adviser to Indira Gandhi. He also served as the media adviser to Rajiv Gandhi, during Rajiv's tenure as Prime Minister.
18. Wajahat Habibullah is the former chairperson of the National Commission for Minorities. Prior to this, he held the position of the first Chief Information Commissioner of India. He was an officer of the Indian Administrative Service from 1968 until his retirement in August 2005.
19. Mani Shankar Aiyar is a politician and former career civil servant diplomat. He is a member of the Congress Party. He was a nominated Member of Parliament from Rajya Sabha from 2010 to 2016.
20. First published as *The Rubaiyat of Sarmad*, published by ICCR, 1991. Reissued as *His Miracle, Not His Sin: The Rubaiyat Of Sarmad*, translated by Syeda Saiyidain Hameed and Reyaz Ahmad, Speaking Tiger Books, 2024.
21. Jahiliyyah is a polemical Islamic and Arabic term that refers to the period of time and state of affairs in pre-Islamic Arabia before the advent of Islam in 609 CE. It is usually referred to as the Age of Ignorance.
22. *Beautiful Country: Stories From Another India* by Syeda Saiyidain Hameed and Gunjan Veda, published by HarperCollins India, 2012.
23. *The History of the Sikhs, Vol. 1 - 1469-1839*, and *The History of the Sikhs, Vol. II - 1839-2004,* published by Oxford University Press (OUP), 2004.

Index

Abbas, Khwaja Ahmad, 3–4, 11–12, 89, 116, 199
- communalism and, 11–12
- films of, 12
- on Jinnah, 4
- "Sardarji" story by, 116, 199

Abbas Tyabji, 11
Abdelrazik, Abousufian, 61
Abdul Qaiyum Ansari, 28
Abu Ayyub Ansari, 26–27, 29
- descendant of, 27
- as host to the Prophet, 26
- munajaat of, 27

Abu Hanifa, 23
Abu Nasr Aah, 96, 98, 100
Achar, 126
Acharya, Kamla, 42
Acid attacks, 112
Activism, 114, 117, 122, 129
- MWF and, 114

Advani, L.K., 13, 16, 17, 158
- at Babri Masjid demolition, 13
- on Rath Yatra, 16

Afendi, Najam, 189
Afghanistan, 28
Africa, 30, 148
Afrazul Islam, 18
Agha Khan, 4, 11
Ahmed, Nuruddin, 96–100
Ahmed Saeed Malihabadi, 98
Ahl-e-Bait, 189, 192
Ahluwalia, Montek Singh, 51, 119–21
- on Gadchiroli Report, 119
- as Planning Commission Deputy Chairman, 119–20
- at St Stephen's College, 119–20

Ahimsa, 40
Aiyer, Mani Shankar, 87
Akbar Road, 86
Akhtar Khan, 46–47
Akhter, Javed, 139
Albanese, Anthony, 214
Alexander, P.C., 86
Alexandra School, 34
Aligarh Muslim University, 3, 4
- Jinnah's portrait controversy at, 4–5
- right-wing violence at, 5

Ali Asghar, 190–91
Ali Imam, 4
Ali, Salmana, 65
Ali, Ursila, 65, 175
Allama Iqbal. *See* Iqbal, Allama
Altaf Husain Hali. *See* Hali, Altaf Husain
Al-Tabari, 11
Alwar, 110
Amarnath pilgrimage, 204
Amar Singh, 182
Ambagouda, 70
Ambedkar Bus Terminal, 228
America. *See* United States
American Airlines, 81
Ammi. *See* Begum, Aziz Jahan
Amroha, 154, 179
Anarchy, 25
Andaman and Nicobar Islands, 123, 124–25, 20
- tsunami in, 124–25

Anglo-Oriental College, 4
Anis, Mir, 174, 189
Anantnag, 110, 201, 207
Ansari, Hamid, 5, 13
Ansari, Iqbal, 13
Ansari, Qutubuddin, 15
Antioch College, 49
Anushilan, 101
Anwar Anwar, Abbas, 9
Arora, Gopi, 86
Asians, 75, 76, 80
- South, 72, 73, 81, 83, 143, 144, 148, 156, 160, 218, 223
- West, 30

ASHA, 134
Ashraaf, 28
Ashura, 190, 192

Assam, 23, 119, 127, 128, 161, 162, 199
tea gardens of, 130
Atish e Chinar (Abdullah), 149
Atma Manthan, 21
Aurat Foundation, 48
Awadhi, 191, 192
Ayodhya, 14, 17
judgment (2019), 14
Azad, Maulana Abul Kalam, 11, 12, 13, 32, 37, 38, 86, 90–92, 94, 96, 100–102, 131, 150–51, 174, 186
biography of, 90, 101, 151
centenary volumes on, 90
and education, 32
essay on Sarmad by, 94
on Indian Muslims, 11
at Jamia Millia Islamia, 12, 38
library of, 91
on Sarmad, 94, 95
and Sufism, 93
Tarjuman-ul-Quran, 90, 93, 151, 174
on women, 11
Azamgarh, 21
Azmi, Kaifi, 21
Azmi, Shabana, 183

Bachchan Sahib. *See* Khan, Murtuza Ali
Bachchan, Amitabh, 44
Badshah Khan, 11, 38
Bagjri, 105
Baghdad, 79
Bajrang Dal, 19, 158
at Kandhamal, 19
and Staines, 19
Bajrangi mob, 15
Bakerwal, 162
Balban, Sultan Ghiyasuddin, 28
Balochistan, 75, 235
Bangalore, 110, 137, 198, 219
Bangladesh Rifles (BDR), 128
Bang, Abhay and Rani, 119
Banihal, 200
Bano, Ambreen, 162
Bano, Afsana, 162
Bano, Bilkis, 164–65
case of, 165
Bano, Hazrat Shehr, 189
Baqal, Rafiq Ahmed, 199
Baramulla, 202
Barooah, D.K., 88
Barpeta, 161
Barve, Sushobha, 204
Bastis, 10, 20, 21
Batla House encounter, 21, 20, 21, 86
BDR (Bangladesh Rifles), 128
Beck, Dr, 58
Bedar, Abid Raza, 40
Beerwah, 202
Begum, Aziz Jahan, 11, 32, 33, 41, 46–47, 90, 166, 168–71
background of, 166, 168–69
death of, 47, 170
and daughter's marriage, 41
on daughter's schooling, 34
and Moharrum, 188
personality of, 169–70
Begum, Fatima, 96
Begum, Hanifa, 96
Begum, Qaisar Zamani, 168, 169
Begum, Saliha Abid Husain. *See* Husain, Saliha Abid
Begum, Sultan Jahan, 168
Begum, Zuleikha, 96, 98, 101
Bheja, 71
Bhil, 17
Bhoodan (Land Gift) Movement, 197
Bhubaneshwar, 19, 86
Bhulle Shah, 144, 155
Bhutto, Zulfikar Ali, 218
Bihar, 106, 191
Bijli-pani, 21
Bilaspur, 17
Billimoria, Niloufer, 153
Bin Aqeel, Muslim, 190
Bindi, 179, 221
Birindra, 40
Bismillah Khan, 126–27
Black, Algernon D., 49
Blacks, 72, 199
African Americans, 49, 82
"Blossoms in the Dust" (Nair), 117
Blue, 28
Boaten, Ernest, 49–50
Bobby, 171
Bokhara, 61, 199
Bombay, 9, 32–33
Alexandra School, 34
Gamadhiya School, 34
J.B. Petit School, 34
Bombay State, 33
Bondage, 163
Bongaigaon, 164
Border Security Force (BSF), 128, 207
Borewells, 85
Brahmin, 110
Breach delivery, 59

Bright Street, 96, 100
British, 11, 32, 38, 40, 153, 167, 201
  in India, 4, 32
Bronx, 49, 50
Bruyere Street, 61
BSF (Border Security Force), 128, 207
Buddha Jayanti Park, 154
Budgam, 202
Buenos Aires, 35
Bulandshahar, 23
Bulhe Shah, 144, 155
Burney, S.M.H., 90
Burqa, 33, 112, 174
Buzurgs, 6, 34, 56, 173
By-election, 5
Byron, 42

Cachar kings, 238
Caesarean section, 58
Calicut, 110
Calcutta, 96, 101, 110, 137, 214
  Circular Road, 97
Calendulas, 154
Caliph, 79
Caliphates, 168
Canada, 13, 46–52, 55, 57, 58–62, 65–68, 69, 72–78, 81, 139, 140, 141, 154, 163, 168, 177, 178, 211, 212, 229
  author's children born in, 58
  author's homes in, 68
  author's life in, 60, 65–68, 72–78
  author's move to, 55, 57, 65
  author's returns to, 67, 68, 81
  author's visits to, 69, 79, 229
  communalism in, 76, 77, 78
  Dominion Day, 60
  East West Centre, 48
  Encampment for Citizenship, 48–50
  General Hospital, 50, 61
  Greyhound bus journeys in, 48, 51
  Harry Ainlay High School incident, 75–76
  and India–Pakistan relations, 55, 67, 68, 69
  and Islam, 174
  Laurentian Mountains, 58
  and Mubashir Hasan, 136
  racism in, 75, 76
  and Ramadan, 174, 185
  Social Credit Party (SOCRED), 74
  University of Alberta, 49, 51, 65, 75, 178
  University of Hawaii, 48, 51
  visa for, 55
Canadian Security Intelligence Service (CSIS), 61
Canning Lane, 120, 121
Canyon City, Colorado, 50
Capitalism, 142
CDR (Centre for Dialogue and Reconciliation), 115
CEDAW (Convention on the Elimination of All Forms of Discrimination Against Women), 158
Censorship, 147
Centre for Advanced Studies, 48
Centre for Dialogue and Reconciliation (CDR), 115
Chador, 30
Chai, 231
Chakbast, Brij Narayan, 215
Chakmas, 128
Chakravarty, Nikhil, 225, 228
Chakla, 14
Chamans, 10
Chapman, Marsha, 49–50
Charity, 184, 198
Charminar, 56
Charles Campbell Hospital, 62
Chattari, Rahat, 66
Cheema, 29
Chennai, 110
Chettur, June, 42
Chhatari, Rahat, 66
Chhatarpur, 161, 162
Chidambaram, P.C., 87
Chikmanglur, 20
Child-carers, 118
Children, 1, 3, 6, 11, 19, 30, 32, 35, 36, 37, 38, 43, 58, 60, 62–64, 66, 67, 68, 70–71, 73, 85, 103, 105, 106, 116, 118, 119, 123, 124, 125, 127, 129, 130, 131, 134, 136, 139, 146, 162, 164, 171, 173, 174, 187, 188, 190, 192, 194, 197, 199, 202, 211, 212, 213, 220, 221, 234, 235
  abuse of, 105, 132
  and communalism, 35
  education of, 11, 32, 38, 130
  of freedom fighters, 1
  future generations of, 1, 3, 116
  and gender, 32
  and Gujarat massacre, 103
  health of, 19, 118, 119
  and India-Pakistan relations, 1, 34, 67

and Kashmir, 194, 197, 199, 202, 212, 213, 234
and Malegaon, 130
malnutrition of, 19, 118
missing, 124, 213
and Moharrum, 188
of sex workers, 126
and theatre, 62
and WIPSA, 196
and work, 130
Child sex ratio, 195
China, 135
University of, 49
Chinese Room, 180
Chittagong, 127
Chittisinghpura massacre, 201
Chughtai, Ismat, 90
Chrungo, Ashwini Kumar, 209
Citizenship Amendment Act (CAA), 24, 145
protests against, 24, 145
City Council elections, 65, 72–74
in Edmonton, 65, 72–74
Civil society, 87, 111, 115, 122, 219, 236
in India-Pakistan relations, 219, 236
and MWF, 111
and Planning Commission, 122
Classes, 20, 78, 181
deprived, 111
middle, 17, 20, 38, 74, 77, 111, 169, 199
serving, 78
working, 14
Clerics, 111
Clovis, Dr. *See* Maksoud, Dr Clovis
CM. *See* Chief Minister
Cochin, 110
Coffee, 44, 45
Coleridge, 42
Colleges
Aligarh Muslim University, 3, 4
Anglo-Oriental College, 4
Antioch College, 49
DAV College, 234
Doaba Arya College, 234
Engineering College (Patiala), 43
Goddard College, 49
Jamia Millia Islamia, 12, 10, 11, 12, 20, 21, 38, 86, 89, 90, 91, 112, 144, 171, 173, 174, 177
Khalsa College, 234
Lady Shri Ram College (LSR), 55, 177
Miranda House, 41–42, 43, 45, 119–20
Modern School, 9, 34, 36, 37, 38, 86, 121, 149, 150
Mount Saint Vincent University, 51
North Patterson School of Carleton University, 60
St Stephen's College, 41, 119, 120
Colombo, 138
Colonialism, 37–38, 40, 168, 181, 217, 238
British, 4, 11, 32, 38, 40, 153, 167, 201
Colour, 30, 42, 75, 76, 78, 83, 191, 236, 240
consciousness, 49
prejudice, 49, 148
Communalism, 9–11, 13, 14, 24, 34, 38, 56, 76, 77, 78, 86, 100, 101, 114, 130, 132, 144, 150, 160, 164, 173, 178, 199, 203, 209, 240, 241
and Abbas, 11–12
author's childhood experience of, 34–36, 38
author's experiences of in Canada, 76, 77, 78
and Babri Masjid demolition, 13
and Batla House encounter, 21
and children, 35
and Gujarat riots, 14–16
and identity, 9–11, 24
and India-Pakistan relations, 10, 115, 217–218
in Kashmir, 200
and Malegaon, 130
and MWF, 114
in Panipat, 33
and Planning Commission, 122
post-partition, 9
and right-wing regime, 11, 17, 24, 101, 112
and violence, 11, 17, 24, 101, 112
Community, 11, 17, 21, 47, 60, 111, 112, 148, 149, 160, 162, 164, 173, 191, 194, 200, 201, 215, 221, 222, 233, 235
development, 60
health, 119, 126
Hindu, 15
Islamic, 4
and Islam, 11, 112, 173
Jewish, 218
medicine, 60

Muslim, 3, 5, 11, 15, 21, 112, 160, 164, 219, 221, 233
Sikh, 15, 116
and social reform, 173
work, 163
Congress, 15
colleagues, 16
Congress Member of Parliament, 15
Conscience, 24
Constantinople, 27
Constitution, Indian, 208
Article 35A, 208, 210
Article 370, 207–208, 210, 214
Four Corners of the, 200
Convent of Jesus and Mary, 34
Copyrights, 122
Corporal punishment, 56
Corporates, 122, 133, 134
Cotton, 42, 45, 64, 180, 189
hand-spun, 180
Council of State, 11
Country, 8, 17, 109, 147, 148, 149, 150, 160, 164, 180, 195, 206, 208, 210, 212, 219, 221, 227, 229, 234, 235, 238, 240
of author's birth, 8, 13, 17, 147, 149
developed, 13
and homeland, 8, 13, 17, 47, 147, 149
post-colonial, 37–38, 40
Western, 49
Courtesans, 150
CRPF, 200
CSIS (Canadian Security Intelligence Service), 61
Culture, 33, 40, 147, 209, 214, 220, 239, 240
Indian, 33, 214
Muslim, 33
Punjabi, 33
Western, 42

Dadhi-topi, 18
Daghistani, Valeh, 95
Dahr, Surah, 65
Dair, 146
Dal, Dhannu Bagh, 71
Dal, Jalandhari, 26
Dalit Foundation, 161
Dalit Shakti Kendra, 161, 162
Dalits, 17, 114, 181
of Dharmapuri, 17
Dal, Vishva Hindu Parishad, 19
Dandavate, Pramila, 181
Dara Shikoh, 94
Daragam, 200
Daraar, 233
Darshan, 126
Das, Nandita, 183
Davidar, David, 101
DAV College, 234
Dawn, 185, 206, 215, 227, 231
Dayal, Shankar, 92
Deb Burmans, 128
Delhi, 9, 11, 12, 13, 20, 21, 23, 32, 33, 34, 38, 40, 50, 55, 57, 58, 61, 66, 67, 68, 69, 70, 86, 87, 90, 91, 97, 101, 112, 113, 117, 120, 121, 122, 127, 137, 150, 154, 156, 158, 159, 161, 164, 180, 197, 202, 208, 212, 214, 222, 223, 225, 227, 228, 232, 234
10 Janpath Road, 87
Akbar Road, 86
author's life in, 9, 12, 33, 34, 38, 55, 57, 61, 66, 67, 68, 69, 86, 87, 90, 91, 97, 101, 112, 113, 117, 120, 121, 122, 127, 137, 150, 154, 156, 158, 159, 161, 164, 180, 197, 202, 208, 212, 214, 222, 223, 225, 227, 228, 232, 234
Buddha Jayanti Park, 154
communal killings in, 12, 33, 38
India Gate, 127
King Edward Road, 39, 91, 97
Lutyens', 40, 124, 139, 176, 202
Modern School, 9, 34, 36, 37, 38, 86, 121, 149, 150
National Archives, 99
Partition of, 12, 33, 38, 146
Pragati Maidan, 88
resettlement colonies in, 159
Sujan Singh Park, 35, 36, 48, 66, 146
Delhi Gymkhana Club, 180–81
class and caste bias at, 180–81
Delhi Sultanate, 28
Sultan Ghiyasuddin Balban of, 28
Democracy, 217, 229, 233, 234
Indian, 181
Desai, Jatin, 232
Deshpande, Nirmala, 10, 115, 197, 219, 223, 230
at 2000 bus journey, 219
at 2001 peace march, 223
and Kashmir, 197
peace song by, 197, 230
and WIPSA, 115, 197
Devyani Krishna, 12

Dhar, Bhushanlal, 197
Dharma, 110
Dharmapuri, 17
Dharti, 8, 12
Dhawan, Prem, 83
Dickens, Charles, 37
Dignity, 98, 100, 113, 114, 160, 162, 175, 180, 181, 203, 223
  of labor, 12
  of women, 113, 114, 175
Dilip Kumar, 47
Dilkashi, 224
Dirges, 163
  lyrical, 174
Divan-e-Ghalib, 3
Doda, 202
Doaba Arya College, 234
Dolittle, Eliza, 66
Donne, John, 42
Doordarshan, 92, 151, 183
Dowry, 105, 111, 188, 202
  murder, 105
Dreams, 17, 54, 70, 144, 154, 196, 222, 223
  of ancestors, 114
  bad, 50
  and community, 17
  of Hameed, 54
  of Maimun, 70
  and youth, 144, 196, 223
Dryden, 42, 43
Dukhayal, Hunduraj, 197
Dukhtaran-e-Millat (Women's Wing of the Jama'at), 197
Dumka, 106
Dupatta, 35, 42, 120, 130
Dyer, Colonel, 226

Earth, 11, 83, 145, 146, 239
  inheritance of the, 146
East, 30
East West Centre, 48
Eclecticism, 6
Economic development, 209
  and women, 133
Economics, 117
Editors, 199
Education, 11, 12, 32, 33, 34, 37, 38, 56, 60, 89, 90, 97, 116, 130, 131, 146, 167, 169, 170, 172, 173, 193, 194, 198, 202
  Department of, 4, 46
  Director of, 32
  of girls, 130
  and identity, 12, 56
  and Islam, 11, 56, 112, 172, 173
  in Kashmir, 193, 194, 214
  Minister of, 32, 37, 90
  Ministry of, 193
  Secretary of, 91, 131, 170
  and women, 11, 33, 112, 172, 173
Edmonton, 48, 58, 60, 61, 68, 69, 71, 72, 73, 75, 139, 147, 177
  author's home in, 60, 68, 71, 139
  author's life in, 60, 61, 68, 71, 72, 73, 75, 139, 177
  Charles Campbell Hospital, 62
  City Council of, 65, 72–74
  General Hospital, 50, 61
  Harry Ainlay High School, 75–76, 81
  Lansdowne Drive, 68
  Miseracordia Hospital, 67
  University of Alberta, 49, 51, 65, 75, 178
  Urban Reform Group (URGE), 73, 74
Edmonton Journal, 72
Educationists, 12
Egypt, 237, 238, 242
Eid, 21, 39, 91, 186, 209, 210
  Khutbas, 28
  -ul-Fitr, 39, 91
Eisaloff, Mrs., 42
Elders, 6, 34, 37, 56, 69, 116, 148, 173, 174, 176, 181, 220, 224, 229
  advice from, 88
  and communalism, 9
  respect for, 34, 173
Elections, 17, 74, 142
  by-election, 5
  City Council, 65, 72–74
  general, 17, 142
  parliamentary, 75
Eliot, T.S., 34
Elia, Jaun, 179
Emblems, 64, 170, 188
Emissaries of Peace (Safiraan-e-Aman), 229
Empire, British, 40, 153, 167
  Order of the, 152
Empire, Mughal, 94, 96
Encampment for Citizenship, 48–50
  description of, 49
  impact of, 49–50
Encounter, 20, 21, 23, 199
  killings, 199
England, 4, 30, 148, 217, 238
English, 9, 21, 89, 90, 92, 93, 96, 141,

144, 149, 150, 152, 156, 172, 174, 177, 218, 238
newspapers, 10, 21
short stories, 90
Environment, 73, 117, 123, 206, 210, 223
degradation, 125
Epithets, 8, 17, 49, 76, 199, 203
for dark complexion, 49
Ethnicity, 17, 114, 144, 220
Europe, 83
Exile, 140, 144, 179, 236

Facts are Facts: The Untold Story of India's Partition (Khan), 90
Fadaeian, Majid, 28
Faith, 6, 11, 14, 17, 25, 26, 29, 34, 63, 64, 93, 94, 118, 122, 159, 160, 162, 164, 166, 173, 174, 184, 185, 186, 187, 188, 190, 194, 218, 238, 241
and community, 17, 191
Hindu, 6
and identity, 14, 26
Islamic, 6, 26, 64, 173, 190
and marriage, 34
Muslim, 159
and writers, 6
"Faith and Inquiry" (Gandhi), 14
Families, 9, 12, 27, 32, 33, 34, 50, 53, 55, 56, 65, 66, 67, 68, 71, 81, 98, 100, 107, 108, 110, 137, 146, 147, 148, 149, 159, 163, 167, 168, 169, 171, 172, 173, 176, 177, 180, 182, 188, 190, 197, 199, 201, 211, 213, 214, 218, 221, 238
and communalism, 9, 33, 159
displaced, 200
extended, 168, 173
feudal, 56, 168
and identity, 53
and India-Pakistan relations, 34, 55, 67, 68, 146, 159, 221, 224, 229, 230
and Islam, 173, 190
joint, 173
Kashmiri Pandit, 200, 210
Muslim, 9, 66, 116, 146, 159, 210
patriarchal, 56, 65
and Partition, 34, 146
Sikh, 9, 116, 199
of Yawar Ahmed Bhat, 211
Family, 11, 12, 27, 28, 32, 33, 34, 37, 38, 41, 47, 50, 53, 55, 56, 59, 60, 65, 66, 67, 68, 70, 71, 86, 89, 90, 91, 96, 97, 100, 102, 106, 112, 116, 126, 136, 137, 140, 143, 146, 149, 151, 152, 155, 159, 160, 166, 167, 168, 169, 170, 171, 172, 173, 174, 176, 177, 178, 181, 182, 186, 188, 189, 190, 192, 197, 199, 200, 201, 204, 210, 211, 212, 213, 214, 215, 218, 221, 229, 230, 231, 233, 234, 235, 238
and community, 11
ethos, 56
history, 27, 149, 169
honor, 109
and identity, 53
and Islam, 56, 190
patriarchal, 56, 65
and Partition, 146
of Yawar Ahmed Bhat, 211
Fan mail, 36
Farooq, Syeda, 202
Farooq, Maulvi Mohammad, 213, 214, 215
assassination of, 213, 214
family of, 214
Fasaad, 5
Fashion, 41, 42
Fatiha, 59, 64, 99, 126, 200
Fatwa, 94
Fazil, Shaikh Badrul Islam, 28
Fazli, Shaikh Badrul Islam, 28
Faiz, Alys, 139, 140
Faiz, Faiz Ahmed, 2, 11, 115, 139–46, 157
"Hum Dekhenge", 144–146, 145
and India-Pakistan relations, 115
influence of, 143–44
at Jawaharlal Nehru University, 139
"Lab pe aati hai dua ban ke tamanna meri", 12
and Mehdi Hassan, 140
and Pakistan, 144
poetry of, 2, 12, 115, 139, 140, 141–43, 144–46, 157
prison poetry of, 141–43
on speaking out, 2, 11, 115
and Urdu, 144
"Yaas", 142
Zindan Nama, 140, 141, 142, 154, 157
FEG (Feminist Economists Group), 132–33
achievements of, 133
FEG (Feminist Economists Group), 132–33
achievements of, 133
Feminism, 183, 233

Feminist Economists Group (FEG), 132–33
Festivals, 34, 149, 210
Feudal outlook, 34
Feudalism, 78, 176, 178, 204
Fidelity, 186, 187
Films, 12, 14, 44, 78, 177, 183, 199, 210, 216, 220
  Char Dil Char Rahein, 12
  "Dharti ke Lal", 12
  "Do Boond Painni", 12
  Fire, 183
  "Kashmir Files", 210
  Khoon diy Baarav (On a Trail of Vanished Blood), 216
  "My Fair Lady", 66
  "Naya Shivalaya", 8
  "Rahi", 12
  Rajnigandha, 177
  "Saat Hindustani", 44
  "Sheher aur Sapna", 12
  and social reform, 12
  The Naxalites, 12
Finance Minister, 27, 218
Firaaq Gorakhpuri. *See* Sahay, Raghupati
Fire, 15, 16, 17, 51, 183, 185, 189, 191, 210, 211, 215, 225, 234
  all-consuming, 3
  communal, 5
  in the heart, 3
  and Sarmad, 95
"Flames of the Chinar" (Abdullah), 149
Floods, 17
Folklore Research Academy Amritsar, 231
Food, 18, 60, 105, 124, 126, 132, 147, 185, 187, 200, 231, 235, 240
  security, 12
  sharing, 38
  street, 130
Foreign climes, 13
Forelock, 7
Frankfurter, Brigitte, 35–36
Frankfurt, 78
Freedom, 4, 11, 13, 24, 34, 55, 83, 144, 145, 146, 186, 197, 199, 206, 210, 219, 236
  fighter, 86, 127
  fighters, 1, 11, 19, 101, 197
  movement, 4, 101
  of speech, 2, 11, 144
  struggle for, 4, 11, 83, 101, 197, 201, 219, 236
French, 78
Friendship, 50, 91, 115, 120, 137, 151, 156, 160, 163, 178, 197, 199, 203, 219, 222, 224, 225, 227, 228, 231, 232, 234, 235, 238
  and India-Pakistan relations, 115, 137, 219, 222, 224, 227, 231, 232, 234, 235
  in Kashmir, 194, 197
Frost, Robert, 41
Fulcrum, 4, 114, 137
Fulbright student, 54
Future generations, 1, 3, 116

Gabbey, Dr., 32
Gadchiroli, 118, 119, 134
  Report, 119, 134
Gaddi, 167
  Nasheen, 96, 97
Gamadhiya School, 34
Gandhi, Indira, 22, 86, 87, 88, 90, 117, 120, 122, 158
  assassination of, 86
  and communalism, 13
  and education, 12, 90
  and Mohammad Yunus, 88
  at Planning Commission, 117, 120, 122
  portraits of, 22
  and Saiyidain, 12
  and Saliha Abid Husain, 12
Gandhi, Mahatma, 12, 14, 18, 37, 38, 101, 117, 130, 180, 197
  at Aligarh Muslim University, 12
  assassination of, 37
  grandson of, 14
  and Indian Muslims, 11
  influence of, 33
  and nationalism, 18
  portraits of, 22
  and Saliha Abid Husain, 12
Gandhi, Ramchandra, 14
Gandhi Samadhi, 22
Gandhi, Sonia, 117, 158
  at Planning Commission, 117
  and Gujarat massacre, 158
Ganga-Jamni tehzeeb, 12, 75, 160, 233, 239
Ganguly, Enakshi, 213
Gang rape, 105, 107, 164, 181
Garibon, 38
Garrulousness, 154
Gautam, Manjulika, 117
Gautam Navlakha, 146

Gauhar, Madeeha, 222, 232
Gayatri Devi, 13
G20, 213, 214
G7, 214
Geelani, Syed Ali Shah, 200–201
Gems, 240
Gender, 10, 17, 22, 32, 41, 69, 83, 90, 111, 112, 113, 114, 122, 131, 132, 133, 173, 174, 175, 178, 179, 180, 181, 182, 183, 195, 197, 212, 213, 233, 241
 abuse, 105
 and children, 32
 equality, 108
 and Islam, 112, 113, 173, 174, 175
 issues, 110, 111, 114, 195
 justice, 41, 176, 183
 lens, 175
 roles, 105
 and South Asia, 115, 220, 233
 and violence, 132
General Elections, 17, 142
Generator, 85
Gentamicin, 119
George Floyd, 76, 81
Germany, 89, 148, 217, 238
Ghaibana Namaz, 21
Ghalib, 3, 137, 152, 153, 156, 205, 240
 poetry of, 3, 10, 45, 152, 153, 156
Ghariban, 192
Ghettos, 15, 16, 122, 129
Ghiyasuddin Balban, Sultan, 28
Giri, Mohini, 10, 104–105, 107, 115, 178–83, 180, 182, 197, 219, 230
 and Babri Masjid demolition, 10
 at Delhi Gymkhana Club, 180–81
 on Hathras gang rape case, 181
 and India-Pakistan relations, 115, 219
 and Kashmir, 197
 at NCW, 104–105, 107, 180, 182
 and PWDVA, 10
 and WIPSA, 115, 197
Girls, 23, 32, 33, 35, 37, 41, 118, 125, 127, 130, 173, 202, 209, 212, 220, 227, 235, 241
 education of, 32, 130, 198
 at Miranda House beauty contest, 41
 and violence, 23, 125, 202
Glasgow, 153
God, 29, 31, 64, 94, 95, 126, 146, 155, 162, 164, 237
 house of, 31
Goddard College, 49
Godhra, 16
Golden Jubilee, 4
 Debate, 4
Golwalkar, Guru, 17
Gonds, 17
 of Bilaspur, 17
Goering, Hermann, 217
Gotra, 108
Gowda, Deve, 121, 179
Grandchildren, 1, 3
Grand Jubilee Debate, 4
Grandparents, 1, 3, 59
Graves, 13, 29, 98, 99, 100, 126, 197, 201, 210, 215
 of Maulana Azad's family, 99, 100
Graveyards, 13, 47, 195, 198
Grey Nuns, 20
Greyhound Bus, 48, 51
Grover, Karen, 51
Grover, Vrinda, 165
Growth, 133
Gubbthi, 207
Gujral, I.K., 104, 121, 219, 223
 and NCW, 104
 and PIPFPD, 219
 and WIPSA, 219
Guild of Service, 104
Gujarat, 11, 14–16, 18, 24, 103, 158, 161, 164, 209, 210, 228, 230
 carnage, 164
 ghosts of, 15
 massacre (2002), 11, 14–16, 103, 158
 middle class, 24
 riots, 14–16
 Sandesh, 16
Gulley, 176
Gulmohars, 154
Gulsitan, 10
"Gulzar" (Naqvi), 92
Gupta, Shobha, 165
Gupta, Suman, 197
Guria Sansthan, 125, 126
Gursharan Ji, 117
Guru Nanak Dev Ji, 232
 birth anniversary of, 232
Guru Nanak, 7, 146, 232
 poems on, 7
Gwadar, 235, 236

Habib Ibn Muzahir, 190
Hadith, 113
 women's rights in, 113
Haj, 184, 229

Consulate, 30
pilgrims, 29
Hali, Altaf Husain, 90, 93, 102–103, 152, 154, 169, 172, 176, 189, 238
"Chup ki Daad", 57, 169
influence of, 172
Musaddas, 103, 152
and Muslim women, 103, 172
on patriarchy, 57
on widow remarriage, 57
Halams, 128
Hali Muslim School, 28
Hali, Saliha Abid, 12, 27, 33, 56, 90, 96, 137, 166, 172–78, 181, 238
and Abid Hussain, 173
biography of, 172
books of, 172, 175
and communalism, 12
on gender and Islam, 175
and India-Pakistan relations, 137
influence of, 172, 174, 176
and Islam, 173, 174, 175
at Jamia Millia Islamia, 12, 173
Jhoot Sach, 177
Kitna Hai Khush Naseeb Zafar, 177
Miladun Nabi gatherings, 173
and Moharrum, 12, 174
on Muslim Personal Law, 174, 175
on Muslim women, 172, 174, 175
Niraas Mein Aas, 174
on polygamy, 175
Purdah, 172
Rah-e-Amal, 175
and Shah Bano case, 172–73
Silsila-e-Roz-o-Shab, 172
on triple talaq, 174–75
Yaadgaar-e-Hali, 28, 176
Hameed, Syed Mohammad Abdul, 48, 51, 54–60, 61, 65, 66, 67, 68, 73, 139, 140, 177, 188, 204, 212
ambitions of, 65
background of, 56
death of, 67, 71, 140, 212
and India-Pakistan relations, 55, 67, 68
and Islam, 64, 65
and Moharrum, 64
personality of, 65
as Pygmalion, 66
and Ramadan, 185
visa for, 55
Hamida Apa, 168
Handloom weavers, 134
Hand pumps, 85
Hanifa Begum, 96
Haram, 31
Sharif, 29
Haru Tai, 230
Haryana, 60, 106, 108, 118, 180, 228, 230, 232
Nuh district, 106, 180
Hasan, Dr. Shubbar, 27, 175
Hasan, Masood, 178
Hashim Ansari, 13
Hashimpura, 25
"Hathras gang rape case", 181
death of institutions and, 181
Hathras, 181
Haveli, 33
Hawwa, Hazrat, 27
Hayne, Ernie, 74
Hazelton, Lesley, 27
Health, 12, 19, 57, 118, 119, 123, 134, 172, 173, 218
care, 199
insurance, 134
Ministry of, 119, 134
Mission, National Rural (NRHM), 19, 118
public, 60
workers, 119
Hejrat, 26
Helen Keller, 39, 236
Hemant, 70, 71
Heptullah, Najma, 93
Herat, 27, 28
Yesterday Today (Fadaeian and Reza), 28
Herat Deroz Imroz (Herat Yesterday Today) (Fadaeian and Reza), 28
Higgins, Professor, 66
Hijab, 23, 78, 112, 220
Himachal Pradesh, 123
Hind, 6, 8, 17, 29
Hindi, 44, 73, 92, 111, 112, 147, 156, 233
films, 44, 73, 177, 220
and Islam, 112
newspapers, 9
and Urdu, 9, 21, 111
Hinduism, 17, 19, 155
and Islam, 12, 19
Jagran Manch, 5
Muslim fasaad, 5
Muslim riots, 5
Rashtra, 17
right wing, 11, 17, 24, 101, 112
scriptures, 12

tradition, 19
Yuva Wahini, 23
Hindus, 5, 7, 11, 19, 21, 23, 25, 106, 108, 125, 179, 186, 188, 191, 210, 226, 232
deities, 7, 25
and Islam, 7, 19, 108
and Muslims, 5, 11, 21, 23, 25, 106, 108, 179, 186, 188, 191
Muslim riots, 5
and partition, 11
Muslim fasaad, 5
paani, 38
subjects, 7
and the tsunami, 125
tribals, 19
and WIPSA, 21
Hindutva, 11, 17, 24, 101, 112, 160
brigades, 11
Hindustan, 6, 8, 33, 200, 220
Times, 92, 147
Hindustan Times, 92, 147
Hira, 29
History, 4, 11, 14, 17, 27, 48, 49, 66, 89, 90, 95, 143, 146, 149, 150, 151, 167, 169, 172, 190, 198, 208, 214, 217, 220, 228, 235
of Aligarh Muslim University, 4
communal, 4
family, 27, 149, 169
of India, 11, 17, 37, 146, 208, 214, 228
of Islam, 11, 27, 95, 190, 217
of Jamia Millia Islamia, 89
of Kashmir, 194, 208, 214
of Modern School, 149
of Muslim Personal Law, 111
snippets of, 37, 38, 53
of Sikhs, 155
of women in Islam, 176
Hitler, Adolf, 128
HIV, 122
Holmes, Joan, 79
Holy Family Hospital, 25
Homeland, 7, 8, 13, 17, 33, 47, 147, 149, 160, 208, 230
author's return to, 13, 47, 208
and country, 8, 13, 17, 47, 147, 149
loss of, 33
Homes, 100, 159, 168, 197, 203, 205, 218, 220
ancestral, 53
destroyed, 200
of elders, 34
family, 16, 67, 86
of friends, 21, 38
of Maulana Azad, 39, 91, 97
middle-class, 38
ransacked, 16
ravaged, 9
of relatives, 198
of writers, 89
Honolulu, 48, 48
Honour killing, 105, 106, 109, 180
at NCW, 105
Hope, 24, 106, 124, 125, 130, 140, 160, 163, 174, 197, 205, 219, 221, 226, 227, 234, 235, 242
and despair, 130
and India-Pakistan relations, 140, 219, 221, 226, 227, 234
in Kashmir, 195, 205
Hors d'oeuvres, 80
Horses, 190, 193, 214
Hospitals, 46, 47, 67, 171
Charles Campbell, 62
Holy Family, 25
Miseracordia, 67
SMHS, 211
Hostility, 78, 132, 200, 218, 223, 230
towards Muslims, 78
towards Pakistan, 230
Houseboats, 205
Howrah station, 99
Human Rights Award, Robert F. Kennedy, 160
Human Rights Commission, National, 165
Human Rights Watch, 160
Human rights, 12, 17, 57, 83, 113, 115, 123, 160, 161, 165, 176, 218, 236, 241
activists, 15, 160
and communalism, 17, 218
crusaders, 61
and education, 57
and gender, 110, 113
and India-Pakistan relations, 115, 218
and Islam, 57
violations, 18, 132, 222
and women, 104, 113, 165, 172–73, 176
"Hum Dekhenge" (Faiz), 144–46, 145
as anthem of non-cooperation, 144–45
interpretation of, 145–46
and youth, 144–45
Hunger, 19, 185, 186, 196, 218, 234, 240

Project, The, 79
strike, 19
tribunal, 19
Husain, Abid, 12, 96, 98, 100, 171, 173
Husain, Imam, 64, 174, 188, 189, 190–92, 192
family of, 189, 192
Husain, Khwaja Sajjad, 3
Husain, Saliha Abid, 12, 27, 33, 56, 90, 96, 137, 166, 172–78, 181, 238
and Abid Hussain, 173
biography of, 172
books of, 172, 175
and communalism, 12
on gender and Islam, 175
and India-Pakistan relations, 137
influence of, 172, 174, 176
and Islam, 173, 174, 175
at Jamia Millia Islamia, 12, 173
Jhoot Sach, 177
Kitna Hai Khush Naseeb Zafar, 177
Miladun Nabi gatherings, 173
and Moharrum, 12, 174
on Muslim Personal Law, 174, 175
on Muslim women, 172, 174, 175
Niraas Mein Aas, 174
on polygamy, 175
Purdah, 172
Rah-e-Amal, 175
and Shah Bano case, 172–73
Silsila-e-Roz-o-Shab, 172
on triple talaq, 174–75
Yaadgaar-e-Hali, 28, 176
Husain, Zakir, 12, 13, 33, 35–36, 38, 89, 90, 131, 169, 173
and Aligarh Muslim University, 12
and communalism, 12
on education, 35–36
influence of, 33
at Jamia Millia Islamia, 12, 38, 89
Hyderabad, 12, 13, 56, 66, 110, 150, 159, 164, 199
MIM attack on Taslima Nasrin in, 11
Maulana Azad Institute of Oriental Studies, 150
Sind, 141
Hyder Ali Aatish, 118

ICDS (Integrated Child Development Scheme), 132
ICCR (Indian Council for Cultural Relations), 91, 92, 97, 98, 151
library, 91
Identity, 3, 8, 9, 12, 14, 17, 23, 24, 26, 37, 53, 56, 75, 77, 90, 112, 114, 147, 148, 149, 160, 169, 177, 199, 203, 214, 227, 233, 241
Asian, 75
and communalism, 9–11, 24
and education, 12, 56
and family, 53
and faith, 14, 26
Indian, 8, 17, 214, 228
markers, 23
and marriage, 53
Muslim, 8, 9, 24, 112, 148, 160, 169, 214, 221, 227, 229
national, 6, 39, 147, 149, 229
and Partition, 9
question of, 3
religious, 37, 148, 149
Sikh, 8, 148
and South Asia, 17, 220
Iftaar, 129, 186
Ijtihad, 175
Illustrated Weekly of India, The, 147
Illiteracy, 144
Imam, 4
of Hind, 6
Imambara, 64, 188
IMR (Infant Mortality Rate), 119
Immigration, 218, 229
officials, 78
India, 1, 3, 5, 7, 8, 10, 11, 12, 13, 14, 17, 18, 19, 20, 21, 22, 23, 24, 25, 28, 29, 32, 33, 34, 37, 38, 39, 40, 47, 53, 55, 56, 57, 58, 59, 60, 61, 62, 63, 65, 66, 67, 68, 69, 70, 71, 72, 75, 76, 78, 79, 81, 82, 83, 85, 86, 87, 88, 89, 90, 91, 92, 94, 96, 97, 98, 99, 100, 101, 102, 103, 104, 105, 106, 107, 108, 110, 111, 112, 113, 114, 115, 116, 117, 118, 119, 120, 121, 122, 123, 124, 125, 127, 128, 130, 131, 132, 133, 134, 136, 137, 139, 140, 144, 145, 146, 147, 148, 149, 150, 151, 152, 154, 155, 156, 158, 159, 160, 162, 163, 164, 168, 169, 172, 173, 174, 176, 178, 179, 180, 181, 182, 183, 186, 187, 188, 193, 195, 196, 197, 198, 199, 200, 201, 202, 204, 206, 207, 208, 209, 210, 212, 213, 214, 215, 216, 217, 218, 219, 220, 221, 222, 223, 224, 225, 226, 227, 228, 229, 230, 231, 232, 233, 234, 235, 236, 238, 239, 240, 241

author's decision to return to, 66
author's life in, 12, 67, 68, 69, 78, 85, 86, 89, 110, 112, 113, 114, 117, 118, 120, 121, 122, 123, 124, 125, 127, 130, 131, 132, 134, 140, 144, 146, 149, 150, 151, 154, 155, 158, 160, 162, 163, 164, 168, 174, 176, 178, 179, 180, 181, 182, 183, 186, 187, 188, 193, 195, 196, 197, 198, 199, 200, 201, 202, 204, 206, 208, 209, 210, 212, 213, 214, 215, 216, 217, 218, 220, 221, 222, 223, 224, 225, 226, 227, 228, 229, 230, 231, 232, 233, 234, 235, 236, 239, 240, 241
author's love for, 8, 34, 159, 160
Constitution, 208
Article 35A, 208, 210
Article 370, 207–208, 210, 214
Four Corners of the, 200
-Pakistan relations, 10, 11, 34, 53, 55, 66, 67, 68, 69, 83, 115, 128, 137, 140, 146, 149, 159, 173, 174, 195, 196, 197, 198, 200, 201, 217–236, 230
animosity in, 54, 115, 217
and children, 34, 67
and communalism, 10, 115, 217–218
peace efforts, 115, 218–236
and Partition, 10, 11, 34, 146, 199
and war, 195, 217, 221, 230
Partition of, 1, 9, 10, 11, 12, 33, 34, 38, 56, 83, 89, 90, 99, 146, 149, 159, 174, 186, 188, 193, 199, 218, 224, 225, 232, 234
post-partition, 9, 11, 12, 34, 38, 146, 199
Supreme Court, 19, 29, 103, 111, 112, 134, 207, 209, 213
Indian Council for Cultural Relations (ICCR), 91, 92, 97, 98, 151
Indian Express Group, 233
Indira Gandhi National Centre for the Arts (IGNCA), 169
Indore, 110, 124
Infant Mortality Rate (IMR), 119
Inquilab, 144
Institute of Social Sciences, 36
Institutions, 20, 181
death of, 181
Integrated Child Development Scheme (ICDS), 132
Integrated Child Protection Scheme, 132
Intellectual
capital, 38
exchanges, 91
property, 122
Intelligentsia, Muslim, 4
International
community, 201
fora, 83, 165
stage, 177
Writing Contest, 36
Internet, 208
Invective, 18
Invocations and Prayers of Khwaja Abdullah Ansari (Saiyidain), 27
Iqbal, Allama, 6–7, 8, 11–12, 39, 58, 90, 112, 152, 154, 165, 176, 206, 238
influence of, 11, 12
on Islam, 11, 112
"Lab pe aati hai dua ban ke tamanna meri", 12
"Naya Shivalaya", 8
poems of, 6–7, 8, 12, 39, 58
on Ram, 6–7
"Ram", 6–7
and Saliha Abid Husain, 12
and Urdu, 12
Iraq, 96, 237, 238
Iran, 28, 94, 237, 238, 242
e-Sagheer, 215
Irani Shehzada, 40
Isha prayer, 226
Islamabad, 138
Ismail, Hazrat, 30
Ismail, 108
Istanbul, 27
Iyengar, Ananthasayanam, 179

Jabalpur, 20, 110
Jafri, Ali Sardar, 141
Jafri, Ehsan, 15–16
lynching of, 16
Jahangir, Asma, 115, 218, 219, 222, 223, 225, 229, 232
at 2000 bus journey, 219, 222
at 2001 peace march, 223
and India-Pakistan relations, 115, 218, 219, 222, 223, 229, 232

Jahangir, Asma, 115, 218, 219, 222, 223, 225, 229, 232
at 2000 bus journey, 219, 222
at 2001 peace march, 223

and India-Pakistan relations, 115, 218, 219, 222, 223, 229, 232
Jaitly, Jaya, 42
Jalaluddin, Mrs., 33
Jalandhar, 26, 230, 232, 233
Jalpaiguri, 124, 130
Jama'at, 197
  Women's Wing of the (Dukhtaran-e-Millat), 197
Jama Masjid, 95
  demolition of, 7
Jamia Millia Islamia, 12, 10, 11, 12, 20, 21, 38, 86, 89, 90, 91, 112, 144, 171, 173, 174, 177
  CAA protests at, 24
  history of, 89
  and Moharrum, 174
  Nagar, 20
  Okhla, 89
  Qabristan, 59, 126
Jammu, 193, 197, 216
  and Kashmir, 193, 194, 197, 198, 199, 213, 214, 215, 232
  Arts Emporium, 205
  Democratic Freedom Party, 199
  High Court, 213
  Juvenile Justice Committee, 213
  and Kargil war, 219
Jammu and Kashmir Democratic Freedom Party, 199
Jammu, 193, 197, 216
  and Kashmir, 193, 194, 197, 198, 199, 213, 214, 215, 232
  Arts Emporium, 205
  Democratic Freedom Party, 199
  High Court, 213
  Juvenile Justice Committee, 213
  and Kargil war, 219
Jantar Mantar, 21
Jansatta, 233
Jan, Maulvi Mohammad, 193
Jan, Safia, 194
Jansatta, 233
Japan, 110
Jarawas, 134
Jaswant Nai, 164
Jawahar Bhawan, 87
Jawaharlal Nehru University (JNU), 139, 186, 215, 222
Jawaharlal Nehru, 12, 13, 33, 37, 38, 101, 117, 186, 197, 215
  at Aligarh Muslim University, 12
  assassination of, 37
  at Bismillah Khan's performance, 127
  and education, 12
  and Indian Muslims, 11
  influence of, 33
  at Jamia Millia Islamia, 12, 38
  and nationalism, 18
  portraits of, 22
  and Saliha Abid Husain, 12
  and secularism, 18
Jayanti Park, Buddha, 154
Jeddah, 29, 31
Jeypore, 70
Jhelum, 210
  River, 86, 205, 210
Jinnah, Mohammed Ali, 4, 11, 13, 89
  Abbas on, 4
  at Aligarh Muslim University, 4
  portrait controversy, 4–5
JNU (Jawaharlal Nehru University), 139, 186, 215, 222
Johnson, Howard, 48
Joshi, Murli Manohar, 13
  at Babri Masjid demolition, 13
"Jhoot Sach" (Husain), 177
  as LSR inaugural play, 177
Jugantar, 101
"Julam dha le tu sitam dha le" (Dhawan), 83–84
Jumna, 224
  River, 86, 239, 240
  Ji, 179
June Chettur, 42
"Junoon, Dil hai mera mulk, meri jan, janan-e-jan", 226
Juzar S. Bandukwala, 16

Ka'aba, 29, 31
Kababs, 38
Kabul, 27, 28
Kachchi abadis, 7
Kadhi, besan ki, 38
Kafan, 18, 100, 192
Kakinara, 100, 101
Kalaam, 169, 179
Kale, Bhai, 170
Kalima, 94, 95
  recitation of, 94–95
Kalidas Marg, 13
Kalium, 61
Kalpur, Mr., 12, 37, 38, 40, 50, 119–120
Kamla Bhasin. *See* Bhasin, Kamla
Kamorta Island, 125
Kandhamal, 19–20, 20

killing fields of, 19
Kanjivaram, 179
Kannauj, 173
Kanwal Krishna, 12
Kapur, Mr., 12, 37, 38, 40, 50, 119–120
Karachi, 9, 10, 23, 66, 67, 97, 101, 102, 137, 138, 154, 218, 228
Jail, 141
Oxford University Press (OUP), 101–102
Karbala, 189, 190–92, 192, 174
Day of Ashura, 190
grief of, 189
pain of, 189, 191
story of, 189–91
Kargil war, 219, 130
and Kashmir, 195, 219
Kargil, 130, 209
Kar Sevaks, 13
Kashan, 94
Kashmir State Human Rights Commission (SHRC), 207
Kashmir Welfare Centre, 198
Kashmir, 10, 17, 55, 112, 124, 193–216, 218, 221, 222, 229, 232, 235, 236, 241
Abdullah Bridge, 205
Aijaz, custodial death of, 198–99
Amira Kadal Bridge, 199
author's birthplace, 193, 214
author's visits to, 10, 195, 197–205, 209, 214
chashmdeed gawahi in, 204
communalism in, 200
conflict in, 17, 195
custodial killings in, 197
education in, 193, 194, 214
and Faiz Ahmed Faiz, 215
families, 124
and filmmaking, 216
"ghaddar" (traitor), 203
and human rights violations, 198–201, 211–13, 216
and the Hunger Project, 79
and identity, 17
and India-Pakistan relations, 55, 195, 196, 197, 198, 200, 201, 218, 221, 222, 229, 232, 236
and the "Indian State", 210
and Islam, 17, 194, 202
and "Islamic State", 17
and "Islamic State", 17
Jammu and Kashmir Arts Emporium, 205
Jammu and Kashmir Democratic Freedom Party, 199
and Kargil war, 195, 219
Kashmiri Pandits, 10, 200, 210, 214
Kashmiriyat, 195, 210
killings in, 12, 195, 197, 199, 201, 211
kidnapping in, 198
and Kuldip Nayar, 229
Kupwara, 194, 241
landmines in, 197
lockdown in, 208, 212
and militancy, 202, 205, 209
"Moo-e-Mubarak" theft, 216
and Moharrum, 194
mountains of, 123
Muralia Village, 197
and Mushirul Haq, 215–16
Muslim women of, 10
Nagbal, 209
Nagrota, 197
Nund Reshi, 194
and "ordinary people", 206
Pahalgam, 203–205
"Paki" color, 81
Pari Mahal, 206
and the Planning Commission, 118
poetry of, 214, 216
and polygamy, 112
Poonch border, 116
and "prudes", 155
Purdah, 112
Raj Bagh, 193
Ranbir Singh Pora, 197
and the "Sachar Committee Report", 114
saffron fields of, 197
and Sarmad, 94, 95
schools in, 193, 198, 209
security forces in, 197, 198, 200, 204, 212
Sher-i-Kashmir Conference Centre, 206
and Sheikh Abdullah, 149
Srinagar, 32, 193, 197, 198, 199, 204, 205, 211, 212, 214, 215, 216
and state subject status, 194–95
as "stone age", 209
story of Sago, 127–28
and Sufism, 194

"The Country Without a Post Office", 216
torture in, 198, 199, 200, 212
tourism in, 213
and triple talaq, 112
turmoil in, 195
University of Kashmir, 204
unrest in, 202
Vice Chancellor Lodge, 204
violence in, 195, 197, 199, 200, 201, 208–13, 216, 221
WIPSA and, 115, 195, 196, 197
"Women's Voice" report, 212
Zero Bridge, 205
"Kashmir Files", 210
Kasauli, 152–54, 153
Khushwant Singh Literary Festival in, 153
Raj Villa, 152
Kathuria, Deepak, 230
Kathodis, 17
of Udaipur, 17
Kaur, Rajkumari Amrit, 37
Kaur, Tirpat, 221
Kavalji, 152–54
and Ghalib, 152–53
Kazim Zaheer, 67
Keats, John, 22, 42, 140
Keema, 71
Keller, Helen, 39, 236
Keonjhar, 19
Kher, B.G., 33
Kheda, 15, 158, 204
Khichri, 127
Kidwai, Rafi Ahmed, 11, 12, 90
King Edward Road, 39, 91, 97
Kitchlew, Saifuddin, 11
"Kitna Hai Badnaseeb Zafar" (Zafar), 177
"Kitna Hai Khush Naseeb Zafar" (Husain), 177
debut of, 177
Kitabon ki Duniya, 151
KSA (Kingdom of Saudi Arabia), 30
mini world of, 30–31
Kufr, 95, 242
Kulgam, 207
Kuldip Nayar, 137, 197, 219, 222, 223, 224–28, 229, 232, 233
at 1996 and 2000 peace initiatives, 228
at 2001 peace march, 223
death of, 229
and Hind-Pak Dosti Manch, 223, 226, 228
and India-Pakistan relations, 137, 219, 223, 224–28, 229
and Kashmir, 197, 229
and peace activism, 224–28
and Wagah border, 137, 223, 225, 226, 228, 229
Kumar, Nitish, 209
Kumar, Sunita, of India Imports, 178
Kumar, Tang, 125
Kupwara, 194, 241
Dolphin School, 194
Kurian, Miss, 44
Kurta, 20, 162, 181
pajama, 19
churidar, 78, 81, 162
Kusum Nair, 117
Kyaas, 221
Kyrgyzstan, 191

Lahore, 10, 66, 137, 138, 218, 219, 220, 221, 222, 224, 228, 229, 231, 235
Aurat Foundation, 48
bus journey to, 10, 219–22
Fort, 141
Shalimar Gardens, 156
Women's Solidarity Conference, 221
Lailat-ul-Qadr (Night of Blessing), 186
Lala Doctor, 164
Lala Shri Ram, 39
Lala Vakil, 164
Lal Ded (Lalla), 194
Lal, Anuradha, 44
Land Gift (Bhoodan) Movement, 197
Landmines, 197
Landscapes, 3, 37, 51, 128, 230
mental, 37
Lankesh, Gauri, 146
Lathis, 5, 106
Latin, 177
Laurentian Mountains, 58
"Lab pe aati hai dua ban ke tamanna meri" (Iqbal), 12
Lady Shri Ram College (LSR), 55, 177
dramatic society at, 177
Leaders, 11, 13, 17, 37, 148, 195, 200, 217, 218, 219, 223, 234
communal, 24
and education, 37
of India, 37
Islamic, 11
Muslim, 11, 24, 176
national, 11, 37, 148

political, 11, 17, 13, 37, 101, 148, 195, 200, 217, 218, 223, 234, 236
right-wing, 17, 112
women, 176
Leadership, 11, 13, 146
and MWF, 160–61
Project, 161
Leaf, 8
Lebanon, 186
Leh, 130
Leprosy, 19
Ashram, 19
Home, Mayurbhanj, 19
Letters, 34, 45, 50, 54, 57, 61, 63, 90, 97, 100, 153, 182, 199, 241
fan mail, 36
from prison, 90
love, 54, 61
to the PM, 119
Libraries, 89, 91, 100, 147, 150, 151, 237
Lidder, 203, 205
River, 203, 205, 210
Life, 1, 2, 3, 6, 8, 9, 11, 12, 13, 14, 17, 22, 24, 34, 36, 37, 38, 41, 44, 45, 50, 51, 52, 54, 55, 57, 59, 60, 62, 63, 65, 66, 67, 68, 69, 70, 72, 73, 74, 76, 85, 86, 88, 90, 91, 94, 95, 96, 102, 103, 104, 110, 112, 114, 115, 117, 120, 121, 125, 126, 129, 130, 137, 139, 140, 141, 142, 144, 150, 152, 153, 154, 159, 160, 162, 163, 165, 166, 170, 172, 173, 174, 175, 176, 177, 178, 181, 182, 183, 185, 186, 188, 189, 190, 191, 192, 194, 195, 196, 197, 198, 199, 200, 201, 202, 203, 204, 205, 206, 209, 210, 211, 212, 213, 214, 215, 216, 217, 218, 221, 222, 224, 225, 229, 230, 231, 232, 234, 235, 236, 237, 238, 239, 240, 241, 242, 242
and communalism, 24
long friend, 178
prison, 95, 141, 144, 145, 212
rural, 126, 162
simple, 192
long struggle, 120, 222, 236
after trauma, 9
urban, 126
way of, 173, 174
Limcas, 154
Lineage, 27, 28
Linguistics, 48, 169
Literature, 6, 12, 34, 140, 144, 147, 152, 154, 172, 174, 177, 209, 240
children's, 172, 174
English, 140
Urdu, 90, 149, 150, 152, 154, 156, 177
Western, 152
Lockdown, 208, 212, 213, 214
Lodestar, 160
Looms, 124, 130
power, 129, 130
Loretto, 20, 183
Love, 1, 2, 3, 7, 10, 22, 34, 41, 42, 44, 53, 54, 57, 58, 59, 60, 66, 68, 71, 76, 94, 95, 98, 106, 108, 117, 120, 140, 142, 148, 149, 153, 154, 156, 157, 159, 167, 170, 171, 172, 173, 174, 186, 189, 194, 202, 203, 215, 216, 224, 234, 235
affair, 42
and communalism, 7, 24, 101
and death, 3, 47
hate relationship, 159
and hate, 18, 101, 109, 209, 210
and homeland, 8, 13
and identity, 9, 53
and India-Pakistan relations, 34, 115, 224, 231, 234
letters, 54, 61
for one's country, 8, 13, 34, 147, 148, 160, 195
and Partition, 10
and peace, 38, 197, 225, 234
stories, 24
spells, 43
and truth, 2, 22
Lucknow, 13, 111, 175, 178, 189, 199, 235
Darul Uloom University, 111, 175
Lula da Silva, 214
Lungi, 30, 128
Lungis, 101
Lushai, 128
Lutyens' Delhi, 40, 124, 139, 176, 202
Lyallpur, 141
Lynching, 14, 16, 23, 81, 109, 164, 241
of Ehsan Jafri, 16
in Malegaon, 132
of Muslims, 16, 81, 132, 164
of "cattle stealers", 23

Macwan, Martin, 160, 161, 162, 163
and Dalit Shakti Kendra, 161, 162, 163

on human rights, 160–61
and MWF, 160, 163
Madras, 138
Magrey, Justice Ali Mohammad, 213
Maharaja S. Sayajirao University of Baroda, 16
Maharaja Hari Singh, 193
invitation from, 193
Maharashtra, 118, 124, 129, 132, 230
Gadchiroli, 118, 119, 134
Malegaon, 21, 129–30, 132, 134
Mahaul, 24, 38, 229
Mahmood, Saman, 48
Mahmood, Shahla, 48
Mahmud, Dr. Satnam, 116, 183
Mahmud-o-Ayaz, 176
Maikhana, 157
Mainstream, 12
Majaz Lakhnawi, 141
Majlis, 64, 155, 188, 189, 191, 192, 194
e-Ittehadul Muslimeen (MIM), 11
Majrooh Sultanpuri, 225
Makkah (Mecca), 30, 31, 93, 95, 152
Malerkotla, 130
Malegaon, 21, 129–30, 132, 134
communal violence in, 132
development deficit in, 130
Hospital, 134
Saman Habib compound, 129
Malhotra, Rajiv, 140
Malik Ali, Khwaja, 28
Malini Ghosh, 158
Malnutrition, 19, 71, 118
in Koraput, 71
Malviya, Amit, 181
Manak, Satnam, 229, 232, 233
Mander, Harsh, 121
Mangalore, 20
Maniktala graveyard, 98, 100
Maniktala, 98, 99, 100
description of, 99
Mankind, 184
Manmohan Singh, Dr., 116–21, 117, 119, 126, 133, 134, 186
and author's appointment to Planning Commission, 116
on Gadchiroli Report, 119
and inclusive planning, 134
on Kusum Nair, 117
personality of, 117
and Voluntary Sector, 133
Mansion, 153
Manual scavenging, 162
Marape, James, 214
Mardana, 170
Mardon, 57
Marg, Kalidas, 13
Mari Thekekara, 158
Marrakesh, 33
Marriage, 34, 53, 55, 56, 65, 76, 111, 173, 175, 177, 199, 202, 221
arranged, 169
child, 189
and communalism, 53, 55, 221
dowry-less, 202
and faith, 34
forced, 19
and identity, 53, 56
and India-Pakistan relations, 55, 221
inter-caste, 12, 65
and Islam, 56, 111, 173, 175, 177
within Islam, 53, 173
love, 108
multiple, 111
of Maimun and Idris, 106–109
of Saliha and Abid Hussain, 173
and societal norms, 56
and women's status, 111, 175
Marsha Chapman, 49–50
Marsiyas, 63, 188, 192
Martin Luther King Jr., 83
Martyrdom, 13
Martyrs, 95, 164
Marx, Karl, 135
Masalas, 126
Masjid, 7, 13, 14, 16, 56, 95, 112, 155, 214, 238, 242
-e-Nabavi, 29, 146
-e-Shah, 238
Masnad, 146
Massachusetts, 48
Maternal Mortality Rate (MMR), 119
Matam, 64, 174
Matriarch, 168
Maulana. *See* Azad, Maulana Abul Kalam
Maulana Azad Institute of Oriental Studies, 150
Maulvis, 175
Mauj Bi, 108
Mauritius, 44
Mayawati, 182
Mayurbhanj Leprosy Home, 19
Mayurbhanj, 19
story of Graham Staines, 19
Mazdoor, 125, 162, 179
McIsaac, Paul, 51

Mecca, 11, 26, 30, 31, 93, 95, 146, 152
Media, 11, 15, 21, 23, 91, 93, 97, 112, 130, 142, 145, 151, 158, 182, 209, 210, 213, 222, 223, 228, 234
  persons, 13, 15
  print, 11, 15, 90, 93, 151, 222, 228
  social, 82, 175
  Urdu, 21, 23, 112
  visual, 11, 15, 222, 228
Medina, 26, 27, 31, 237, 238
  Haram, 31
Mehdi Hassan, 140, 140
Mehdi, Dr. Sughra, 90, 110, 112
Mehfil, 140, 233
Mehta, Deepa, 183
Mehr, 190
Memoir, 3
Memories, 3, 7, 13, 37, 42, 45, 50, 61, 66, 75, 80, 81, 96, 127, 140, 153, 156, 171, 178, 183, 192, 194, 204, 205, 221, 224, 229, 237
  collective, 18
  and communalism, 13, 24
  of death, 47
  of family, 13, 33
  of friends, 45
  of Ghalib, 153
  of Gujarat, 15
  of homeland, 13
  of India-Pakistan relations, 221, 224
  of Kashmir, 194, 204
  of Malegaon, 130
  of Maulana Azad, 90, 91, 96, 100, 150
  of Moharrum, 188
  of mothers, 171
  of NCW, 110
  of Partition, 9, 13, 34, 224
  of school, 34
  of student days, 52
  and trauma, 9, 13, 24, 33
  of Wagah border, 225, 228
Men, 3, 4, 5, 11, 12, 20, 21, 30, 32, 33, 38, 41, 42, 53, 54, 57, 64, 76, 80, 94, 95, 103, 106, 109, 113, 114, 118, 122, 123, 124, 125, 129, 133, 136, 137, 140, 144, 146, 159, 160, 163, 166, 167, 169, 170, 173, 174, 175, 176, 177, 178, 180, 181, 183, 188, 190, 192, 194, 196, 197, 199, 201, 202, 203, 204, 206, 209, 211, 212, 214, 215, 216, 217, 218, 219, 220, 221, 222, 224, 225, 226, 228, 231, 232, 235, 236, 237, 238, 239, 241
  and communal violence, 5, 21, 23, 101, 106, 109, 181
  and domestic violence, 105
  education of, 32, 57
  employment of, 133
  and gender, 3, 57, 113
  and Hinduism, 19, 108
  and identity, 3, 9, 12, 24, 53, 56, 114, 214
  and India-Pakistan relations, 224
  and Islam, 11, 112, 113, 173, 175, 190
  and marriage, 53, 111, 175, 177
  and Moharrum, 188, 190
  of Muslim community, 112, 233
  Muslim, 3, 5, 9, 11, 12, 21, 23, 24, 53, 81, 101, 106, 108, 109, 112, 113, 116, 132, 159, 160, 164, 169, 170, 173, 175, 176, 179, 181, 186, 191, 199, 200, 202, 210, 214, 215, 217, 221, 227, 233, 235, 236, 239, 241
  and Muslim Personal Law, 111, 113
  and the Planning Commission, 122
  rights of, 57
  and the Sachar Committee Report, 114
  Sikh, 116, 199
  and social reform, 173
  status of, 57
  and theatre, 177
  and violence, 5, 21, 23, 101, 106, 109, 181, 202, 211
  and WIPSA, 196
  and women, 3, 57, 113
  and work, 124, 133
Menon, Vasantha, 42
Mentors, 12, 17, 86, 90, 107, 116, 136, 159, 160, 162, 165, 172, 174, 181, 183, 187, 222, 229, 230
  women, 12, 183
Meos, 108
Merak Shah, 28
Mewat, 17, 118
  Muslims of, 17
Michener, Roland, 58
Michener Park, 63
Micro, Small and Medium Enterprises (MSME), 123
Middle East, 238
Miladun Nabi, 173
Militancy, 202
Militants, 20, 197, 200, 201, 203
Millennium School, 234
Milton, 42

MIM (Majlis-e-Ittehadul Muslimeen), 11
  attack on Taslima Nasrin, 11
Minds, 3, 18, 37, 99, 144, 175, 180, 200, 209, 218, 222, 229, 238, 241
  closed, 208
  -scape, 3
  set, 81
Minister of Education, 32, 37, 90
Minister of Finance, 27, 87, 218
Minister of Information and Broadcasting, 200
Minister of State, 77, 120
Minorities, 123
  cell, 123
  women, 103, 158
Mir Anis, 174, 189
Mir, Mir Taqi, 242
Mirwaiz Maulvi Mohammad Farooq. *See* Farooq, Maulvi Mohammad
Mirwaiz, 216
Mishra, Devi Prasad, 239
Mitra, Amit, 236
Mittal, Devika, 235
Mittal, Devika, 235
Mithesh Bhatt, 164
MNK, 12
Mobs, 13, 15, 16, 24, 101, 159
Modern School, 9, 34, 36, 37, 38, 86, 121, 149, 150
  alumni of, 149
  author's children at, 67, 86
  author's time at, 36–38
  eclecticism of, 37
  history of, 149
  and identity, 37, 149
  influence of, 37–38
  and secularism, 38
  75th anniversary of, 149
Modi, Narendra, 15, 82, 164
  and Gujarat massacre, 15
Modasa, 21
Mofussil, 43
Mohammad Yunus, 86, 88
  Letters from Prison, 90
Mohammedan Anglo-Oriental College, 4
Mohan, 70, 71
Mohan Roy, Ram, 137, 197, 230
  and India-Pakistan relations, 137, 230
  and Kashmir, 197
  and peace activism, 230
Mohallas, 20, 129, 130, 126
Mohini Giri. *See* Giri, Mohini
Monogamy, 175
Montgomery (Sahiwal) Jail, 141
Montreal, 61
Monuments, 28
  of Herat, 28
Moplah, 148
Morad, 58–60, 62, 67, 68, 69, 71, 139, 140, 188
  birth of, 58–59
  description of, 59, 60
  and Fatiha, 59
  and Moharrum, 188
  personality of, 59
Morbidity, 57
Motherland, 7, 8, 17, 24, 47, 147, 149, 160, 208, 230
  author's return to, 13, 47, 208
  and country, 8, 13, 17, 47, 147, 149
  loss of, 33
Mothers, 32, 34, 44, 53, 56, 60, 62, 67, 71, 103, 105, 110, 124, 130, 140, 162, 166, 169, 171, 172, 174, 176, 183, 188, 189, 192, 199, 200, 201, 212, 213, 218, 219, 221
  and communal violence, 5, 103, 200
  and education, 34, 53
  expectations for children, 32
  and gender, 110
  and identity, 53, 114
  and India-Pakistan relations, 221
  and Islam, 174, 188, 190
  and Kashmir, 212, 213
  and Malegaon, 130
  and Moharrum, 64, 188, 192
  and peace, 219
  of sex workers, 126
  and the tsunami, 125
  and work, 130
Mughalpura, 221, 222
Mujahideen, Indian, 21
Mujeeb, Prof Mohammad, 12, 38, 89, 173
  at Aligarh Muslim University, 12
  at Jamia Millia Islamia, 12, 38, 89
Mukherjee, Geeta, 181
Mullahs, 95
Multinationals, 222
Munir Niazi, 3
Murmu, Bitiya, 106
Murals, 154
Murli Manohar Joshi. *See* Joshi, Murli Manohar
Musaddas-e-Hali, 29, 103, 152
Mushaira, 39, 226, 233
  Indo-Pak, 39

Shankar-Shaad, 39
Musharraf, Pervez, 220
Music, 126, 127, 143, 156, 177, 205, 220, 222, 227, 233, 239
classical, 191
and Maulana Azad, 93
Sufi, 233
Muslims, 3, 4, 5, 7, 9, 10, 11, 12, 13, 15, 16, 17, 18, 19, 20, 21, 22, 23, 24, 25, 26, 27, 28, 33, 34, 35, 36, 38, 53, 55, 56, 57, 64, 66, 67, 83, 89, 90, 93, 94, 98, 99, 101, 102, 103, 106, 108, 109, 110, 111, 112, 113, 114, 115, 116, 129, 130, 132, 146, 148, 150, 155, 158, 159, 160, 162, 164, 165, 169, 170, 173, 174, 175, 176, 177, 178, 179, 180, 182, 183, 186, 188, 189, 191, 192, 193, 194, 197, 198, 199, 200, 201, 202, 203, 204, 206, 209, 210, 214, 215, 218, 221, 222, 226, 229, 232, 233, 234, 236, 239, 241
bastis, 10
and communal violence, 5, 15, 16, 21, 23, 101, 103, 106, 109, 112, 129, 130, 132, 158, 159, 164, 180, 200
divines, 94
education of, 11, 57, 112, 173
and gender, 113
and Hinduism, 7, 19, 108
-Hindu riots, 5
and identity, 8, 9, 24, 112, 148, 160, 169, 214, 221, 227
-Indian relations, 11, 115
and India-Pakistan relations, 34, 53, 55, 66, 67, 217, 218, 221, 224, 227, 229, 230, 232, 233
intellectuals, 4, 215
and Islam, 11, 112, 113, 173, 175, 190
and Kashmir, 10, 17, 195, 197, 198, 199, 200, 201, 202, 203, 206, 209, 210, 214, 215
leaders, 11, 176
lynching of, 16, 81, 132, 164
massacre of, 11, 15, 16, 18, 81, 103, 132, 158, 164, 200, 241
and marriage, 53, 55, 111, 175, 221
middle-class, 20
and Moharrum, 174, 188, 190, 191
and the Muslim Personal Law, 111, 113
Personal Law, 23, 111, 112, 113, 174, 175
and the Planning Commission, 118
politicians, 4, 11
and polygamy, 112
post-partition trauma of, 12
-residents of Medina, 27
rights of, 57
and the Sachar Committee Report, 114
and secularism, 3
- women, 10, 15, 16, 23, 103, 104, 105, 110, 111, 112, 113, 114, 123, 158, 159, 160, 162, 164, 172, 173, 174, 175, 176, 183, 191, 200, 222
and activism, 114
and communalism, 23, 158, 200
condition of, 103, 111, 112, 172
and education, 11, 112, 173
and gender, 113
and Gujarat massacre, 103, 158
and identity, 23, 24, 112, 221, 227
and India-Pakistan relations, 222, 228
and Islam, 112, 113, 173, 174
and marriage, 111, 175
and Moharrum, 191, 192
and the Muslim Personal Law, 111, 113
and the NCW, 110, 112
and the Planning Commission, 118
and the Sachar Committee Report, 114
and violence, 23, 103, 158, 200
and WIPSA, 222, 228
and status of women, 57
students, 5
and Sufism, 94
and the tsunami, 125
and triple talaq, 112
- writers, 6
and violence, 5, 15, 16, 21, 23, 101, 103, 106, 109, 112, 129, 130, 132, 158, 159, 164, 180, 200
and WIPSA, 21, 196, 219
and work, 124, 133
Muslim Women Act (1986), 173
Muslim Women's Forum (MWF), 112–14, 160–64
activism and, 114
and communalism, 114
financial difficulties of, 160
and gender in Islam, 113
and Gagan Sethi, 160, 163
goals of, 112, 114
and India-Pakistan relations, 163
and Islam, 112, 113
Leadership Project, 160–62

and "My Voice Shall be Heard" report, 113–14
and the Sachar Committee Report, 114
and Understanding Islam workshops, 163–64
Mustafa Lodge, 168
Mustafa, Seema, 142
Mutanabbi, 216
Mutarjim Nizam, Agha, 238
Muttoo, Maya, 42
Muzaffarnagar, 17, 25, 144
carnage, 17

Naach gaana, 92
Nadvi, Maulana Abul Hasan Ali (Maulana Ali Miyan), 111, 114
and MWF, 111, 114
and Muslim Personal Law, 111, 114
Nagbal, 209
Naga Mother's Association, 132
Nagaland, 123, 132
Nagar, Jamia, 20, 97
Nagpur, 230
Nainital, 168
Nair, Kusum, 117
Naish Hasan, 175
Nanak Dev University, Guru, 225
Nancowrie, 125
Nanking, 236
Nanna, 50
Nannies, 168
Naqvi, Tahira, 90
Naqvi, Azra, 131
Naqvi, Farah, 158, 164
and Gujarat massacre, 158, 164
Naqvi, Gulzar, 91–92, 93
and Azad's bibliography, 92
Naqvi, Zehra, 218
Narasimha Rao, P.V., 13, 121
and Babri Masjid demolition, 13
Narang, Professor Gopi Chand, 55, 87
Narendra Sharma. *See* Sharma, Narendra
Nasrin, Taslima, 11
MIM attack on, 11
Nasturtiums, 154
National Archives, 99
National Commission for Women (NCW), 10, 104–10, 112, 113, 114, 117, 120, 132, 160, 163, 178, 181, 182, 183
achievements of, 132
author's experience at, 104–10, 110, 178–83
Chairperson, 104, 110, 181, 182
and communalism, 114
and gender issues, 110, 114
goals of, 112
and "Hathras gang rape case", 181
hearings on Muslim women, 110–11
and "My Voice Shall Be Heard" report, 113–14
and the Sachar Committee Report, 114
and violence against women, 104–109, 180, 182, 183
National Register of Citizens (NRC), 24, 145
protests against, 24, 145
National Rural Health Mission (NRHM), 19, 118
Nationalism, 18, 40, 222, 236
false, 18
and India-Pakistan relations, 222, 236
- Urdu, 144
National Policy for the Voluntary Sector, 133
writing of, 133
Nativity, 153
"Naya Shivalaya" (Iqbal), 8
Nazarahari, Reza, 28
Naxalites, The, 12
Nayar, Kuldip. *See* Kuldip Nayar
Nazi, 209, 217
leader, 217
Trials, Nuremberg, 217
NCW (National Commission for Women), 10, 104–10, 112, 113, 114, 117, 120, 132, 160, 163, 178, 181, 182, 183
Need for a New Religion in India (Singh), 17, 155
Neera, 40
Nehru, Jawaharlal. *See* Jawaharlal Nehru
Nehruvian, 38, 114, 117, 135
India, 40
principles, 38
Nehru, Pandit. *See* Jawaharlal Nehru
Nepal, 115
and SAHR, 115
Netherlands, 153
New Delhi, 154, 182, 199, 213
New York, 20, 47, 48, 49, 50, 79, 80, 81, 83, 163, 212, 221, 229
City, 80, 81, 221
Police Department (NYPD), 81
Nigah, Zehra, 39
Nigam, Dr Srishti, 62, 68
Niazi, Munir, 3
Nikah, 55, 175, 202

nama, 108
Niloufer Billimoria, 153
Niraas Mein Aas (Husain), 174
Nirbhaya case, 110
Nitesh, Ravi, 60, 230, 235
Niti Aayog, 134–35
  structure of, 134
Nobel Prize, 183
"no man's land", 225, 226, 234
Non-Alignment, 40
Non-Muslims, 7, 112
Non-violence, 38, 197
Norman, Dr Marion, 20, 183
North East, 127, 214
North Patterson School of Carleton University, 60
Nova Scotia, 51
NRC (National Register of Citizens), 24, 145
NRHM (National Rural Health Mission), 19, 118
Nuh district, 106, 180
Nukkad-nataks (street plays), 230
Nuremberg Trials, 217
Nursery, 62
Nuruddin Ahmed, 96–100
Nusrat Fateh Ali Khan, 192, 233, 234

Obituaries, 237–38
Obscenity, 185
Obscurantism, 241
Ocean, 11, 25
Odetta, 144
"Ode to a Nightingale" (Keats), 22, 140
Of Human Bondage, 163
Okhla, 89
Odisha, 19, 118
  Koraput district, 70, 71, 124
  Mayurbhanj district, 19
O'Neill, Katherine, 72
One Thousand and One Nights, 79
Ontario, 178
Oprah Winfrey, 110
Oppression, 8, 11, 18, 25, 40, 145, 201
  by the "Indian State", 210
  of Muslims, 11, 83, 201
  of women, 40, 57, 104, 110, 172, 173, 176
Orient Longmans, 99
Oriya, 144
Orissa, 19, 118
  Koraput district, 70, 71, 124
  Mayurbhanj district, 19
Ostracism, 35
Ottawa, 50, 54, 58, 60, 75, 81, 178
OUP. *See* Oxford University Press

"Paigham-e-Aman", 228
Pakistan India Peoples Forum for Peace and Democracy (PIPFPD), 137, 219, 232, 236
Pakistan India Women's Solidarity Conference, 221
Pakistan Tourism, 222
Pakistan, 1, 9, 10, 11, 17, 18, 23, 24, 33, 34, 53, 54, 55, 56, 57, 61, 66, 67, 68, 69, 78, 81, 83, 85, 86, 89, 90, 91, 92, 93, 96, 97, 98, 99, 100, 101, 102, 103, 104, 105, 106, 107, 108, 110, 111, 112, 113, 114, 115, 116, 117, 118, 119, 120, 121, 122, 123, 124, 125, 127, 128, 130, 131, 132, 134, 136, 137, 139, 140, 141, 142, 144, 145, 146, 147, 148, 149, 150, 151, 152, 154, 155, 158, 159, 160, 162, 163, 164, 165, 168, 169, 172, 173, 174, 176, 178, 179, 180, 181, 182, 183, 186, 187, 188, 193, 195, 196, 197, 198, 199, 200, 201, 202, 204, 206, 208, 209, 210, 212, 213, 214, 215, 216, 217, 218, 219, 220, 221, 222, 223, 224, 225, 226, 227, 228, 229, 230, 231, 232, 233, 234, 235, 236, 238, 239, 240, 241
  Air Force, 54
  author's relatives in, 33, 55, 66, 90, 159
  author's visit to, 53, 136, 229–30
  and communalism, 10, 115, 217–218
  -India relations, 10, 11, 34, 53, 55, 66, 67, 68, 69, 83, 115, 128, 137, 140, 146, 149, 159, 173, 174, 195, 196, 197, 198, 200, 201, 217–236, 230
  animosity in, 54, 115, 217
  and children, 34, 67
  and communalism, 10, 115, 217–218
  peace efforts, 115, 218–236
  and Partition, 10, 11, 34, 146, 199
  and war, 195, 217, 221, 230
  and Islam, 17, 23, 90, 144, 174, 233
  -India Women's Solidarity Conference, 221
  Oxford University Press (OUP) Karachi, 101–102
  "Paigham-e-Aman", 228

Partition and creation of, 1, 9, 10, 11, 33, 34, 146, 159, 174, 199
-India Peoples' Forum for Peace and Democracy (PIPFPD), 137, 219, 232, 236
Rangers, 225, 226
and Ramadan, 174
students, 9, 54
visa for, 55, 67
"Women's Initiative for Peace in South Asia", 10, 219–22
Women's Solidarity Conference, 221
"Pakistani" pigeon, 228
Palisades, 50
Palo Alto, 51
Pampore, 197
Panchmahals, 15, 158
Panchsheel, 40
Panda, G.B., 117
Pande, Jyoti, 191
Pandey, Devenendra, 115
and SAHR, 115
Pandits, Kashmiri, 10, 197, 200, 210, 214
Panipat, 28, 33, 37, 90, 137, 149, 170, 172, 176, 220, 230, 231, 234
author's ancestral home, 33, 137, 149, 159
communal killings in, 33, 159
family, 170
and Hinduism, 33
and Islam, 33
and Muslim culture, 33
and Partition, 33, 159
and primacy of women, 33
Ram Mohan Roy from, 137, 197
women, 33–34
Panipatwallah, 137, 197
Papa. *See* Saiyidain, K.G.
Papa One, 212
Papa Two, 212, 216
Paradise Lost (Milton), 42
Parikrama, 23
Parliament, 104, 110, 112, 180, 217, 232
Hill, 81
Parliamentary election, 75
Parsi, 191
Partition, 1, 9, 10, 11, 12, 33, 34, 38, 56, 83, 89, 90, 99, 146, 149, 159, 174, 186, 188, 193, 199, 218, 224, 225, 232, 234
and communalism, 10, 218
and creation of Pakistan, 1, 9, 10, 11, 33, 34, 146, 159, 174, 199
and family, 34, 146
and homeland, 33
and identity, 9
impact on families, 1, 9, 12, 33, 34, 38, 56, 146, 159
and India-Pakistan relations, 10, 11, 34, 146, 199, 218
literature on, 90, 99
- riots, 116, 199
trauma of, 9, 12, 34, 35, 83, 90, 199, 224
and violence, 11, 12
witnesses to, 12, 146
and women, 11, 103
Pathway to India's Partition (Prasad), 186
Patiala, 43
Engineering College, 43
Patriotism, 222, 236
and India-Pakistan relations, 222, 236
- Urdu, 144
Patna, 164, 235, 237
Pattan, 238
Pantsuits, 74
Parvaaz (Soaring), 90
Parveena, 130
Parveena Ahangar, 216
Khoon diy Baarav, 216
Passion, 7, 73, 143, 162
in Iqbal's poetry, 7
for peace, 115
for social justice, 162
for work, 46
Passport, 77, 78, 229
official, 77
personal, 77
Pathan, 89
way, 89
"Pathway to India's Partition" (Prasad), 186
Patriarch, 56, 65, 111, 113, 166, 170, 175, 188, 222
and Islam, 111, 113, 175
and Moharrum, 188
-al family, 65, 172, 173
-al setup, 56
PCR, 180
Peace, 10, 11, 12, 13, 21, 25, 38, 40, 83, 115, 137, 144, 160, 163, 173, 174, 180, 192, 195, 196, 197, 198, 203, 206, 214, 218, 219, 220, 221, 222, 223, 224, 225, 226, 227, 228, 229, 230, 231, 232, 233, 234, 235, 236, 241
activists, 10, 21, 115, 137, 160, 218,

219, 220, 222, 223, 224, 225, 227, 229, 230, 232, 235, 236
bus to Lahore, 10, 219–22
and communalism, 115, 218, 236
efforts, 115, 218–236
and Faiz, 144
and friendship, 38, 197, 225, 234
and Gagan Sethi, 160
and gender, 233
and India-Pakistan relations, 115, 137, 140, 218–236, 230
initiatives, 196
and Islam, 11, 112, 113, 163, 173, 174, 201
and Kashmir, 195, 196, 197, 198, 203
march, 223
message of, 227
and Moharrum, 192
movement, 219
-loving, 112
-makers, 227
and Partition, 11, 199
-niks, 218
and Satyagraha, 12
and the "second abyss", 11
-shagirds, 232
song, 197, 230
and Sufism, 93
- talks, 201
- treaty, 218
through dialogue, 202, 218, 228
and WIPSA, 10, 115, 195, 196, 197, 219, 222, 223
Pedantic, 95
Peg, 129
Peshwar, 61, 219, 235
Persian, 78, 94, 237, 238
Empire, 94
Gulf, 238
Personal Law, Muslim, 23, 111, 112, 113, 174, 175
Board, All India Muslim (AIMPLB), 111, 114
and MWF, 113
Phupi, 170
Philip, 19
Philosophers, 6, 17, 145, 146, 241
of the West, 6
Sufi, 146
Philosophy, 6, 154, 156, 236, 241
Greek, 144
Indian, 6, 156
of Islam, 93
of Khushwant Singh, 147–49
Sufi, 93, 146
Western, 6
Phool Mandi, 21
Photographs, 61, 64, 75, 91, 93, 97, 109, 112, 149, 183, 193, 199, 202, 222, 228
Pickaxe, 13, 14
PIPFPD (Pakistan India Peoples Forum for Peace and Democracy), 137, 219, 232, 236
Pir, 187, 232
-e-Herat, 28
s, 198, 227
Planning Commission, 17, 116–35, 123, 124, 160, 163, 178, 180, 181, 229
and Abhay and Rani Bang, 119
achievements of, 131–34
author's appointment to, 116–17
author's experience at, 117–24
Chairperson, 120, 134
and child rights, 131
Civil Society Window, 122, 133
and communalism, 122
Deputy Chairman, 119–21
and FEG, 132–33
goals of, 123
and Gadchiroli, 118–19
and handloom weavers, 134
and human context, 123
inclusive planning, 134
Internal Planning Commission (IPC), 121
and Island Development Authority (IDA), 123
and Jarawas, 134
and MGNREGA, 118
and Mewat, 118
and "ordinary people", 117, 123, 124, 134
and policy change, 118
reports, 117, 119, 123
structure of, 121, 134
and women, 133
Plays, 34, 90, 172, 177, 230
"Importance of Being Ernest", 177
about Peter Rabbit, 36
"Pygmalion", 66, 177
school, 6, 34, 62
street (nukkad-nataks), 230
"Towards Women's Agency and Child Rights", 131
Poetry, 6, 7, 11, 22, 34, 37, 39, 42, 60, 63,

89, 93, 95, 103, 115, 126, 139, 140, 141–44, 145, 149, 150, 152, 154, 156, 157, 172, 174, 177, 189, 191, 192, 194, 195, 197, 203, 206, 214, 215, 216, 218, 225, 226, 231, 233
about compromise, 39
erotic, 154
of Faiz Ahmed Faiz, 2, 12, 115, 139, 140, 141–43, 144–46, 157, 215
on homeland, 7
of Hyder Ali Aatish, 118
of Iqbal, 6–7, 8, 12, 39, 58, 152, 206
on Islam, 115
of John Keats, 22, 140
and Kashmir, 194, 214, 215
love, 142
of Mir Anis, 174
of Mir Taqi Mir, 242
on Moharrum, 63, 126, 188, 189, 191, 192, 194
of Munir Niazi, 3
on nationalism, 6
patriotic, 7, 37
prison, 141–43
Punjabi, 191, 195, 233
on Ram, 6–7
recitation of, 12, 34, 37, 63, 188, 189, 191, 192
romantic, 142
on Sarmad, 95
Sufi, 145, 156
on the Taj Mahal, 38
of Valeh Daghistani, 95
Vaakhs, 194
on women, 57, 172
Poets, 11, 12, 34, 37, 38, 89, 90, 102, 115, 126, 131, 137, 139, 140, 141, 142, 144, 146, 150, 152, 154, 156, 157, 169, 172, 174, 176, 179, 186, 189, 191, 197, 203, 206, 207, 214, 215, 218, 225, 231, 233, 239
of the West, 6
feminist, 169, 172
Hindu, 126
of India, 102, 126, 239
Islamic, 6, 11, 39, 144
and Kashmir, 194, 214, 215
marsiya, 188
Muslim, 126
of Panipat, 35
Sufi, 145, 146, 156
Urdu, 38, 39
women, 174, 176
of the West, 6
feminist, 169, 172
Hindu, 126
of India, 102, 126, 239
Islamic, 6, 11, 39, 144
and Kashmir, 194, 214, 215
marsiya, 188
Muslim, 126
of Panipat, 35
Sufi, 145, 146, 156
Urdu, 38, 39
women, 174, 176
Police, 5, 21, 23, 81, 105, 125, 191, 199
action, 21
brutality, 24
and communal violence, 5, 21
and custodial deaths, 197
firing, 14
harassment, 202
and India-Pakistan relations, 226
and Kashmir, 197, 198, 199, 202, 204, 209, 212
lathi-charge, 5
moral, 103
- registration, 202
state, 24
tear gas, 5
torture, 212
- stations, 5, 10, 198
vans, 25
violence, 21, 24, 81, 125
Politicians, 4, 11, 13, 17, 24, 37, 101, 121, 148, 182, 196, 209, 217, 218, 219, 223
and education, 37
and India-Pakistan relations, 196, 219, 223
Muslim, 4, 11, 182
Politics, 9, 43, 72, 74, 117, 158, 208, 219, 233
electoral, 74
of Gujarat, 16
and identity, 9
as theatre, 73
Pollitzer, Alice K., 49
Polygamy, 112, 175
Poonch border, 116
Poverty, 19, 38, 110, 111, 118, 119, 123, 127, 130, 133, 169, 170
line, 122
Prabhavati, 121
Prabhash Chandra, 210
Pragati Maidan, 88

Prajapati, 16
Prasad, H.Y. Sharada, 86, 90, 92

Prasad, H.Y. Sharada, 86, 90, 92

Prayer, 3, 5, 21, 23, 27, 112, 170, 175, 184, 186, 187, 226
  mat, 60, 188
  s, 3, 184
  fajr, 3
  Friday, 204
Prayers
  from Khwaja Abdullah Ansari, 27
Prejudice, 49, 147, 148, 174, 229
  color, 49, 148
Prem Dhawan, 83
President of India, 5, 13, 55, 86, 115, 179, 181, 207
  former, 5, 13
  Dr Zakir Husain, 115, 179
President Karzai, 28
Prime Minister, 13, 14, 16, 86, 116, 117, 120, 121, 123, 158, 179, 182, 214, 218, 233
  former, 86, 115
  and Babri Masjid demolition, 13
  and Gujarat massacre, 14, 16, 158
  Indira Gandhi, 13, 22, 86, 87, 88, 90, 117, 120, 122, 158
  I.K. Gujral, 104, 121, 219, 223
  Dr. Manmohan Singh, 116–21, 117, 119, 126, 133, 134, 186
  Narendra Modi, 15, 82, 164
  Rajiv Gandhi, 22, 86, 87, 90, 117, 120, 122
Prison, 21, 93, 97, 110, 140, 144
  Ahmednagar, 97, 100
  letters from, 90
  life, 95
  - poetry, 141
  terms, 140, 141, 144, 236
  virtual, 61
Pritpal of Asia Import House, 178
Privy purses, 122
Progressive Writers Movement, 139, 141
Prophet Muhammad, 11, 26, 27, 63, 64, 95, 108, 146, 175, 186, 189, 190, 192, 241
  life of, 11
  sunnah of, 11, 56, 175, 186
Prose, 90, 143, 174
  and poetry, 139, 143
Protest, 4, 5, 21, 24, 141, 145, 201, 208, 209, 222
  against CAA and NRC, 24, 145
  march, 201
  and youth, 141, 145, 222
Prufrock, J. Alfred, 34
Punjab, 12, 33, 116, 159, 195, 197, 219, 224, 225, 230, 231, 232, 234, 235
  East, 35
  killings in, 12, 159
  Natshala, 232
  Partition of, 12, 33, 159, 234
  and peace, 219, 224, 225, 231, 232, 234, 235
  - Jagriti Manch, 232
  -India relations, 221
  West, 35
Punjabi, 78, 130, 146, 148, 152, 156, 195, 220, 233
  - Muslim, 52
  Sufis, 155
Pune, 11, 12, 174, 188
  author's childhood in, 11, 12, 174
  Moharrum in, 188
Puncture, 76
"Pygmalion" (Shaw), 66, 177

Qabristan, 13, 18, 21, 59, 197, 209
  Jamia, 59
Qadri, 56
Qafilas, 39
Qasim, 190
Qasmi, Maulana Mujahidul Islam, 113
Qayamat, Surah, 65
Quraish, 26
Qureshi, Dr. Aziz, 112, 160
  and MWF, 112, 160
Qureshis, 108
Qutubuddin Ansari, 15

Race Course Road, 13
Racism, 75, 76, 238
Radio, 32, 159
  gram, 159
Rafi Ahmed Kidwai. *See* Kidwai, Rafi Ahmed
Rafi, Mohammed, 118
Raghupati Sahay, 39
Rahat Chhatari, 66
"Rahi", 12, 83
Rahman, Gibran Rehan, 175
Rahmani, Maulana Khalid Saifullah, 114
Rahul, 153
Rah-e-Amal (The Practical Path) (Husain), 175
Rain, 3, 106, 20, 128, 153

Rajasthan, 18, 123, 191
  Rajsamund, 18, 18
Rajiv Gandhi, 22, 86, 87, 90, 117, 120, 122, 219
  and communalism, 13
  and education, 12, 90
  and Mohammad Yunus, 88
  at Planning Commission, 117, 120, 122
  portraits of, 22
  and Saiyidain, 12
  and Saliha Abid Husain, 12
Rajkamal Prakashan, 36
Rajnigandha, 177
Rajsamund, 18, 18
Raj Villa, 152, 153
Ramadan, 20, 21, 65, 174, 184–88, 185, 186, 204
  beauty of, 185
  and cleansing, 185
  daily routine during, 185
  description of, 185
  and eitedaal, 185
  and empathy, 186
  and fasting, 184, 185
  Iftar, 129, 185, 186, 187
  and Islam, 185, 186
  Lailat-ul-Qadr, 186
  month of, 20, 21
  and Moharrum, 184
  - observance, 155
  - prayers, 155
  and Pakistan, 174
  and Quran, 186
  and work, 185
"Ram" (Iqbal), 6–7
Ram, 6–7, 25
  -i-Hind, 6
  Mandir, 17, 13, 14, 17
  Setu, 17
Ramoowalia, B.S., 180
Rampur, 166, 167, 168, 170, 188
  family, 166, 168, 169
  Nawab of, 167
  royal family, 166, 168
  - and Moharrum, 188
Ranbir Singh Pora, 197
Rangers, 225, 226
Rangoon, 177
Rape, 7, 125, 181, 192, 200
  and communal violence, 15, 16, 103, 164, 200
  gang, 105, 107, 164, 181
  revenge, 109, 180
  - and MWF, 112
  and patriarchy, 111
Rapprochement, 137
Rassoul, Zelmai, 27
Rath, 16, 158
- Yatra, 16, 158
Ravi Nitesh, 60, 230, 235
Ravi, 45
Ray, Ranesh, 169
Razia Apa, 139
Razia, 162
Reangs, 128
Reason, 20
Regar, Shambhu Lal, 18
Regar, Shambhu Lal, 18
Regime, 5, 11, 15, 112, 145, 209, 241
  anti-Muslim right-wing, 11, 17, 24, 101, 112
  change of, 133
  Hindu right-wing, 19
  military, 144
  right-wing, 5, 15, 112
Regressive genes, 59
Regar, Shambhu Lal, 18
Regar, Shambhu Lal, 18
Regime, 5, 11, 15, 112, 145, 209, 241
  anti-Muslim right-wing, 11, 17, 24, 101, 112
  change of, 133
  Hindu right-wing, 19
  military, 144
  right-wing, 5, 15, 112
Regressive genes, 59
Regressive genes, 59
Related terms, 1
Relationships, 68, 166, 173, 208
  familial, 238
  love-hate, 159
Relief camps, 15, 19
Religion, 35, 37, 53, 110, 147, 148, 155, 156, 160, 172, 173, 174, 176, 185, 186, 187, 188, 189, 192, 229, 233, 238, 241
  and communalism, 35, 144
  and education, 37
  freedom of, 147, 148
  and gender, 110
  and identity, 37, 148
  and India-Pakistan relations, 229, 233
  and Islam, 172, 173, 174, 176, 186, 187, 188, 189, 238, 241
  - and "prudes", 155

and Moharrum, 188, 189, 192
of peace, 108
and violence, 108
and women, 172, 173, 176
Religious
beliefs, 49
- bigotry, 147
- identity, 37, 148
- persecution, 94
places, 13
practices, 168, 173
- sentiments, 145
- traditions, 224
Reno, 49
Repression, 40
Reshi, Nund, 194
Resettlement colonies, 159
Result Framework Document, 135
Reva, 45
Revolution, 25, 144, 145, 173
and Faiz, 141
Reyazuddin Ali, 23
Right wing, 3, 5, 11, 15, 17, 19, 24, 101, 112, 118, 144, 160, 241
forces, 5
regime, 5, 11, 15, 17, 24, 101, 112, 160
violence, 5
Rights, 57, 90, 104, 127, 131, 172, 173, 176, 195, 207, 241
of children, 131
fundamental, 207
of Muslim women, 57, 104, 172–73
of women, 57, 104, 172, 173, 176, 182
Rijz, 190
Riots, 5, 14, 159, 174, 241
anti-Sikh, 116
communal, 5, 14, 159, 174
Gujarat (2002), 14–16
Hindu-Muslim, 5, 14
Partition, 116, 199
Ripon Street, 101
Circular Road, 101
"Rip Van Winkle", 5
Ritual, 23, 29, 43, 95, 188, 205
-s, 43, 64, 174, 188
River, 127, 179, 203, 205, 210, 224, 235, 239, 240
Baan, 179
Dajla, 239, 240
Ganga, 12, 179, 224, 239, 240
Jhelum, 205, 210
Lidder, 203, 205, 210
Yamuna, 86, 239, 240
Roads, 31, 193, 231
dirt tracks for, 193
empty, 208
to Lahore, 10
lined with defecators, 148
and peace, 224
snow-covered, 76
village, 187
Robert F. Kennedy Human Rights Award, 160
Rohit, Indu, 161
Roll of Honour, 3
Romance, 142, 22
s, 54, 42
Roman Urdu, 152
Romantic, 140, 154
-ism, 22, 140
Rome, 238
Rosa, 184, 185, 186
kushai, 185
Roshini, Nai, 12
Ross, Izena, 72, 75
Roy, Aruna, 11, 121
Roy, Bidhan Chander, 101
Roy, Ram Mohan. *See* Mohan Roy, Ram
"Rubaiyat of Sarmad, The", 95
Rukh, 206
Rum, 116
Russia, 217
-n, 42, 238

Sa'aba, 205
Sabeels, 191
Sabrum, 127
Sachar Committee Report, 114, 130, 134
and Muslim communities, 114, 130
and MWF, 114
Sachar, Justice Rajinder, 114, 223
Sadhus, 94
Sadiq, 109
Sadeqain, 154–55
erotic verses of, 154
Saeeda Khurshed, Begum, 112
and MWF, 112
Safa, 30, 146
Safiraan-e-Aman (Emissaries of Peace), 229
SAFMA (South Asia Free Media Association), 232
Sahay, Raghupati (Firaaq Gorakhpuri), 39
Sahla, 161, 162
Sahib, Bachchan. *See* Khan, Murtuza Ali

Sahib, Khushwant. *See* Singh, Khushwant
Sahib, Larkana, 187
Sahib, Maulana. *See* Azad, Maulana Abul Kalam
Sahib, Jhamtani, 187
Sahibzada, 167
Saiyad, Amina, 102
Saiyidain Manzil, 85
Saiyidain, K.G., 3, 11, 12, 32, 33, 35, 37, 38, 41, 46, 47, 52, 55, 57, 66, 86, 89, 90, 97, 121, 131, 139, 150, 169, 173, 176, 214, 238
  as Educational Advisor (Bombay), 33
  at Education Department, Aligarh Muslim University, 4
  and education, 32, 33, 35, 37, 90, 131, 169, 214
  and Golden Jubilee Debate, 4
  on Indian Muslims, 11
  influence of, 33, 52
  and Islam, 56, 176
  at Jamia Millia Islamia, 12, 38, 89, 97, 173
  library of, 89
  and Moharrum, 188
  and Nai Roshini, 12
  - personality of, 169
  and Saliha Abid Husain, 173
Saiyidain, Saliha Abid. *See* Husain, Saliha Abid
Sajid, 20, 21
Sajoni Kisku, 105–106
  treatment of, 105–106
Sakina, 221
Salamis, 63
Saleha, 164
Saleem, Sunny, 233
Salman, 220
Salt Lake City, 49
Saloni Sehgal, 42
Samajwadi Party, 182
Saman Habib compound, 129
Saman Mahmood, 48
Samarkand, 239
Samina ("Driver Ben"), 161
Samosa, 153
Sanand, 161, 162, 163
Sangam, 12
Sangli, 164
Sanskrit, 92, 94
Santa Cruz airport, 148
Santhal Adivasis, 106
Santhal woman, 105
Saqlain, Khwaja Ghulamus, 3, 237, 238, 239
  travelogue of, 237, 238
Sarabhai, Mallika, 110
Sarabhai, Mridula, 37
Saraswati Vandana, 105
Sardar, 116, 120
  Sobha Singh, 149, 150
  Teja Singh, 152
  ji, 116, 150
"Sardarji" (Abbas), 116, 199
Sardars, 116, 120, 183
Saris, 41, 42, 74, 75, 77, 80, 81, 162, 179, 183
  cotton, 41
  silk, 75, 183
  tussar, 58
Sarisht, 6
Sarod, 126
Sarover Zaidi, 163
Sarvodaya, 38
  philosophy, 38
Sasural, 221
Sati, 35
"Saat Hindustani" (Abbas), 44
Saudi Arabia, Kingdom of (KSA), 30
Sauda, Mir Mohammad Rafi, 118
Savarkar, Vir, 17
SC. *See* Scheduled Castes
"Scandal", 44
Schools, 6, 9, 12, 32, 34, 35, 37, 38, 41, 44, 53, 56, 60, 62, 66, 103, 110, 116, 120, 124, 129, 130, 140, 147, 149, 166, 167, 168, 169, 170, 172, 176, 177, 188, 193, 194, 198, 202, 209, 212, 234, 235
  Alexandra, 34
  bridge, 130
  co-educational, 34, 177
  convent, 34, 166
  curriculum, 6, 34
  - functions, 6, 37, 130
  Gamadhiya, 34
  and gender, 32
  girls', 32, 33, 34, 41, 130, 168, 202
  Harry Ainlay High, 75–76, 81
  Hali Muslim, 28
  and identity, 37, 56
  -Inspectress, 33
  and Islam, 56, 172, 173
  J.B. Petit, 34
  Jamia Millia Islamia, 12, 10, 11, 12,

20, 21, 38, 86, 89, 90, 91, 112, 144, 171, 173, 174, 177
Khalsa, 234
in Kashmir, 193, 198, 209
and love-hate, 159
in Malegaon, 13, 130
Millennium, 234
Modern, 9, 34, 36, 37, 38, 86, 121, 149, 150
North Patterson School of Carleton University, 60
of old Panipat, 33
principal, 56
- principals, 16
Qasba, 170
- stage, 62, 188
St Stephen's College, 41, 119, 120
in Sudaka, 107
and the tsunami, 125
village, 130, 202, 209
and violence, 202
and WIPSA, 219
Sculptor, 65, 94
Seattle, 81
Second Coming, The, 25, 141
of Christ, 25
Secular, 3
Divine, 7
state, 17
Secularism, 12, 13, 14, 18, 38, 99, 194
at Aligarh Muslim University, 12
and Babri Masjid demolition, 13
and Batla House encounter, 21
at Jamia Millia Islamia, 12, 38
and Kashmir, 194
and MWF, 114
and Partition, 12
at Planning Commission, 122
Security forces, 197, 198, 199, 200, 201, 202, 204, 208, 212
in Kashmir, 197, 198, 199, 200, 201, 202, 204, 208, 212
Security guard, 78
Sedition, 116, 199
charges, 116, 199
Sehgal, Saloni, 42
Sehra, 58, 157, 210
Sehri, 186, 187
Sehgal, Saloni, 42
Sehgal, Saloni, 42
Sehra, 58, 157, 210
Sehri, 186, 187
Self-confidence, 13, 77
and humility, 13
Self-control, 185
Self-esteem, 77
Sen, Abhijit, 121, 122
Senwal (silk cotton), 154
Serge Augustin, 50
Seth, Padma, 105, 108, 181
and Hathras gang rape case, 181
at NCW, 105, 108
Sethi, Gagan, 158–65, 163, 183, 235
and Bilkis Bano case, 164–65
and Dalit Shakti Kendra, 161, 162, 163
on human rights, 160–61
and Gujarat massacre, 158, 164
and "Justice for Bilkis" movement, 165
and Kashmir, 195
and MWF, 160, 163
and "Understanding Islam" workshops, 163
Sethi, Neeraj, 117
Seth, Padma, 105, 108, 181
Shah Bano case, 172–73, 176
and Saliha Abid Husain, 172–73
Shahadat, 13
Shaheed, Sarmad. *See* Sarmad, Shaheed
Shaheen Bagh, 144
Shaheen, 206
Shah, Hazrat Makhdum, 28
Shah, Shabbir Ali Khan, 167, 168, 169
and education, 169
Shah, Merak, 28
Shah, Shabbir Ali, 169
Shahryar, Adil, 59
Shahjahanabad, 94
Shajra, 27
Shakeel, Rubina, 221
Shakespeare, 117, 142, 174
Shalimar Gardens, 156
Sham-e-Ghariban, 192
Shambhu Lal Regar, 18
Shankar Dayal Sharma. *See* Dayal, Shankar
Shankar's Weekly, 35, 36, 39, 146
International Writing Contest, 36
Sharma, Narendra, 12
Sharma, Rekha, 181
Shawl, Pashmina, 78
"Sheher aur Sapna", 12
Shelley (Shahla Mahmood), 48, 48, 50, 52
Sherbet, 191
Sher e Kashmir, 149
autobiography of, 149
Sher-i-Kashmir Conference Centre, 206

"Shikwa Jawab e Shikwa" (Iqbal), 152, 154
Shimr, 191
Shireen, 156
Shireen, Phupi, 170
Shishu Rakshaks, 118
Shivdaspur, 125, 127, 191
  Mohalla, 127
Shivalaya, 8
Shobha Gupta, 165
Schools, 9, 12, 32, 34, 35, 37, 38, 41, 44, 53, 56, 60, 62, 66, 103, 110, 116, 120, 124, 129, 130, 140, 147, 149, 166, 167, 168, 169, 170, 172, 176, 177, 188, 193, 194, 198, 202, 209, 212, 234, 235
  Alexandra, 34
  bridge, 130
  co-educational, 34, 177
  convent, 34, 166
  curriculum, 6, 34
  functions, 6, 37, 130
  Gamadhiya, 34
  and gender, 32
  girls', 32, 33, 34, 41, 130, 168, 202
  Harry Ainlay High, 75–76, 81
  Hali Muslim, 28
  and identity, 37, 56
  Inspectress, 33
  and Islam, 56, 172, 173
  J.B. Petit, 34
  Jamia Millia Islamia, 12, 10, 11, 12, 20, 21, 38, 86, 89, 90, 91, 112, 144, 171, 173, 174, 177
  Khalsa, 234
  in Kashmir, 193, 198, 209
  and love-hate, 159
  in Malegaon, 130
  Millennium, 234
  Modern, 9, 34, 36, 37, 38, 86, 121, 149, 150
  North Patterson School of Carleton University, 60
  of old Panipat, 33
  principal, 56
  principals, 16
  Qasba, 170
  stage, 62, 188
  St Stephen's College, 41, 119, 120
  in Sudaka, 107
  and the tsunami, 125
  village, 130, 202, 209
  and violence, 202
  and WIPSA, 219
Shovelling, 60
  snow, 60, 140
Siddhrath Varadarajan, 232
Siddique Kappan, 182
Sikhs, 21, 25, 38, 116, 178, 188, 191, 199, 210, 226
  and Hinduism, 19, 108
  and identity, 8, 148
  and Islam, 19, 108, 155
  and Moharrum, 191
  and Partition, 11
  and WIPSA, 21
Silk, 64, 152, 170
  cotton, 154
  saris, 75
Silver, 64, 91, 96, 170
  alams, 64
  Jubilee, 12
Sind, 94, 141, 191, 227, 233
  Thatta, 94
Sindbad, 206
Singh, A.P., 133
Singh, Kalyan, 13
  and Babri Masjid demolition, 13
Singh, Khushwant, 17, 36, 90, 92, 93, 101, 116, 146–57, 183, 186, 228
  on author's writing, 36, 90
  at Babri Masjid demolition, 36
  and communalism, 17
  death of, 147
  "A Dream Turns 75", 149–150
  Facts are Facts: The Untold Story of India's Partition, 90
  and Faiz Ahmed Faiz, 154
  on Ghalib, 156
  "History of the Sikhs", 36, 155
  and identity, 147–49
  and "Islamic Seal on India's Independence", 101
  on "Kitabon ki Duniya", 151
  and Kashmir, 195
  Khushwant Singh Literary Festival, 153
  and Maulana Abul Kalam Azad, 93, 101, 150–51
  on "Musaddas e Hali", 152
  Need for a New Religion in India, 17, 155
  on "Nawabs and Courtesans", 150
  and "ordinary people", 146
  - personality of, 155
  - and "prudes", 155

relationship with author, 146–47, 149–51
and Sadeqain's erotic verses, 154–55
- story of "Sardarji", 116
and translation, 90
- on Urdu, 149
on "You Have to Learn to Make Friends", 36
and "Why I Am an Indian", 147–49
- writing style of, 228
Singh, Montek. *See* Ahluwalia, Montek Singh
Singh, N.K., 120, 120
Singh, V.P., 92
Sinha, Dhananjai, 164
Sinha, Shanta, 213
"Sirr-i-Akbar (The Great Secret)", 94
Sistan, 239
Sita, 14
'*s Kitchen: A Testimony of Faith and Inquiry*, 14
Sitam, 23, 143, 235
Sitar, 93, 126
Siyaasat, 233
Skein, 207
Skyline, 50
Slogans, 18, 101, 129, 220, 226
Slums, 131
clusters, 131
Smithereens, 16
SMHS hospital, 211
Sniper, 81
Snow, 60, 76, 139, 140, 153, 211
-bound, 139
-covered, 76
Social reform, 12, 57, 173
Socialism, 17
Society, 24, 56, 106, 109, 111, 125, 126, 133, 222, 240, 241
for Eastern Art & Literature (SEAL), 177
for Education, Action and Research in Community Health (SEARCH), 119
- of old Panipat, 33
- patriarchal, 56, 65, 113
rigid structures of, 176
SOCRED (Social Credit Party), 74
Sofie, 48
Soil, 8, 47, 100, 190, 211
fertile, 28
Somnath, 242
ka, 242
Songs, 37, 83, 140, 144, 158, 197, 219, 220, 226, 227, 230, 234, 239
about unity, 40
devotional, 40
love, 34, 44, 142
of Mohammed Rafi, 226
peace, 197, 230
protest, 21
soz-salaams, 63, 191
of unity, 40
Sorrow, 3, 39, 45, 152, 157, 202
and love, 36
and peace, 224
Soura, 209, 214
South Asia Free Media Association (SAFMA), 232
South Asian Association for Regional Cooperation (SAARC), 229
South Asian Perspective, 10
South Asians, 76, 137, 140, 178, 218, 220, 223
South Asians for Human Rights (SAHR), 115, 137
founding of, 115, 137
South Block, 86, 87
South, 30
Asia, 10, 17, 110, 113, 143, 144, 148, 156, 160, 218, 220, 223, 233, 234, 235, 240
and gender issues, 110
and India-Pakistan relations, 220, 223, 233
and Islam, 113
and partition, 218
Perspective, 10
Asian Perspective, 10
Soviet, 135
SP, Anantnag, 201
Speaking out, 2, 11, 18, 115, 175, 181, 208, 236
and Faiz Ahmed Faiz, 2, 11, 115
importance of, 2, 11, 18, 115, 181, 208, 236
Saliha Abid Husain and, 175
Special Task Force (STF), 200
Speech, 2, 3, 5, 11, 60, 66, 176, 182, 238
death of, 2
freedom of, 2, 11
persuasive, 4
public, 4, 5
short, 4
and truth, 2
Springdales School, 234

Srinagar, 32, 193, 197, 198, 199, 204, 205, 211, 212, 214, 215, 216
Raj Bagh, 193
SMHS hospital, 211
Zero Bridge, 205
Srishti Nigam, Dr., 62, 68
Sri Lanka, 115
and SAHR, 115
ST. *See* Scheduled Tribes
Stage, 4, 11, 20, 41, 43, 66, 95, 113, 150, 154, 177, 178, 189, 192, 216
international, 177
Staines, Reverend Graham, 19
and Bajrang Dal, 19
burning of, 19
work of, 19
Stalwarts, 225, 232
Stamp paper, 195
Stanford University, 48, 51
Stains, Graham. *See* Staines, Reverend Graham
Starvation, 71, 125, 234
and malnutrition, 71
State, 13, 17, 24, 25, 34, 111, 122, 148, 159, 160, 165, 170, 200, 201, 207, 210, 214, 221, 225, 234, 236
subject, 32, 194–95
subjects, 32
Women's Commission, 181
Statements, hostile, 217
STF (Special Task Force), 200
Stephen's College, St, 41, 119, 120
Stories, 1, 3, 5, 12, 24, 35, 36, 37, 38, 66, 89, 90, 91, 94, 95, 96, 98, 99, 102, 103, 105, 106, 110, 112, 113, 114, 116, 117, 118, 119, 120, 121, 122, 123, 124, 125, 127, 129, 130, 131, 132, 134, 136, 137, 139, 140, 141, 142, 144, 145, 146, 147, 148, 149, 150, 151, 152, 154, 155, 158, 159, 160, 162, 163, 164, 165, 168, 169, 172, 173, 174, 176, 178, 179, 180, 181, 182, 183, 186, 187, 188, 193, 195, 196, 197, 198, 199, 200, 201, 202, 204, 206, 208, 209, 210, 212, 213, 214, 215, 216, 217, 218, 219, 220, 221, 222, 223, 224, 225, 226, 227, 228, 229, 230, 231, 232, 233, 234, 235, 236, 238, 239, 240, 241
of Abu Ayyub Ansari, 26
of Bilkis Bano, 164
children's, 35, 36, 62, 172, 174
of Ehsan Jafri, 16
fading, 24
family, 24, 27, 159, 167, 168, 169, 211
fictional, 56
of Graham Staines, 19
and Gujarat, 24
of Imam Husain, 189
of India, 117
of India-Pakistan relations, 217, 228
of Islam, 11, 190
of Jamia Millia Islamia, 89
of Juzar S. Bandukwala, 16
of Kashmir, 195, 198–200, 202–204, 206, 211–13, 215–16
of Khwaja Abdullah, 27
of Khwaja Malik Ali, 28
love, 24, 171
of Maimun and Idris, 106–109
of Malegaon, 129–30
of Maulana Azad, 90, 93
of Moharrum, 188–92
of Nuruddin Ahmed, 96–100
of "ordinary people", 102, 117, 118, 123, 124, 125, 134, 151, 226
of Partition, 34, 83, 99
of Prophet Muhammad, 11
of Qutubuddin Ansari, 15
of Rafiq Ahmed Baqal, 199
of Sago, 127–28
of Sajoni Kisku, 105–106
"Sardarji", 116, 199
of Sarmad, 94
from Shankar's Weekly, 35
short, 89, 90, 103, 168, 172, 174, 177
of Sindbad, 206
of Sufi philosophy, 93
of the tsunami, 124–25
true, 36
from Urdu, 90, 149
of women, 103, 105–109
"You Have to Learn to Make Friends", 35, 146
Storytelling, 178
ST (Scheduled Tribes), 110, 111, 114, 118, 123, 181
women, 111, 114
Students, 5, 12, 20, 21, 24, 27, 38, 41, 43, 44, 49, 50, 51, 53, 54, 60, 62, 66, 75, 76, 77, 89, 119, 121, 125, 130, 163, 177, 186, 190, 220, 225, 227, 231, 232, 234, 235, 236, 238
Union, 5, 4
-led movement, 24

- activism, 24, 121, 227
and communalism, 24, 76
- demonstrations, 25
and education, 38, 119, 130
Fulbright, 54
and gender, 110, 220
and identity, 56
and India-Pakistan relations, 220, 221, 225, 227, 231
and Islam, 56, 173, 190
and Kashmir, 198, 202, 209
at Miranda House, 41, 43
and Moharrum, 190
movements, 101
and peace, 219, 227, 231, 235
strikes, 20
and violence, 24, 76
Subalterns, 83, 241
Subhashini Ali, 165
Sudaka, 5, 106, 107, 108, 109, 180
story of Maimun, 107–109
Sufi, 27, 28, 93, 94, 95, 144, 152, 156, 165, 169, 194, 242
dominated town, 33
music, 233
philosophy, 93, 146, 152
philosophy, 93, 146, 152
philosopher, 145, 146
saint, 194
scholars, 93
Tariqah (Sufi way), 28, 93
way (Tariqah), 28, 93
Sufism, 93, 94, 156
contemporary relevance of, 93
and Sarmad, 94
Sujan Singh Park, 35, 36, 48, 66, 146
Sukru, 71
Sultanate, 28, 94
period, 94
Sultan, 28
Ghiyasuddin Balban, 28
Sultans, 168
Sumo, 204
Sunak, Rishi, 214
Sunnah, 11, 56, 113, 170, 175, 177, 186
of the Prophet, 11, 56, 175, 186
women's rights in, 113
Supreme Court, 19, 29, 103, 111, 112, 134, 207, 209, 213
Commission on Right to Food, 19
Surat, 235
Surveillance, 202
Swayamvaras, 54
Swat, 235
Synonyms, 1
Syria, 237
Syed Farooq, 202
Syed Mazharul Haq Society, 202

Tabla, 126, 178
maestro, 178
Tabarruk, 188
Tabari, Al-, 11
Tadi, 106
Tagore, Rabindranath, 37
Taj Mahal, 38
poem on, 38
Taj, 157
Takbeer, Nara-e-, 199
Takia kalaam, 169
Taliban, 236
Tallies, 142
Tamil, 144, 232
Nadu, 110, 232
Thiruvanthapuram, 110
Tanhai, 47
Tanner, Ches, 74
Tanvir, 16
Taqi Zade, Agha, 238
Tariqah, 28, 93
Tarjuman-ul-Quran (Azad), 90, 93, 151, 174
Taslima Nasrin. *See* Nasrin, Taslima
Tawaaf, 29, 30
Tea, 187
estate, 130
gardens, 124, 130
Tears, 15, 16, 25, 49, 76, 80, 97, 109, 125, 126, 147, 153, 159, 162, 174, 183, 188, 189, 191, 194, 205, 212, 222, 228, 229, 231, 233, 237
gas, 5, 24
Tehzeeb, Ganga-Jamni, 12, 75, 160, 233, 239
Television, 13, 92, 110, 234
cameras, 13, 24, 151
personality, 110
Temple, 18, 95, 146, 162, 242
-s, 94, 155, 226
donations for, 18
Hanuman, 199
of Somnath, 242
Ten Commandments, 181
Terror, 17, 18, 20, 21, 110, 144, 199
attacks, 9/11, 11, 17
cells, 212

-ism, 21, 144
-ists, 17, 20, 21, 201
modules, 17
Tesu (Flame of the Forest), 154
Thatta, 94
Thathari, 203
The Citizen, 142
Thekekara, Mari, 158
Theology, 111, 163
The Hunger Project (THP), 79–80
and discrimination, 79–80
and Joan Holmes, 79
Third Reich, 78
Thiruvanthapuram, 110
Thomas, Dylan, 141
Thomson, Polly, 39
THP. *See* The Hunger Project
Tiffin, 38
Timothy, 19
Tirpat Kaur, 221
Tirupati, 236
Tiryaq, 215
Toba Tek Singh, 235
Toilets, 43, 78, 104, 176, 187
Indian, 104
Western, 104
Tolerance, 11, 12, 110, 187, 219, 233
and community, 11
and Islam, 11, 110, 187
and peace, 12
taught by parents, 173
Torii, Chiyoka, 110
Toronto, 60, 78, 81, 229
airport, 78
Torture, 14, 61, 78, 189, 192, 199, 200, 201, 212, 216, 222, 230
chambers, 212
photographs of, 199
Touch, 157, 192
gentle, 157
stone, 29
Tourism, 18, 134, 213, 222
eco-, 134
and Kashmir, 213
in Rajsamund, 18
working group, G20, 213
Tradition, 6, 12, 33, 64, 90, 93, 143, 144, 148, 167, 168, 173, 174, 188, 191, 215
community, 6, 33, 148, 221
eclectic Indian, 6
family, 63, 64, 167
Hindu, 19
and identity, 12, 169
Islamic, 3
Shia, 188
of Moharrum, 64, 188, 191
nawabi, 166, 167, 169, 170
oral, 93, 143, 144
Shia, 64, 188
Sufi, 28, 93
Train to Pakistan (Singh), 156
Translation, 90, 92, 93, 95, 100, 110, 149, 150, 151, 152, 154, 155, 172, 174, 189, 218, 224, 237
of Azad's work, 90, 92, 93, 150, 151
of Chughtai's work, 90
of "Ebb and Tide in Islam", 152
of Hali's work, 103, 152, 174
of Iqbal's work, 152
of Khan's work, 90
of the Quran, 65, 151
of Saqlain's work, 237
of "Sarmad Shaheed", 96
of "The Rubaiyat of Sarmad", 100
of Sadeqain's work, 154
of Sheikh Abdullah's work, 149
from Urdu to English, 90, 149
Translators, 93
Traumatic, 9
experiences, 24
Trauma, 9, 12, 24, 33, 35, 36, 55, 56, 159, 195, 202, 221
of communalism, 13, 24, 35
of Partition, 9, 12, 34, 35, 83, 90, 199, 224
of "You Have to Learn to Make Friends", 36
Travel, 13, 29, 51, 53, 67, 77, 115, 117, 118, 124, 196, 204, 221, 229, 234, 237
by Greyhound bus, 48, 51
-ogues, 237
to Kashmir, 194, 204
to Lahore, 10
to Pakistan, 53
restrictions, 147
to the US, 10
to Wagah border, 225
writers, 28
Treaties, 240
Trees, 8, 13, 32, 118, 128, 130, 140, 146, 152, 154, 203, 206, 210, 234
deodars, 32
flowering, 140, 154, 205
and peace, 224

Trials, 103, 168, 172
  Nuremberg, 217
Tribal, 19, 70, 118, 119, 134, 162
  belt, 70, 124
  children, 19
  district, 19, 124
  women, 118, 119, 134
Tribes, 128, 197
  nineteen, of Tripura, 128
Triple talaq, 111, 112, 174–75
  and MWF, 112
Tripura, 124, 127, 128
Trishuls, 101
Trust, 91, 149, 228
  Navsarjan, 160
Truth, 2, 6, 22, 24, 57, 93, 109, 112, 145, 162, 176, 182, 204, 209, 218
  and communalism, 109
  distortion of, 218
  wine of, 6
Tsunami, 70, 124–25
  in Andaman and Nicobar Islands, 124–25
  and community, 125
  devastation of, 124
  and hope, 124
  and life, 124, 125
  stories of, 124–25
Turkey, 237, 238
Turquoise, 28
Tussar, 58
Tyabji, Abbas, 11

Udaipur, 17, 123
  Kathodis of, 17
Ulema, 113, 175
  and MWF, 113
Uma Bharati, 13
  at Babri Masjid demolition, 13
Umardin of Shikarpur, 107
Ummah, 21, 113, 191
Umar Farooq, Mirwaiz, 200–201
  assassination of father, 200
  on Chittisinghpura massacre, 201
  and Hurriyat, 200
  personality of, 200
UNESCO, 28, 36
  Courier, 36
Union, 3, 165
  no memory of the beloved, 3
  desire for, 3
  of India, 165
  Territory, 193
  Minister of, 182
United Nations (UN), 209, 217, 229
  anti-terrorism listing, 61
  CEDAW, 158
United States (US, America), 10, 11, 13, 46, 47, 48, 49, 50, 51, 55, 57, 58, 60, 66, 67, 68, 69, 75, 76, 79, 81, 83, 87, 90, 93, 102, 110, 141, 152, 153, 154, 158, 159, 163, 165, 166, 169, 172, 175, 177, 178, 183, 186, 188, 193, 195, 196, 197, 198, 199, 200, 201, 202, 204, 206, 208, 209, 210, 212, 213, 214, 215, 216, 217, 218, 219, 220, 221, 222, 223, 224, 225, 226, 227, 228, 229, 230, 231, 232, 233, 234, 235, 236, 237, 238, 239, 240, 241
  author's trips to, 10, 46, 48, 50, 55, 57, 65, 66, 67, 68, 69, 75, 79, 81, 140, 154, 158, 163, 165, 172, 175, 229
  author's daughter in, 216
  Special, No. 9 University, 43
  author's time in, 46–52, 65–67, 140, 154, 172, 175
  Canyon City, Colorado, 50
  civil rights in, 236
  communalism in, 18, 80–81, 221
  Department of Education, 46
  discrimination in, 79–80
  East West Center, 48
  Encampment for Citizenship, 48–50
  English Department, 46
  George Floyd incident, 76, 81
  Goddard College, 49
  Greyhound bus journeys in, 48, 51
  and "Hathras gang rape case", 181
  and India-Pakistan relations, 55, 66, 67, 69, 140, 229, 236
  JFK Airport, 81
  Madison campus, 46
  and Moharrum, 191
  and Muslim women, 110, 112, 113
  New York City, 47, 48, 49, 50, 79, 80, 81, 83, 163, 212, 221, 229
  North, 81, 209, 214
  racism in, 75, 76, 81, 241
  Salt Lake City, 49
  Scholar in Residence, 48
  Stanford University, 48, 51
  student visa for, 55
  University of Alberta, 49, 51, 65, 75, 178

University of California, 51
University of Chicago, 49
University of Hawaii, 48, 51
University of Wisconsin, 46, 48
Vice-President, 72
violence in, 80–81, 221
Visiting Professor, 46, 48
West Coast, 47
and WIPSA, 228
Universities. *See* Colleges
University Special, No. 9, 43
Untouchability, 176
-in Lutyens' Delhi, 176
Upanishads, 7, 94
and Iqbal, 7
UP, 5, 23, 108, 110, 111, 173, 180, 182, 191, 230, 239
by-election, 5
Governor, 112
weavers, 125
Urban
areas, 15
development, 74
elite, 38
ghettos, 129
Reform Group Edmonton (URGE), 73, 74
Urdu, 8, 12, 21, 23, 39, 78, 89, 90, 92, 93, 96, 99, 100, 110, 111, 112, 139, 140, 142, 144, 145, 149, 150, 151, 152, 154, 156, 168, 172, 174, 177, 178, 199, 215, 224, 233, 237
books, 90
couplets, 205
Drama Club, 177
journals, 96
Literature, 90
media, 21, 23, 99
newspapers, 21, 90, 100
papers, 97
poetry, 12, 38, 39, 139, 140, 149, 150, 151, 152, 154, 156, 177, 214, 215, 224
press, 21
Professor of, 90, 110, 112
Roman, 152
and translation, 90, 149
writers, 35, 90, 174, 178, 215
URGE (Urban Reform Group Edmonton), 73, 74
Usmani, Nisar, 218
Uttarakhand, 112
Vadodra, 15, 158, 204
Vajpayee, Atal Bihari, 22, 233
Vakil, Lala, 164
Valley. *See* Kashmir
Vandana, Saraswati, 105
Varanasi, 124, 126–27
Varadarajan, Siddarth, 232
Varavara Rao, 146
Vedas, 7
and Iqbal, 7
Veda, Gunjan, 117, 229
Ved Vyas, 12, 40
Veena, 43, 45
Mago, 43
Venkataraman, R., 92
Venice, 204
Vice Chancellor Lodge, 204
Vice Chancellor, 5, 13, 204, 215
former, 5, 13
Mushirul Haq, 204, 215–16
Vice President, 5, 13, 92, 117
former, 5, 13
Hamid Ansari, 5, 13
Vidarbha, 119
tribal district of, 119
Vidya Rao, 191–92
Vijay Chowk, 108
Vijay Maurya, 164
Villages, 19, 70, 105, 106, 107, 109, 118, 121, 122, 123, 124, 127, 128, 132, 162, 173, 180, 187, 191, 197, 199, 202, 203, 219, 221, 224, 227, 230, 235, 238
global, 241
headmen, 109
pradhans, 107
schools, 130
health workers, 119, 134
Violence, 5, 11, 15, 16, 17, 18, 19, 20, 21, 23, 24, 25, 59, 62, 81, 83, 95, 101, 103, 105, 106, 107, 108, 109, 110, 112, 113, 125, 127, 130, 132, 144, 145, 158, 162, 163, 173, 178, 180, 181, 182, 183, 188, 191, 192, 195, 197, 199, 200, 201, 202, 208–213, 216, 221, 222, 227, 233, 234, 236, 241
Against Women, 10, 14, 24, 110, 132, 158, 162, 180, 183, 200, 222
Act (PWDVA), 10, 132
against children, 105, 132
at Aligarh Muslim University, 5
and communalism, 11, 17, 24, 101,

112, 130, 132, 158, 164, 173, 180, 199, 203, 209, 210, 240, 241
domestic, 105, 132
and faith, 14
and gender, 132
in Gujarat, 14–16, 103, 158
and hate, 18, 101, 109, 209, 210
and identity, 23
and India-Pakistan relations, 217, 222, 230, 236
and Islam, 11, 14, 17, 108, 112, 113, 173, 190
in Kashmir, 195, 197, 199, 200, 201, 202, 208–213, 216, 221
in Malegaon, 132
and MWF, 112
and the NCW, 104–109, 180, 182, 183
against women, 10, 14, 24, 104, 110, 112, 113, 132, 158, 162, 180, 183, 200, 222
police, 21, 24, 81, 125
and right-wing regime, 11, 17, 24, 101, 112
sexual, 15, 16, 103, 164, 200, 202
by the state, 24
and students, 24
and the tsunami, 125
Vinoba Bhave, 8, 38, 197, 230
and peace, 38, 197
song of, 197, 230
yatra of, 230
Visa, 55, 67, 220, 229, 236
refusal, 236
Vishva Hindu Parishad, 19
at Kandhamal, 19
Voters, 74
Vyas, Ved, 12, 40

Wagah border, 10, 137, 219, 222, 223, 224, 225, 226, 228, 229, 231
Aghaz e Dosti at, 229
author's visits to, 137, 225, 229
"Baab-e-Azadi", 230
bus to Lahore, 10, 219–22, 225
candle lighting ceremony at, 224–28, 229
check-post, 225, 227
closing of, 10
concert, 227
crowds at, 225–26
"Hind Pak Dosti Manch", 223, 227, 228
and India-Pakistan relations, 10, 219, 222, 223, 224, 225, 228, 229, 231
Joint Declaration at, 227
langar, 228
midnight at, 137, 224, 225, 227
mushaira, 226
"no man's land", 225, 226
peace initiatives at, 225, 228, 229
retreat ceremony, 226
Swarna Jayanti Dwar, 231
"- Women's Initiative for Peace in South Asia", 219–22
Women's Solidarity Conference, 221
Wah, West Punjab, 52
Wahini, Hindu Yuva, 23
Waikikki Beach, 48
Wali Khan, Facts are Facts: The Untold Story of India's Partition, 90
Wali Khan, Khan Abdul, 90, 232
Wali Khan, Naseem, 90
Wali, Shaikh Nuruddin, 194
War, 11, 17, 25, 32, 110, 140, 145, 190, 195, 196, 197, 199, 201, 209, 212, 217, 219, 221, 222, 226, 230, 233, 234, 236, 238, 239, 241
and children, 130
widows, 104
cries of, 138
Kargil, 195, 219
low-intensity, 217
news, 32
rhetoric, 195, 217, 234
of 1947, 11, 12, 32, 193
of 1965, 45, 54, 221
of 1972, 217
of 1999, 217
Ward 1, 73, 74
Watan, 33, 159, 195, 179
Water, 12, 21, 23, 38, 60, 85, 106, 123, 124, 129, 130, 148, 156, 185, 187, 189, 191, 198, 205, 239, 240
scarcity, 12
supply, 85
Weavers, 125, 134
UP's, 125
Weddings, 170, 199
West, 6, 30, 35, 48, 49, 110, 141, 191, 236
Asia, 30
Bengal, 18, 99, 100, 110, 214, 236
Coast, 47
Nepean, 75
philosophers, 6
Punjab, 35, 52, 159

Whitemud Freeway, 74
Wilde, Oscar, 177
    Importance of Being Ernest, 177
Wilderness, 89
    with zero amenities, 89
Wildernesses, 165
Winfrey, Oprah, 110
WIPSA (Women's Initiative for Peace in South Asia), 10, 115, 195, 196, 197, 219, 222, 223
    2000 bus journeys, 10, 219–22, 225
    demands of, 195
    founding of, 115, 195
    and peace initiatives, 196
Wisconsin, 46, 48, 51, 53, 55
    University of, 46, 48, 55
    Graduate School, 48, 55
Witnesses, 10, 14, 24, 29, 91, 123, 169, 178, 188, 190, 195, 204, 206, 210, 238
    to communal violence, 10
    to Partition, 12, 146
    to the tsunami, 125
Women, 3, 4, 5, 7, 9, 10, 11, 12, 13, 15, 16, 17, 18, 19, 20, 21, 23, 24, 25, 26, 27, 28, 30, 32, 33, 34, 35, 36, 37, 38, 39, 40, 41, 42, 43, 44, 45, 46, 47, 49, 50, 52, 53, 54, 56, 57, 58, 59, 60, 62, 64, 65, 67, 68, 69, 70, 71, 72, 73, 76, 80, 81, 83, 86, 89, 90, 93, 96, 97, 98, 99, 100, 101, 102, 103, 104, 105, 106, 107, 108, 109, 110, 111, 112, 113, 114, 115, 116, 118, 119, 121, 122, 123, 124, 125, 126, 127, 129, 130, 131, 132, 133, 134, 136, 137, 139, 140, 141, 144, 146, 148, 149, 150, 151, 152, 154, 158, 159, 160, 162, 163, 164, 165, 166, 168, 169, 170, 171, 172, 173, 174, 175, 176, 177, 178, 179, 180, 181, 182, 183, 186, 187, 188, 191, 192, 193, 194, 196, 197, 198, 199, 200, 201, 202, 203, 204, 206, 209, 211, 212, 213, 214, 215, 216, 217, 218, 219, 220, 221, 222, 223, 224, 225, 226, 227, 228, 229, 230, 231, 232, 233, 234, 235, 236, 238, 239, 241
    and activism, 114, 132, 219, 222, 227, 233
    and communal violence, 5, 15, 16, 103, 106, 132, 158, 164, 200
    and community, 11, 17, 112, 160, 162, 164
    and domestic violence, 105, 132
    driver, 71
    education of, 11, 33, 57, 112, 130, 172, 173, 198
    employment of, 133
    empowerment of, 106, 112
    and faith, 14, 188
    and family, 34, 56, 65, 168
    and filmmaking, 216
    and gender, 3, 4, 10, 17, 22, 57, 110, 113, 114, 122, 132, 133, 175, 178, 179, 180, 181, 182, 183, 195, 197, 212, 213, 233, 241
    and Hinduism, 19, 108, 188
    and identity, 3, 9, 12, 23, 24, 53, 56, 114, 214, 221, 227, 241
    and India-Pakistan relations, 34, 53, 55, 66, 67, 69, 217, 219, 220, 221, 222, 223, 224, 225, 227, 228, 229, 230, 232, 233, 234, 235, 236
    and Islam, 11, 14, 17, 56, 108, 112, 113, 173, 174, 175, 188, 190, 191, 200
    in Kashmir, 10, 17, 195, 197, 198, 199, 200, 202, 203, 206, 209, 212, 213, 214, 215
    killings of, 12, 159, 200
    kidnapping of, 108
    leaders, 176
    lynching of, 16, 81, 132, 164
    and marriage, 53, 55, 111, 173, 175, 177, 221
    middle class, 18, 20, 111
    mistresses, 175
    and Moharrum, 64, 174, 188, 190, 191, 192
    and the Muslim Personal Law, 111, 113
    of Muslim community, 112
    National Commission for, 10, 104–10, 112, 113, 114, 117, 120, 132, 160, 163, 178, 181, 182, 183
    and the Planning Commission, 118, 123, 133, 134
    of Pochampally, 124
    and polygamy, 112, 175
    post-partition trauma of, 12
    poets, 57, 172, 174, 176
    and poverty, 110, 124
    primacy of, 33
    rights of, 57, 104, 172, 173, 176, 182
    and the Sachar Committee Report, 114

and schools, 9, 12, 32, 34, 35, 37, 38, 41, 44, 53, 56, 60, 62, 66, 103, 110, 116, 120, 124, 129, 130, 140, 147, 149, 166, 167, 168, 169, 170, 172, 176, 177, 188, 193, 194, 198, 202, 209, 212, 234, 235
and secularism, 3, 12, 18
in senwal (silk cotton) saris, 154
Sikh, 116
status of, 111, 172, 173, 175, 176
stories of, 103, 105–109, 125–26, 164, 168
and Sufism, 94
and the tsunami, 125
and triple talaq, 112, 174–75
tribal, 118, 119, 134, 162
and violence, 5, 15, 16, 18, 23, 103, 105, 106, 107, 108, 109, 125, 132, 158, 162, 164, 180, 181, 182, 183, 188, 192, 197, 199, 200, 202, 211
and WIPSA, 10, 21, 195, 196, 197, 219, 222, 228
and work, 124, 133, 160, 163, 220
writers, 6, 90, 103, 168, 174
Women's Initiative for Peace in South Asia (WIPSA), 10, 115, 195, 196, 197, 219, 222, 223
Women's Reservation Bill, 180
World, 1, 2, 3, 6, 11, 17, 18, 20, 22, 23, 30, 31, 34, 36, 37, 39, 41, 47, 50, 51, 55, 65, 68, 70, 76, 79, 83, 88, 90, 93, 99, 109, 110, 112, 124, 130, 140, 142, 144, 145, 146, 150, 152, 154, 155, 164, 173, 174, 175, 178, 185, 188, 190, 191, 192, 195, 196, 203, 204, 206, 209, 211, 212, 214, 216, 217, 220, 222, 227, 230, 236, 238, 239, 240, 241
view, 153
Health Organization (WHO), 126
War II, 128
Writers, 6, 7, 90, 102, 144, 155, 172, 174, 177, 207, 214, 215, 218, 235, 237, 238, 240, 242
of children's literature, 35
Hindu, 6
and identity, 6
and Islam, 6
marsiya, 191
Muslim, 6, 35, 103, 174, 177
of Partition trauma, 35
Punjabi, 195, 197
Urdu, 35, 90, 174, 177, 215
women, 6, 90, 103, 174, 215
Writing, 3, 4, 7, 12, 35, 36, 57, 89, 90, 91, 93, 95, 97, 98, 99, 102, 103, 110, 117, 131, 133, 147, 149, 150, 151, 152, 154, 156, 157, 159, 160, 165, 170, 171, 172, 173, 176, 177, 178, 179, 180, 181, 182, 183, 186, 187, 188, 193, 195, 196, 197, 198, 199, 200, 201, 202, 203, 204, 206, 208, 209, 210, 211, 212, 213, 214, 215, 216, 217, 218, 219, 220, 221, 222, 223, 224, 225, 226, 227, 228, 229, 230, 231, 232, 233, 234, 235, 236, 237, 238, 239, 240, 241
of Azad, 93
Contest, International, 36
erotic, 154
of Faiz, 142
on human rights, 165
of Hali, 174
on identity, 3
of Iqbal, 6
on Islam, 113, 165, 174
of Khushwant Singh, 147, 149, 150
morbid, 57
on Muslim women, 112, 113, 172, 174
of Niazi, 3
on Partition, 90, 99
persuasive, 4
style, 228
urge for, 212
on women, 172
style of, 228

Yadav, Ramesh, 224, 232
Yadav, Mulayam Singh, 182
offensive language of, 182
Yaqub Gill, 233
Yaqub, Hazrat, 233
Yaadgaar-e-Hali (Husain), 28, 176
Yamuna River, 86, 239, 240
Yavar, 58, 60–61, 62, 67, 68, 69, 71, 86, 139, 140, 188, 212, 229
birth of, 60
description of, 60, 61
and Fatiha, 59
and Moharrum, 188
personality of, 60
and Quran, 65
Yawar Ahmed Bhat, 211–12

death of, 211
Yawar Abdul Hameed, 211
"Yaas" (Faiz), 142
Yatra, 16, 17, 158, 230
s, 230
Rath, 16, 158
Vinoba Bhave's, 230
Yavar Hameed, 60–61, 62, 67, 68, 69, 71, 86, 139, 140, 188, 212, 229
Yeats, W.B., 8, 25, 37, 40, 80, 141
"Among Schoolchildren", 8
"The Second Coming", 25, 141
Yugandhar, B.N., 121, 122
Yunus, Mohammad, 86, 88, 90, 98, 159
"Facts are Facts: The Untold Story of India's Partition", 90
"Letters from Prison", 90
Yusuf Ali, Abdullah, 65, 151
Yusmarg, 198

Zafar, Bahadur Shah, 177
"Kitna Hai Badnaseeb Zafar", 177
Zaheer, Anwar Abbas. *See* Anwar Anwar, Abbas
Zaheer, Kazim, 67
Zaheer, Sarover, 163
Zaheer, Sajjad ("Banney Bhai"), 139
Zakia, 47, 58, 59, 65, 67, 68, 139, 166, 168, 169
and Ammi's love, 171
Zamir, 24
Zamzam, 30
aab-e-, 30
Zeba, 218
Zero Bridge, 205
Zero line, 128, 234
Zehra Nigah, 39
Zehra, Nasim, 218
Zia-ul Haq, 144
Zindan Nama (Faiz), 140, 141, 142, 154, 157
Zohra, 58, 66, 67, 68, 85, 166, 170
Zothanpuii, 118